Women's Culture in a New Era

A Feminist Revolution?

Edited by
Gayle Kimball

The Scarecrow Press, Inc.
Lanham, Maryland • Toronto • Oxford
2005

SCARECROW PRESS, INC.

Published in the United States of America
by Scarecrow Press, Inc.
A wholly owned subsidiary of
The Rowman & Littlefield Publishing Group, Inc.
4501 Forbes Boulevard, Suite 200, Lanham, Maryland 20706
www.scarecrowpress.com

PO Box 317
Oxford
OX2 9RU, UK

British Library Cataloguing in Publication Information Available

Library of Congress Cataloging-in-Publication Data
Women's culture in a new era : a feminist revolution? / edited by Gayle
Kimball.
   p. cm.
Includes bibliographical references and index.
ISBN 0-8108-4961-5 (pbk. : alk. paper)
1. Feminism—United States—History—20th century. 2. Women
artists—United States. 3. Women musicians—United States. 4. Women and
literature—United States—History—20th century. I. Kimball, Gayle. II.
Title.
HQ1426.W6633 2005
305.4'0973—dc22

                   2005006524

∞™ The paper used in this publication meets the minimum requirements of
American National Standard for Information Sciences—Permanence of
Paper for Printed Library Materials, ANSI/NISO Z39.48-1992.
Manufactured in the United States of America

~

Contents

Part Two: Music

Part Three: Literature

Part Four: Religion

Part Five: Organizations

~

Preface

Women's Culture: The Women's Renaissance of the Seventies was published in 1981 to see if and how women create and organize differently from men. Much of U.S. culture still reflects men's viewpoint and experiences, so our original quest remains a pertinent question. However, that was the only book to explore the topic from a wide-angle lens, looking at women's approach to creating visual arts, music, literature, religion, and all female organizations. It grew out of a Feminist Visions of the Future conference I organized at CSU, Chico (a *Feminist Visions of the Future* videotape with many of the original chapter authors and colorful visuals is available from me). The book became a unique classic, as most publishers are uncomfortable with such a sweeping topic as women's creativity. Susan Suntree told me she'd heard it referred to at various conferences, in the United States and Europe, and urged me to update it.

I wanted to find out how the themes and goals described in the first edition have changed over the past decades. Have feminist goals become mainstream or marginalized? What do young women think about women's issues today? I asked chapter authors to analyze how their field has changed. Some original authors were not able to update their work, so six of the chapter authors are new. Our intention is to stimulate you to think about your own creativity and activism in the context of social construction of attitudes and values. We'd like to hear your comments on what we wrote and the progress of feminism and encourage you to e-mail us (gkimball@csuchico.edu).

Thanks to Irena Praitis for copyediting with me.

~

Overview and Background

Gayle Kimball

Attitude Changes

How have attitudes expressed in *Women's Culture: The Women's Renaissance of the Seventies*, the 1981 book, changed? After answering this question more fully in terms of increased globalism, less anger toward men, less dualism, and a less simplistic view of women's essential nature, in this chapter I outline the highlights in the women's movement since 1980. The last question to be answered in this book is to compare second wave with young feminist third wave activity. In the 1981 introductory essay, I defined the *third wave* as cultural feminism, but that definition was unique to our book. *Third wave* came to refer to young feminists, rather than women's artistic and intellectual creativity, while *second wave* refers to the generation of Betty Friedan and Gloria Steinem, and *first wave* to the movement for women's suffrage.

A major change since the first women's culture book is expansion of global feminism and technological advances in the information age, especially the Internet, enabling us to share information immediately and without censorship. In an era of globalism and infotechnology, we've seen the mushrooming of online women's newsletters. For example, we quickly learned about the African and Pakistani women sentenced to be stoned to death for adultery in 2002.

We wrote the first edition on a typewriter and didn't have immediate, uncensored access to events in other countries. The U.N. Decade on Women, beginning in 1975, helped develop a global feminism and critique of Eurocentricism. Chapter author Robin Morgan encouraged this expansion in her 1984 book *Sisterhood Is Global*, in her *Ms.* magazine articles (while editor), and by founding the Sisterhood Is Global Institute for research. Mary Beth Edelson continues this trend with her European art performances for "Forgiveness" of conflict and for social interaction.

Faith Wilding, the 1981 book cover artist, is a leader in cyberfeminism, which had its first eight-day gathering in 2004. She reports that young women repudiated "old style" (1970s) feminism as antitechnology, antisex, essentialist, guilt inducing, and restrictive in its notions of political correctness. Like many foremothers, she wonders why so many younger activists know so little about past feminist philosophies and are antitheory. Ironically, young cyberfeminists adopted many of the 1970s' strategies of "strategic separatism" of women's groups, feminist cultural theory, creation of new images of women (feminist avatars, cyborgs, genderfusion) to counter stereotyping, strategic essentialism, and the like. She points to the proliferation of "grrrl" groups on the Net in the form of chat groups, zines (sci-fi, cyberpunk, femporn, etc.), antidiscrimination projects, sexual exhibitionism, transgender experimentation, and artistic self-promotion. She advocates building a movement to create a "politicized feminist environment on the Net."[1]

Another change is that anger toward men seems to have softened, as seen in Judy Chicago's *Powerplay* artwork, which sympathetically explores the restrictions of the male role (explained in her chapter). Robin Morgan says now she "wouldn't flinch from writing a male character" and notes that in her recent talks about eroticization of violence against women, men in the audience "get it." She points to the TV images of firefighters sobbing in each other's arms in the aftermath of September 11, 2001, to show that the male role is changing.

We said women's culture opposed patriarchal duality, which simplified concepts into either/or, good/bad, men/women, rather than recognizing a continuum of possibilities and diversity. This theme developed in the last decades with discussions of multiple oppressions, multiracial feminism, multicultural studies, etc. In her chapter, Susan Suntree talks about "no binaries," a blurring of personal and public, art and life, and other dualities. Although major shifts in awareness have occurred, both editions of this book stand alone in taking on the whole arena of women's culture.

We are interested in exploring women's perspective, however, since patriarchal culture expressed the male viewpoint. What are women's particular themes, images, experiences; how would culture look in an egalitarian society rather than our patriarchy, where historically art, literature, philosophy, and religion express the male view as the norm? This focus on femaleness was later negatively labeled "essentialism" (the belief in an innate and natural essence of femaleness and maleness) and used to trivialize and "kill off the

Founding Mothers" of feminist art, reports Mary Beth Edelson, one of the founders. I was interested in female archetypes and universal themes, as in the romanticization of femaleness by Mary Daly and Adrienne Rich, while now Irena Praitis notes "archetypes are not viewed as universal or evidence of a deep structure."

Kay Gardner still maintained in our recent interview that women are more in touch with natural cycles and that nature is female. The chapter on novels also focuses on women's relationship with nature. Robin Morgan observes that women writers notice more detail, as in seeing what work needs to be done around the house, and they "see the magic in the practical." Marge Piercy says hers is an "an alter viewpoint, a femalecentric narrative" and Suntree talks about the focus on intimacy and women's bodies in theater by women. Some of the essentialism remains in the essays in this book.

However, diversity, not essentialism, became the organizing principle. Most contemporary feminists are not interested in defining a basic female nature, however romanticized. Some were influenced by postmodernist deconstruction of the concept of an essential identity by French philosophers like Lacan, Derrida, and Foucault, who maintained that we are constructed by social environment. Feminist scholars of color, and lesbian theorists, took the lead in describing "interlocking systems of domination," to use bell hooks's phrase. Audre Lorde, Gloria Anzalduá, Barbara Smith, Paula Gunn Allen, and Charlotte Bunch are others who view individuals as shaped by the facets of ethnicity, class, religious background, ableism, age, and other social constructions of behavior.

Multiple perspectives are emphasized in the theater chapter (5), Kay Gardner's music chapter (7), chapter 8 ("diversity and proliferation of more perspectives"), and the theology chapter (13). In the latter, Shannon Craigo-Snell writes: "The notion of women's experience, the status of normative ethical claims, and even the belief that women can or should form a stable group, are all questioned by contemporary feminist theologians." In Boden Sandstrom's chapter, even the notion of two innate genders is questioned by transsexual musicians, and Carey Lovelace writes about Queer Theory, which describes the fluid social construction of gender's "performative character."

Women of color have started their own groups, such as The Black Women's Health Imperative, the National Latina Institute for Reproductive Health, Pro-Choice Education Project (NYC), Human Rights Coalition (D.C.), Black Women Organized for Political Action (SF Bay Area), and the National Center for Human Rights Education (Atlanta). Pioneering organizations were Hijas de Cuauhtemoc, a Chicana feminista group begun in

1971; Women of All Red Nations—1974; and the National Black Feminist Organization, founded in 1973. These organizations weren't mentioned in the 1981 edition.

In academia, black studies grew out of the Civil Rights Movement, Black Power Movement, and New Left of the 1960s and produced a proliferation of research and textbooks. Women's studies, Chicano studies, Native American studies, and Asian American studies formed using the black studies model in the 1970s. But women's studies classes are still taught from a primarily white perspective using textbooks with a token chapter on race rather than integration throughout the text, says Megan Seely, who teaches women's studies at a community college. She adds that the National Women's Studies Association has downplayed activism and overemphasized academic worth to prove themselves as a legitimate discipline.

Black feminists (Alice Walker and bell hooks) developed the concept of "womanism" to advocate the need to consider multiple layers of oppression rather than sexism as the essential oppression for white and middle-class women. This expanded into multicultural feminism, which emphasizes global politics. Ella Habiba Shohat, a professor at CUNY, edited *Talking Visions: Multicultural Feminism in a Transnational Age*.[2] As an Arab Jew who has lived in Israel, Iraq, and the United States, she has personally experienced multiculturalism. In Daisy Hernandez's and Bushra Rehman's anthology *Colonize This!*, they maintain that women of color turned feminism upside down, "exposing the '70s feminist movement as exclusive, white, and unaware of the concerns and issues of women of color from around the globe."[3] In the anthology, twenty-two young chapter authors from various backgrounds relate their personal experiences with the intersection of ethnicity, class, gender, and sexuality, similar to other young feminist anthologies.

Feminist theory in the 1970s distinguished between role socialization and biological gender, disavowing gender as essential to one's identity. An understanding of "multiple oppressions" developed in multicultural feminism and lesbian feminism, influenced by the Civil Rights Movement and the Gay Liberation Movement of the 1970s (fomented by the Stonewall Riots in New York City in 1969). Gay/lesbian studies developed in academia in the mid-1980s, followed by Queer Theory, which matured in the United States in the late 1980s, as explained in books like *Feminism Meets Queer Theory*.[4]

Lesbian feminists reacted against the social construction or manipulation of "compulsive heterosexuality," which defined heterosexuality as a biological given. They maintained that it's possible to be a "political lesbian," a "woman-identified woman," who refuses to sleep with the patriarchal oppressor. Like feminist theorists, lesbian theorists view gender as the critical factor. Queer Theory views sexuality as the key factor and wishes to separate it from gender, as in its interest in drag queens, and critiques cultural norms of acceptable sexual practices. Hence gay pride parades and resource centers include in their titles gay/lesbian/bisexual/transgender/intersexual/gender queer. But Queer Theory has been criticized for representing gay male concerns and for not being feminist.

Third-wave feminists have made diversity a central issue; they still focus on women's experiences revealed in writing, music, and art but without trying to define an essential female core. The third wave hasn't been interested in organizing national young feminist groups, although young people have been active in protesting globalism as imposed by the World Trade Organization. However, I'm surprised at their lack of campus antiwar activism about Iraq War. They are critical of large second-wave organizations like the National Organization for Women for disregarding young women's issues, although NOW has a young feminist task force.

Other themes we outlined as feminist goals and causes are still relevant and still under fire, including women's right to reproductive choice, having a self-defined rather than media-defined body image in an era when Marilyn Monroe would be considered fat, and manifesting social and political power. Most chapter authors observe that although much progress has been made, the sexist structure remains intact at its core, something many young women have not yet experienced, but will, as organizations remain patriarchal. Their lack of feminist activism is their blind spot, a view shared by the young feminist coauthors of *Manifesta* (see chapter 12).

Themes in Exploration of Women's Culture

So, have we witnessed a feminist revolution or marginalization in a "postfeminist" era? Many women have disavowed identifying themselves as feminists, but most advocate its goals, so I'm going to call it a gradual evolutionary movement forward along a continuum. Robin Morgan explains, "Women's culture had a huge explosion and then it normalized." She adds, "there's not just a third wave, but a 10,000th wave." She defines feminist energy as making connections, which indicates we won't achieve feminist revolution until governments stop solving their conflicts with war, rather than with negotiation. Z Budapest calls feminism a stealth revolution, in terms of spirituality, which occurs in the popular media, including TV shows about women with magical powers like *Buffy the Vampire Slayer* and *Charmed*.

Let's look at the themes in women's culture analyzed in the introduction to the 1981 edition, comparing and contrasting them with today's attitudes.

The following excerpt includes parts of the beginning and closing sections of that introduction. The excerpt continues to page xvi.

The first wave of American feminism began with the Seneca Falls women's rights convention in 1848. The second emerged in 1963 with Betty Friedan's book *The Feminine Mystique*. The third wave is cultural feminism, the conscious emergence of women's culture.[5] This wave is visible in women's creativity, spirituality, and relationships, and in feminist organizations. Women's culture draws inspiration from the heart and body as well as from the conscious mind. The focus is on women's experiences and expression. Women are subsumed in the cultural concept of "mankind," as history, literature, art history, and religion are about male activities, while women remain outside, classed as the "Other."[6] Female muse for the male artist, mother of a son, and the woman behind the great man: Women were identified according to the men in their lives. Excluded from much of recorded culture, women are now researching their history as well as creating contemporary environments conducive to unhampered creativity, such as women's studies courses or feminist publishing companies. Cultural feminist endeavors are revealing women's themes and images as different from men's, providing a pluralistic worldview more rich and balanced than one seen only through male eyes.

This collection of original essays and interviews explores women's unique culture. These essays are historically possible now because of the essential background of the women's movement, consciousness-raising groups, the rise of a feminist scholarship that considers the study of women vital rather than trivial, and the establishment of women's institutions. In the 1970s, women created their own institutions for publishing, bookselling, teaching women's studies, music production, filmmaking, displaying and teaching art, worship, theater, counseling, rape crisis intervention, refuges for battered women, health care, banking, travel, and farming. The Los Angeles Woman's Building is an example of an organization specifically titled an institution of women's culture—like *Chrysalis*, a magazine of women's culture. Great excitement exists among feminists about the flowering of women's culture, what Robin Morgan calls the new woman's renaissance. Some of the themes in the women's renaissance are egalitarian use of power; choices in forms of love, sexuality, and family; respect for women's experiences; reclaiming control of women's bodies; and integrative thought processes that include more than the knowledge of the conscious mind.

Growing awareness of women's restrictive sex-role socialization and of the fact that traditional studies of culture do not often include women's contributions has led to the development of cultural feminism. Cultural feminists differ from reformist or liberal feminists, who focus on political organizing, and from radical feminists, who broke away from the National Organization for Women (NOW) in 1968 over the issue of organizational structure. Radicals wanted to do away with hierarchies as well as all sex roles and gender distinctions. Writers like Shulamith Firestone and Ti-Grace Atkinson advocated entirely eradicating gender-linked roles of men and women and substituting individuals not defined in terms of their sex organs or biological functions.[7] So that there would be absolutely no roles determined by gender, Firestone advocated a society in which brooding devices would birth infants. Another radical feminist, Brooke Williams, defines cultural feminism as "the belief that women will be freed via an alternative women's culture." She believes that this ideology dominated the women's movement beginning in 1974. She faults it for not being sufficiently political or revolutionary, for selling a "happiness mystique": Goddess worship and reading women's novels do not solve men's oppression of women.[8]

In contrast to radical feminists, cultural feminists are defining differences between men and the concerns and expressions that characterize women. They believe that women have distinctive experiences and values and that these must be studied as unique contributions to culture. Women have their own social system, according to the sociologist Jessie Bernard. In an interview in which she discussed writing her book *The Female World*, Dr. Bernard explained to me:

> It became suddenly very clear to me that men and women live in different worlds. We all live in a one-sex world . . . we have clichés and stereotypes about women, but very little about the world that women live in. So that's what I've been trying to explore—the shape of it, the class structure of it, the group structure of it, the culture of it. . . . The female ethos is one of love and/or duty, one of doing for others. Cooperation rather than competition prevails. I think women are always building up people, women as well as men. They like to build up people rather than throw them down. It shows in all kinds of research in language and interaction. In conversation, the male style is someone says something and he knocks it down, it's a battle, one-upmanship all the time. Women make a statement and the other women will say "uh-huh" and build it up. They build it up together; instead of it being a battle, it's a cooperative venture.[9]

Some cultural feminists believe women have a unique way of thinking that transcends the rational and includes intuition, and draws from the unconscious, from the mystical, and from nature. A persistent theme in cultural feminist descriptions of women's orientation to the world is that it is life affirming, what the theologian Mary Daly describes as "biophilic female energy."[10] This theme stands in contrast to the patriarchal establishment of dualistic vision, which rationalizes rape of the planetary body and of women's bodies. Daly equates patriarchy with necrophilia. A striking parallel in descriptions both of matriarchies of the distant past and feminist visions of an egalitarian future is the perception of women as living in harmony with nature and receiving inspiration by way of their intuition and vision.

Feminist goals for the future are often built on an assumption that there are basic differences between men and women and that women think differently in drawing from a source deeper than the conscious mind or the linear sequential thinking of the left-brain hemisphere. Wholeness and connectedness characterize women's thinking. Whether this assumption about women's thinking process is accurate or provable, based on role socialization or genetic and hormonal differences, is not within the scope of this chapter. It is worth noting what qualities cultural feminists claim for themselves, what qualities they value. The "woman is wonderful" school, as radical Charlotte Bunch calls it,[11] has critics like Bunch, who find it unrealistic and a diversion from political activism. However, we do need to know more about what women value, since culture has been male defined for so long.

Women project their own way of relating to nature because they feel that they are more closely allied to it. "This earth is my sister," says the poet Susan Griffin.[12] "Women are daughters/lovers of the earth," says Mary Daly, asserting that female energy is "life-loving." Their connectedness with nature gives women a deeper thinking process. For example, Daly states that male "ecologists such as Barry Commoner can summarize 'laws of ecology,' but it is something else to intuit the deep mysteries." Daly seems to be affirming the folklore about "women's intuition." She describes men as thinking in a linear way, while women think in spirals, making connections between concepts where men would not be able to see them. Symbols of female ability to make interconnections are "the maze, the labyrinth, the spiral, the hole as mystic center, and the Soul Journey itself."[13]

In 1963, Betty Friedan's The Feminine Mystique named the problem that previously had no name—the malaise of housewives. She wrote that it was not neurotically unfeminine to be unfulfilled by a white wash, a polished floor, and a station wagon full of children. In doing so, she was a catalyst in bringing about the rebirth of the women's movement. One of its main tools is the consciousness-raising (C-R) small discussion group, in which women realize they are a subordinate class, socialized to be affiliational rather than achievement oriented and to fear success as unfeminine.[15] Preoccupation with physical appearance and charm to attract a husband prevents healthy self-identification and saps time and self-esteem. A reaction is seen in the feminist slogan on T-shirts: "Develop Your Brain, Instead of Your Bust."

Yet the notion of woman's happiness as found primarily in her affiliational role as wife has emerged again in the recent movement for *Fascinating Womanhood* and *Total Womanhood*, best-selling books and courses that teach a wife how to keep her man by being seductive, childishly cute and perpetually cheerful, and remaining an angelic domestic goddess. These descriptions of femininity are strikingly reminiscent of nineteenth-century ideology.

Feminists have struggled against the feminine mystique, the fear of success as unfeminine, and *Fascinating Womanhood*. They organized small C-R groups and such large networks as the National Organization for Women (1966) and the National Women's Political Caucus (1971), whose slogan is "Make Policy, Not Coffee." They have established women's studies programs (over 300 programs, 5,000 courses). Consciousness-raising encouraged women to be self-actualizing, and what emerged is the new woman's renaissance.

The rest of the 1981 chapter describes the characteristic concerns and themes that were prominent in women's culture of the 1970s:

Anger about women's powerlessness, a search for alternatives to patriarchal hierarchical power—such as collective decision making; for some, separatism as a means for gaining control over one's life; and the quest for role models of strong women—both historical and mythical.

Reaction against romantic love of the Hollywood variety; the monolith of the nuclear family as the only acceptable way of living; and the glorification of motherhood and child rearing exclusively by the biological mother, as well as a concomitant search for alternative family structures.

Respectful description of women's actual lives and experiences, as in oral histories, diaries, letters, autobiographies, and women's traditional crafts.

Reclamation of sensuality, health care, control over contraception and birthing, and free choice in sexual preference.

Emphasis on knowledge lodged in the unconscious, the right brain hemisphere, spirituality, and the occult.

Concern for wholeness and overcoming duality.

The concept of women's culture is controversial in the women's movement. Some feminists criticize it as being apolitical. All feminist women's creations and organizations, however, are parts of a woman's culture that functions with aims, styles, and images different from patriarchal culture. Women provide alternatives to hierarchical power and to thinking in dualities, which lead to rape of environment and women and to suppression of emotion, the unconscious, and the sensual. Karen De Crow, the fourth president of NOW, warned

xvi ⌢ Overview and Background

against the concept of women's culture, equating it with separatism, in her farewell address to the Detroit NOW convention in 1977. She stated that women should not build exclusive record companies, restaurants, and so on, because they provide a false security and replicate the existing male separatist world. She advocated total integration as the only viable tactic. She warned against a "pie-in-the-sky" retreat to mysticism. Radical and socialist feminists also criticize cultural feminists for retreat from the reality of political struggle.

The feminine Eros principle must provide balance if the Western world is to survive, as the technological rape of Mother Earth threatens life itself. Women's culture is a key to human survival. Awareness of women's culture is so new to us that the definition of its values and styles and the building of its institutions only began again in the 1960s and 1970s. The realization that women often compose paintings, music, and architecture differently; structure organizations differently; and have different religious and spiritual beliefs and rituals, is a far-reaching discovery. Its applications vary from pragmatic advice on how to succeed in the business world by understanding male games and rules, as in Betty Harragan's *Games Mother Never Taught You* (1977; unfortunately still pertinent), to academic analysis of the different worlds of men and women by the sociologist Jessie Bernard, to belief that the integration of women's culture is necessary for the preservation of the planet.

We are witnessing a potentially revolutionary proliferation of women's culture: films, music, magazines, presses, books, and bookstores; coffeehouses, theater groups, and credit unions; health clinics, women's centers, caucuses in academic societies, and women's studies programs; shelters for battered women and centers for displaced homemakers; and political caucuses, minority women's groups, and international feminist groups. The third wave of the women's movement provides an upwelling of the talents of half the population previously silenced by the patriarchy. We are fortunate to live in this era of the woman's renaissance.

Key Events in the Women's Movement since 1980: Mixed Results

When the first women's culture book was published, we thought progress was linear, a revolution. We didn't think the dark ages would follow the renaissance. Let's look at the backward steps, then the progress. Many of the organizations we mentioned as beacons of women's culture are no longer active, such as the Los Angeles Woman's Building, *Chrysalis* and *Heresies* magazines, Olivia Records (producers of feminist music), the Women's Philharmonic Orchestra in San Francisco, and The New England Women's Symphony. The number of women's health centers in the feminist women's health federation has declined, and so has the federation structure, as explained by Dido Hasper in chapter 15. Most of my college students have never heard the term "consciousness-raising group."

We discovered that the president in the White House sets or reflects the tone of the era. The 1980s and 1990s witnessed the ascendancy of the conservative Republican Ronald Reagan and George Bush presidencies, opposed to most of the goals of the women's liberation movement. From 1981 to 1989, the Reagan presidency opposed abortion rights and the Equal Rights Amendment (ERA), tried to restrict Title IX regarding gender equality on college campuses (mainly applied to sports), and restricted EEOC (Equal Employment Opportunity) enforcement by appointing reactionary Clarence Thomas as its head. (Thomas is now one of the most conservative Supreme Court judges.) George Bush's presidency (1989–1993) continued to oppose equality legislation, including family leave. Bill Clinton (1993–2001) didn't have much clout with Congress, although he did sign into law unpaid family leave, vetoed legislation limiting reproductive choice, and appointed Madeline Albright Secretary of State. Two women now serve as Supreme Court justices.

George W. Bush (2001–2008) transferred focus and spending from social programs in the United States to costly postwar reconstruction in Afghanistan and Iraq. His administration opposed national health insurance; U.N. policy against gender discrimination; international policies to educate women about reproductive choice; and efforts to outlaw female genital mutilation, forced child marriages, and "honor" killings as human-rights violations (at the World Summit on Sustainable Development in 2002). Laura Bush focused on reading programs while her husband cut funds for education and increased military spending and the deficit.

Politically, we've seen continued assault on access to abortion—especially for young and poor women hindered by the informed-consent laws in thirty states (they typically require listening to a lecture and waiting twenty-four hours), and 87 percent of counties have no identified abortion provider. We've not seen much change in the number of women in Congress (14 percent: 79 women out of 485 members in 2005, although this was better than the 23 women in 1981), or the top leadership of corporations (5 percent), or in the wage gap (women earned 76 percent of men's wages in 2003). A national guarantee of family leave is unpaid and doesn't apply to about half the workforce, who work for employers with fewer than fifty employees. About two-thirds of women work in traditionally female jobs that are lower paid than jobs with a majority of male workers. Women and their children make up 80 percent of those living in poverty. Sexual harassment continues on the job. Many women who bump into the glass ceiling at work leave to start their own small businesses.

The number of female ordained clergy has risen to about 12 percent, and we have women Episcopal priests; this is an increase but not equitable when women are a majority of the churchgoers. The Southern Baptists went retro and reversed approval of the ordination of women. In 2000, the leadership explained, "The office of pastor is limited to men as qualified by Scripture" (1 Timothy 2:9–14). This is similar to the policy of the Catholic Church, while priest pedophiles make the news and lawsuits drain church coffers.

In the media, popular books still teach women *The Rules* about how to get a man to propose by playing hard-to-get, although the authors claim to be feminists. Women comprise less than one-third of TV characters, fewer in leading roles. A series of films portrayed the childless woman as crazed, in a backlash against independent career women, in *Fatal Attraction, The Hand That Rocked the Cradle, The Nanny,* and *The Last Seduction.* Men bought women in *Pretty Woman, Mad Dog and Glory, Indecent Proposal,* and *Milk Money.* Reality shows like *Who Wants to Marry a Multi-Millionaire* and *Joe Millionaire* assume the man is the millionaire and women are sexy golddiggers. The television shows *The Swan* and *Extreme Makeover* provided horrifying plastic surgery makeovers. Oprah, Roseanne, Xena, Murphy Brown, Madonna, Ally McBeal, and Jennifer Aniston garnered attention, a quirky, often neurotic, set of media role models of achievement. Marge Piercy reports that the *Women's Review of Books* was the only literature review publication with a feminist perspective: "Elsewhere, no way." Susan Suntree agrees with the latter viewpoint in terms of reviews of women playwrights.

Millions of copies of the Boston Women's Health Collective's *Our Bodies, Our Selves* have been sold in eleven languages, teaching women how to be activists in their health care. The rise and fall of magazines like *Working Woman* and *Savvy* may indicate that working women are no longer seen as special. Ms. survives: Begun in 1972, its sixth and latest (2001) owner is the Feminist Majority Foundation, which wanted to make sure the voice for the feminist movement stayed alive and well. Currently, its highest percentage of newsstand sales is on college campuses, and it is sold to over 110,000 "members" who want to further the feminist community. Associate publisher Alicia Daily is a young feminist who estimates that about one-third of Ms. readers are also young. One of her goals is to return circulation to the high point of 300,000 under Robin Morgan's editorship from 1989 to 1993.

Isis Films is still active, as is Women Make Movies in New York, and the archived records of the San Francisco Woman's Building are available up to 2001. Eve Ensley's *Vagina Monologues* and *The Good Body* made millions of viewers think about women's body issues and women's ownership of their sexuality. She helped raise more than $25 million for V-Day to end violence against women. The first feminist science fiction conference occurred in 2004 in Madison, Wisconsin. The Feminist Press is alive and well in New York City, but so is discrimination in academia.

In academia, feminism became institutionalized in women's centers—about half are on campuses, and women's studies programs include graduate degrees as well as women's studies majors and minors. Scholars fussed about the "feminization" of academia as women became the majority of undergraduate students, but women academics still don't make as much as male professors on the average, and few are upper-level administrators.

Culturally, in the music world, Ladyslipper—supplier of feminist music— expanded, there's *Journal of Women and Music*, and an International Alliance for Women and Music. Lilith Fair featured all female recording stars in its concert tours. In the art world, achievements are a Museum of Women in The Arts in Washington, D.C., and Brooklyn Museum added a feminist art wing to house Judy Chicago's *The Dinner Party*. Chicago reports that the feminist art movement has become global. Feminist art radically changed the art world, proclaimed Holland Cotter in *The New York Times*, as quoted by Mary Beth Edelson.

Milestones in Feminism Since 1980

1980: The second UN Conference on Women was held in Denmark. I was there with my baby: He and his dad made local TV news with dad shown caring for his baby by himself. Most of the official U.N. delegates were men, but that had changed by the 1985 Nairobi conference.

1981: Betty Friedan's *The Second Stage* advocated that the family become the new frontier of the women's movement and that institutional restructuring, as by employers providing child care, is required to create equality between men and women. This theme was echoed in Robin Morgan's third anthology, *Sisterhood Is Forever*, to ensure "a total transformation of imbedded estrangement from women." Morgan's call for action in 2003 indicates Friedan's goal has not been achieved.

Sandra Day O'Connor became the first woman Supreme Court justice and astronaut Sally Ride was the first American woman in space.

1982: The Equal Rights Amendment died because it didn't get two-thirds of state legislatures to ratify it.

1984: Representative Geraldine Ferraro became the Democratic vice-presidential candidate. (Barbara Bush characterized her as "a word that rhythms with witch.") Emily's List started raising millions of dollars each year for pro-choice Democratic women candidates.

(continued)

Milestones in Feminism Since 1980 (*continued*)

1986: More than 100,000 marched in Washington to protect abortion rights. The Supreme Court defined sexual harassment as a form of illegal job discrimination under Title VII, which prohibits job discrimination.

1987: Ellie Seal, former president of NOW, founded The Feminist Majority Foundation.

1989: A TIME/CNN poll found the most important issues to women are equal pay, child care, rape, maternity leave, and job discrimination; even now they remain problems.

1991: Anita Hill accused Supreme Court Justice nominee Clarence Thomas of sexual harassment. The negative reaction of the Senate generated feminist activism. Senator Alan Simpson referred to "this sexual harassment crap" and Senator Arlen Specter accused Hill of "flat-out perjury." Senator Orrin Hatch said her allegations didn't "square with what I think is common experience." Representative Pat Schroeder commented, "People saw for the first time what a lot of us have been trying to tell them for years; this place doesn't get it."

1992: Susan Falud's book *Backlash: The Undeclared War on American Women* was a surprise best seller that also renewed interest in feminism.

1993: President Bill Clinton signed off on the Family and Medical Leave Act as his first act. The 103rd Congress passed thirty-three bills for women's rights, due to the presence of forty-eight women in the House and six senators, following "The Year of the Woman" with its high point of numbers of women candidates for political office.

1995: The fourth UN Conference on Women was held in Beijing, including 30,000 representatives of nongovernmental organizations. The platform maintained that women's rights are human rights, which seems obvious but has been another ongoing struggle in international organizations that maintain outsiders should not criticize social rituals such as female circumcision.

2001: President Bush appointed conservative *Bushwomen* (the title of a 2004 book by Laura Flanders, Verso) to important posts, including National Security Adviser Condoleezza Rice (who became Secretary of State in 2005), Karen Hughes as press secretary, and heads of three departments.

2004: March for Women's Lives, with 1.15 million protesters, the largest march ever held in Washington, D.C., was organized by a coalition of women's groups including The Feminist Majority.

Can you think of other recent milestones for equality? I couldn't, which either means the feminist revolution has succeeded or that it has slowed down as people pay lip service to its goals and conservatives marshal attacks on reproductive choice, ordination of female clergy, and other backlash actions.

Young Feminists

My experience with young women rests in the university classroom, teaching decades of women's studies courses. To generalize, most enter the classroom with the attitude, "I'm not a feminist but I believe in equal rights," an observation confirmed by young feminists I interviewed. I don't know of any young women who are going to college to get their "MRS degree," looking for a prince of a husband to take care of them. However, they associate the term feminism with man-hating and unfeminine appearance. Latina Roxanne Damask, age twenty-two, reports that her cousin told her, "I can't believe you're a feminist; they hate being a woman." She replied, "that's what people would like you to think." The exception I see is young women raised by feminist mothers who proudly proclaim themselves feminists. Students usually think the era of gender inequality is over and that women have equal opportunity with men.

Women's unassertive language style indicates lower self-esteem than men. Women, as linguist Deborah Tannen describes in her books, use more tag questions (huh? yeah? OK?), questioning inflection, talk less than men in mixed sex groups, and are less likely than men to monologue. The editor of the *Young Women's Handbook: Beyond Surviving in the 90s*, Naiad Moritz, reported, "If there is one common theme in these essays, it's a fear of our own expression. . . . Because we are young and female . . . we write with many question marks . . . we need to trust ourselves more." That pattern has continued in my women students' oral communication.[14]

The only established organization for young women is The Third Wave, organized by Rebecca Walker (daughter of writer Alice Walker) and Shannon Liss in 1996, with a part-time staff person. Amy Richards was also a leader, tired of not being called on in second wave groups who "weren't necessarily willing to let young women be leaders in the way that I think was needed." Third Wave has led some national activities, starting with a 1992 voter registration drive called ROAMS (Reaching Out Across Movements), adding an annual tour to meet with social justice organizations to share strategies, and public education campaigns such as "I Spy Sexism" and "Why Vote?" But it seems mainly localized in New York City. The Third Wave's mission is to conduct public education campaigns and provide technical assistance and funding to projects for young women, including leadership training, small business loans, and college scholarships. In 1997, it changed its name to the Third Wave Foundation.[15]

Second wave groups realize they need to reach out to young people. NOW is the largest feminist organization, with around 500 chapters and a Young Feminist Task Force (www.now.org.issues.young/taskforce/yf.html). The Feminist

Majority's Campus Leadership Initiative focuses on college students, with the "world's largest pro-choice student network"(www.feministcampus.org). NAR-RAL (National Abortion and Reproductive Rights Action League, founded in 1969) is active as well. Young feminists are leaders in other reproductive choice and health groups, including Choice USA, begun by Gloria Steinem, with campus groups and a young president. This group hosted young women-led groups, which gathered before the 2004 March for Women's Lives and included the National Latino Institute for Reproductive Health, Third Wave, and Pro-Choice Public Education Project.

College students have founded local groups such as Voice, Fearless, Womanish, and Students Organizing Students to confront date rape, biased curricula, eating disorders, violence with self-defense, homophobia, etc. Some high school groups have been formed, including FURY and YELL (see my *The Teen Trip: The Complete Resource Guide*). These groups communicate through a loose network of Internet sites and newsletters.

Holly Morris explains differences between second and third wave feminists on the Internet:

> We were raised on pop culture . . . and pop tarts, not pop political movements. We know computers, not the Dewey Decimal System, divorce not devotion—Email, gang-rape, rage, websites, and the Webster Decision, androgyny and AIDS, Bikini Kill and the battered women's movement. We know there is no one-way to be; we embrace multiplicity and contradiction. We know about harassment and rape. We know how empowering fun can be. We know that feminism lets us know ourselves; and we know it has a history and a legacy. It used to wear petticoats but now it can wear ripped jeans and publish zines, or it can wear reinforced power suits that bust through glass ceilings. It can be heterosexual, homosexual, or bisexual, and most importantly, just plain sexual. Somewhere within this splintered kaleidoscope we exist.[16]

She adds that the media portrayed feminists as "bra-burning, granola dykes in the 70s; power-hungry, ruthless business women in the 80s; and in the 90s we are lipstick lesbians, do-me feminists."

I interviewed young women leaders on the telephone in 2004, asking about differences between second and third wave feminists. They agreed that young women take for granted rights their mothers and grandmothers fought for in the streets, courts, and legislatures, leading to complacency and lack of activism, especially during the Clinton years. Generation Y is not thinking about political change for equality—as indicated by being the age group least likely to vote—but personal change. Perhaps generational rebellion against the mode of the older generation is inevitable.

High school NOW club copresident Alexandra Such (age eighteen) reports: "In many classrooms and homes, students are taught that the fight against inequality has already been waged—and won. They don't see the patent sexism and racism which still afflict our country, and therefore, feel no need to fight against it." Many of Megan Sealy's Sacramento community college students are also apolitical and don't vote. She thinks the power elite wants and manipulates this disengagement.

"It took a few dangerous laws to wake us up," reports a representative to the NOW young feminist task force. George W. Bush's attack on reproductive rights galvanized them, as evidenced by the biggest ever March for Women's Lives (April 2004), many of them young. Three participants I talked with estimated that 20 to 50 percent of marchers were young adults. This was also the most diverse of marches, including a large delegation of people of color. Marchers protested the White House's "war on women," including the 2003 law banning second trimester abortion (where the fetus is removed by dilation and extraction partially intact) even if the health of the mother is at stake. This law was the first to threaten doctors with punishment for a federal crime and was blocked by a court order. The FDA didn't allow teens under sixteen to buy emergency contraception without a prescription in 2004 (mifepristone was finally approved in 2000, after being used in Europe for years).

Other setbacks were cuts in funding for family planning and sex education, withholding funding from the United Nations Population Fund, global gag rules about informing women about reproductive choices, major concern that the five to four majority of Supreme Court judges who favor abortion rights will be switched by the appointment of one new antichoice judge by George W. Bush in 2005, and his support for a constitutional amendment to ban same-sex marriages. More acts undermining women's rights are listed on www.nwlc.org/pdf/AdminRecordOnWomen2004.org.

Increasing global awareness galvanized some young women. Crystal Lander, twenty-nine, Campus Program Director for the Feminist Majority Foundation (FMF), reported that she's surprised at how college students make the connection with global issues, such as health problems and lack of access to birth control, because of college training and the Internet. The campus program began in 1997. Currently Lander works with a staff of nine for 146 campus groups, which she thinks is the largest of any feminist organization. They educate students about feminism by wearing "This is what a feminist looks like" T-shirts, etc. They emphasize leadership and organizing, providing an annual leadership training conference and ongoing support to campus groups. Lander says the main problem for young women is that they don't have organizing tools. Her organization is also working on a "Get Out Her

Vote" campaign. Other "huge" young feminist issues are date rape and campus assault, according to Megan Seely. At twenty-eight, she became the youngest president of California NOW, after serving as the first president of the young feminist committee in 1999.

Young women are critical of second wave leaders for ageism, not listening more, and not being respectful enough, probably a typical reaction of the younger to older generation. Seely explains that an intergenerational conflict exists between second and third wavers as they learn to share leadership: "Young women don't want to be seen as only the future leaders because we are here now with ideas and vision to contribute." Crystal Lander agrees that the biggest problem for young women has been lack of opportunity in feminist leadership and that "a bit of ageism goes on" as young women feel their ideas are left out. She organized a hip-hop event as part of a Feminist Majority conference, to counter the idea that feminists can't have fun. (Roxanne Damask notes that hip-hop includes Queen Latifah and Missy Elliott and has crossed cultural borders, including Spanish feminist musicians.)

An activist who does not want her name used, Ms. X, twenty-three, has friends whose "great ideas for political activism were not what older feminists were used to; they were met with hostility and dropped out. A lot of younger women don't want to be degraded and insulted for being young upstarts; they would rather take abuse from men at work. A lot of younger women are feminists but don't call themselves that, they're not comfortable in an intergenerational movement." She doesn't think there will need to be a fourth wave because the third wave will "tie up the loose ends in the struggle for equal rights, pay equity, child care, and health care."

Marie Hammer attended the NOW annual convention in 2003 and reported on the Internet: "Young feminists stood up to proclaim the feminist movement was not helping them on their college campuses. They complained that NOW's leaders were out of touch with the issues they were facing. . . . [They were] angry because the feminist movement was not giving them the respect and responsibility they felt was deserved."[17] Second wave leaders, such as Kay Gardner, feel young women don't know or appreciate their foremothers who opened the doors for them.

This anger is a "generation war," writes Megan Austin, who explains on the Internet, "There are few generalizations you can make about young feminists, except that our feminism is likely to be idiosyncratic, even contradictory, and we prefer it that way. It isn't just irony and lipstick that separate us from Second Wavers: It's an entire continent."[18]

Young feminists like Ms. X see themselves as more media savvy, more familiar with technology and the Internet, such as Third Wave using the Web to get donations. Some of her friends were working as field organizers for a NOW chapter that used a card system for recruiting. When the younger women suggested creating a database, they were told, "we've always done it this way." Online organizing is so prominent (e.g., moveon.org), because people are so busy, so activism needs to adjust to the realities of people's lives today, says Megan Seely.

To counter this generation gap, NOW established a Young Feminist Taskforce, which held its first meeting in 2004, with twelve representatives, including one high school student. Alexandra Suich cofounded a NOW club at her high school in San Francisco. She reports that only about half the participants in the club refer to themselves as feminists (and about 25 percent are guys), as the label doesn't jive with a "sexy attractive image." They've had to do a lot of education to make people realize "you don't have to be incredibly radical to believe in women's rights." At the national task force, Suich reported, "The goal was to meet each other, to advise the national board in terms of our needs and agenda, and share experiences." They were advised by Megan Seely, head of California NOW, and national officers and discussed "internal racism, ageism, helping NOW to keep young feminism in mind," said Ms. X.

Young feminists fault second wavers for racism, paying lip service by installing some women of color in leadership positions (two of the four NOW leaders, none of the top leaders, but three directors at the Feminist Majority in 2004), but not really listening or being sensitive to the issues of women of color. "They're making steps, but not gigantic ones," reports Ms. X. For example, the first title for the April 2004, march was March for Freedom of Choice. But she says there's no translation of that term in Spanish, and women of color don't have choice about access to good child care, health care, family planning clinics, and economic justice, so they pressed for the title to be more inclusive. That conversation should have happened five months earlier, she said. A lot of her friends are bitter; they don't think there's enough progress, as in getting support from white feminists to challenge hip-hop misogyny or to support the Million Women March.

To attract more members of color, NOW has a diversity coordinator, but Latina Roxana Damas, who began a local chapter in Northern California, feels "they're so busy putting it on paper, there's not enough action." When she brings women of color to local NOW meetings they often say they don't feel acknowledged or included after the initial greeting. Only five women of color were represented on the one-hundred-person contingent to the March, and she didn't feel women of color were included socially. She is a Diversity Delegate to the state NOW's Diversity Committee, and applied for the new

Diversity Field Director position. She believes, "Diversity needs to be included in everything we do, using different languages, until we have the numbers we need, not just talk."

Megan Seely, the state president until 2005, observes, "In terms of multiplicity, young activists don't simplify gay/straight, but include transgender, bisexuality, intrasexuality, queer, and questioning. Being more inclusive, they don't engage in the same power plays." (For example, when The Third Wave Foundation announces scholarship recipients in their newsletter, they are identified by ethnicity, age, and sometimes sexual orientation, as in "Julie is a 21-year-old gender queer/boy-dyke.") "They're not concerned about who is going to be the next Gloria Steinem, but rather support multiple leaderships and varying perspectives. Diversity and multiculturalism is central to third wave feminism, as is the inclusion of men in the movement." See Seely's book *Fight Like a Girl* for more explanation.[19]

When I asked Anastasia Higgingbotham, who works for Girls, Inc., in New York City, if young feminists were as concerned about structure of group dynamics as second wavers, she said:

> We have a continued desire not to have stars. Amy Richards worked with *Ms.* and Gloria Steinem throughout her 20s. She has a column called "Ask Amy" on www.Feminist.com/askamy. She puts people in touch with each other, a little powerhouse in the movement now. She is published with Jennifer Baumgardner as her writing partner (they're in their early 30s). They empower women by connecting people with people other than themselves. A clearinghouse, they let you know someone is doing this same thing in another area. They're very aware of what's going on outside their neighborhood. They started a company called "Soap Box," a speakers' bureau for feminists. They send their acquaintances out to speak. That's the model I want us to follow.

Richards believes that the most important issue for her generation is the lack of participatory democracy in the United States. She would like to see more people voting as a step forward; the swing voters courted by politicians in the 2004 elections were single women nonvoters who say they're too busy to participate.

Culturally, young feminists have written self-published zines (underground self-published, often autobiographical chap books by teens and young adults, including Internet zines; http://grrlzines.net/resources/femorgresources.htm); anthologies of their personal experiences; magazines like *Riot Grrrl*, *New Moon*, *Teen Voices*, *Sassy*, *Bust* (which began as a zine) and *Jane*; and music lyrics by the female bands' Riot Grrrl movement of the early 1990s. Band members wrote song lyrics, and started zines and websites, which dealt with issues like childhood sexual abuse, where teens could share their experiences. A 1990s Washington, D.C., newsletter stated,

> Riot Grrrl is about changes. . . . You don't have to take shit from anyone. Be who you want, do what you want. Don't be pushed to the back of shows if you want to be in the front. Don't stop doing something just because someone says you can't do it, or doesn't encourage you. Go skateboard, write a zine, form a band. Make yourself heard!

Anastasia Higginbotham explained to me in 2003, "Riot Grrrls are not as active, but "grrrls" has taken off. Third Wave and V-day are good at marketing themselves. The website Feminist.com has pretty wide impact; it's linked to all kinds of resources."

Higginbotham reviewed *Girls' Guide to Taking Over the World: Writings from the Zine Revolution* (1997) for the *Women's Review of Books* and wrote a chapter for *Listen Up: Voices from the Next Feminist Generation*, whose essays have similar themes to the zines. When I asked her about zines, she said:

> They're compelling, although hard to get a hold of. Distribution is to their friends, grass roots, underground, word of mouth, Internet sites, their own websites, a lot of word of mouth; "Send a dollar and I'll send you another zine." I see centers of activity in Seattle, San Francisco, and New York City.
>
> Themes include focus on body image, sexuality—including sexual orientation, abuse, incest, and exploration. The revolutionary aspect is challenging the way they were raised, repressed, told to feel shame. Because of second wave accomplishments, the third wave writers have a high level of sophistication about the intersection of various oppressions: class, income level, race, sexual orientation. They understand these concepts as some girls studied feminism in high school, but more in college classes. Mothers also taught their daughters about sexism.
>
> I like that they take equality for granted, but don't like that feminism is still seen as something to distance yourself from, attacked as man hating. This reaction taps into the internalized misogyny of the culture, so that something explicitly pro-female is shameful or embarrassing. We feel embarrassed about how angry we feel about doubting ourselves more, how we work harder for self-confidence, drive, and entitlement that white males feel.
>
> Sexual preference is more fluid, less categorical than for older women. For example, spin the bottle has become a game that girls play, as girls crossed that line within the last 10 years. Media figures have influence, like Ellen De-Generes and Rosie O'Donnell coming out, Madonna's bisexuality, or Ani DiFranco's music about bisexuality.
>
> The authors tend to be older college and post-college women, but the themes still stem from their personal history that emerged in childhood. A significant

number of zines deal with the underbelly: alcoholism, sexuality, sex abuse. In the ones that stand out, the tone is looking straight at the underbelly with a courageous steady eye that people would ordinarily turn away from. They deal with trauma and oppression with a clear confident gaze.

Third wavers have also developed magazines with large circulations, as Higginbotham explains:

> Bust magazine started in the early 1990s. It's feminist but very playful and sexy. It's like Ms. but appeals much more to the daughters of the second wave generation. It's more absurd, more jovial, irreverent. It's more biting, very pro-sex, pro-girl, trying to reclaim pink and sparkly nail polish. You can wear wonderbras and still be a feminist. Bust tries to make feminism palatable by emphasizing health and liking men. I appreciate the fun of it; it highlights that feminism is all about options; you can wear mini-skirts.
>
> They started Bust when they were in their 30s, girlie feminists. Another magazine that I think is better, less slick, funnier and smarter is Bitch. It's been out since 1996. They hate Jane magazine which is an attempt to be a smart, sexy, slick magazine, although it's more expressively feminist than Cosmo, and takes for granted we should be treated as equals, be equally involved. Bitch has a column called "Jane: Petty Criticism Corner." Pamela Anderson does a column for Jane. Jane is successful, Bust is fairly successful, and Bitch has a smaller readership. Bust and Bitch are more political.

A third wave theme is acceptance of a continuum of behaviors rather than a dualistic this or that category, such as bisexuality. Young people were raised with MTV gender-bending music stars, men wearing makeup, and Madonna publicly kissing women. Charlie's Angels star Lucy Liu was quoted in Jane magazine as saying in 2003, "Sometimes you just fall in love with somebody, and you're really not thinking about what gender or whatever they happen to be." Ariel Federow, a feminist at age eighteen, reports on the Internet, "Saying that men have power and women don't is awfully binary, and I'm anti-binary gender construction."[20] She does refer to herself as a feminist.

One of the best-known Generation X authors was Susan Faludi, who wrote Backlash in 1992, while in her twenties. She traces the backlash against women's advancement after every era of success. Naomi Wolf wrote The Beauty Myth (1992), when she also was in her twenties, criticizing the way the popular culture oppresses women with its unrealizable beauty standards (even top models don't look like their airbrushed and carefully lighted photographs). These were familiar themes to second wave activists. Wolf commented on suppression of female sexuality in her 1997 book Promiscuities and on the generational shift from second to third wave, urging young women to assert their power in *Fire: The New Female Power and How It Will Change the 21st Century* (1993).

Third wavers have written a number of anthologies, focusing on the variety of their personal experiences. Again a major theme of third wave books is honoring diversity, refusing to lump women in a category. We read often about the bisecting effects of ethnicity, class, sexual preference, and religious upbringing, in addition to gender. The first anthology was Paula Kamen's *Feminist Fatale: Voices from the "Twentysomething" Generation Explore the Future of the Women's Movement* (1991). Rebecca Walker's *To Be Real: Telling the Truth and Changing the Face of Feminism* (1995), followed. Walker notes in the introduction that she at first felt guilty about editing such an apolitical book of memoirs.

Published the same year was Barbara Findlen's *Listen Up: Voices from the Next Feminist Generation*. The twenty-eight young writers discuss their concerns about underemployment, eating disorders, racism in the women's movement, AIDS, family, etc. Two years later Leslie Heywood and Jennifer Drake edited *Third Wave Agenda: Being Feminist, Doing Feminism*. They include male authors, indicative of the third wave's reluctance to make men the enemy. They explore ways to incorporate beauty and power in activism. *Bitch* magazine commented on the book: "These girls have theory and they know how to use it—while having a good time, of course."

Third wavers have a sense of humor and style that contrasts with the seriousness of second wave leaders, who didn't publicly emphasize having a good time or refer to women as girls. I asked Anastasia Higginbotham about this:

> We take ourselves seriously but have taken it further by trying to adapt the message with more humor and playfulness; this can be subversive. Although the media didn't portray it, second wave feminists were funny with each other; I think of Gloria Steinem, Flo Kennedy, and Bella Abzug, but the default reaction to feminism was to tell them to lighten up.

Third wave feminists have a different sensibility, states Amy Richards, in contrast to the second wave focus on legal equality. In *Manifesta*, excerpted in this book, Richards and Jennifer Baumgardner say they and others call "the intersection of culture and feminism 'Girlie.' Girlie says we're not broken, and our desires aren't simply booby traps set up by the patriarchy."[21] They maintain that reclaiming "girl culture" and "bitch" is empowering. (An appendix to their book contains resources for contemporary feminists, including organizations and publications.) They add, "Although the issues facing the second and third wave are similar [in correspondence to me, Richards gave examples of access to welfare, violence, and birth control], sometimes we differ in our approach and our expectation. Because we grew up in the wake of the second wave, we were afforded more opportunities and feel entitled to want and ask for more." Her generation has great feminist writing and music but is less interested in politics, notes Baumgardner.

This is the deficiency of this generation, from my second wave perspective. But, "We've produced the most uppity generation of young women in history," concludes Gloria Steinem, who adds that her generation should enjoy them and learn from their willingness to deal openly with conflict.[22] Betty Friedan observes, "They take nothing for granted and are advancing the cause with marvelous verve." We can expand our horizons, using third wave non-dualistic kaleidoscopic perspective, one of the goals outlined in 1981. Our concept of women's culture now is much different than the one we defined and explored for the first time in 1981, as young feminists develop "Girlie Culture." Read on to discover the changes and to decide whether a feminist revolution has occurred when women occupy such a small percentage of political and economic power. E-mail your thoughts to gkimball@csuchico.edu.

Biography

Gayle Kimball, Ph.D., taught women's studies courses for decades and is the author of ten books and numerous videotapes. She travels worldwide teaching "energy tools" to develop the power of the mind. Her books include *Essential Energy Tools: How to Develop Your Clairvoyant and Healing Abilities*, *21st Century Families*, *How to Create Your Ideal Workplace*, *50/50 Marriage*, *50/50 Parenting*, *Everything You Need to Know to Succeed After College*, *Women's Culture: The Women's Renaissance of the 70s*, *The Teen Trip: The Complete Resource Guide*, and *How to Survive Your Parents' Divorce*. gkimball@csuchico.edu; www.gaylekimball.info

1. Faith Wilding, *Where Is Feminism in Cyberfeminism?*, www.obn.org/cfundef/faith_def.html.

2. Ella Habiba Shohat, ed., *Talking Visions: Multicultural Feminism in a Transnational Age* (Boston: MIT Press, 2000).

3. Daisy Hernandez and Bushra Rehman, *Colonize This! Young Women of Color on Today's Feminism* (New York: Avalon, 2002).

4. Elizabeth Weed and Naomi Schor, eds., *Feminism Meets Queer Theory* (Bloomington: Indiana University Press, 1997).

5. Ann Pride (editor of KNOW Press). Speech to National Organization for Women Conference, Philadelphia, October 1975.

6. Simone de Beauvoir, *The Second Sex* (New York: Vintage, 1952), 57.

7. Shulamith Firestone, *The Dialectic of Sex: The Case for Feminist Revolution* (New York: Bantam, 1971); Ti-Grace Atkinson, *Amazon Odyssey* (New York: Links, 1974).

8. Brooke Williams, "The Chador of Women's Liberation: Cultural Feminism and the Movement Press," *Heresies* 3, no. 1: 70, 71, 72.

9. Jessie Bernard, interview by Gayle Kimball, May 1979; Jessie Bernard, *The Female World* (New York: Free Press,1981).

10. Mary Daly, *Gyn/Ecology: The Metaethics of Radical Feminism* (Boston: Beacon, 1978), 352.

11. Jessica Benjamin and Lilly Rivlin, "The deBeauvoir Challenge: A Crisis in Feminist Politics," *Ms.* 7 (January 1980): 51.

12. Susan Griffin, *Woman and Nature: The Roaring Inside Her* (New York: Harper & Row, 1978), 219.

13. Daly, *Gyn/Ecology*, 400, 401, 410, 414. See Gayle Kimball, *Feminist Visions of the Future*, videotape.

14. Naida Moritz, *Young Women's Handbook: Beyond Surviving in the 90s* (Washington, DC: Institute for Women's Policy Research Young Women's Project, 1991.)

15. ThirdWaveFoundation@aol.com.

16. At http://mcnary.blogspot.com (accessed September 8, 2003).

17. At www.thestranger.com/2001-05-10/feature2.html

18. At www.wigmag.com/word/holly_morris_3_18_2201.html

19. Megan Seely, *Fight Like a Girl* (New York: New York University, 2006).

20. At www.thestranger.com/2001-05-10/feature2.html

21. Jennifer Baumgardner and Amy Richards, *Manifesta: Young Women, Feminism, and the Future* (New York: Farrar, Straus & Giroux, 2000), 136.

22. At www.virginia.edu/insideuva/2000/31/steinem.html

PART ONE

VISUAL ARTS

∼

CHAPTER ONE

Shaking the Ground: Women's Visual Culture Several Decades Later

Carey Lovelace

No doubt, feminism has changed society—it has changed art absolutely, although some may deny this is true. Veterans of the trenches bemoan that few museums have staged exhibits highlighting 1970s' landmark achievements; they lament how young women seem to be repudiating activism. And given the early pioneers' sweeping goals, a letdown was inevitable—holding that a matriarchal utopia would overthrow corrupt male domination, female deities supersede the male, that women together would forge a kinder, gentler art world.

Yet look around, and everywhere women—and the thought behind the art they make—have changed art-world attitudes in ways subtle and profound. Even in this seemingly reactionary era, the one called "postfeminist," themes whose roots lie in the efforts of early activists have infiltrated work by both genders. In fact, feminism has had an impact much broader than early proponents ever dreamed.

Not that there hasn't been a self-destructive streak. Women with common aims who should have been downplaying differences, joining energies against a common enemy, instead attacked each other. In the 1970s, those who early on committed themselves as "feminist" artists maligned other women working in "neutral" styles; trying in good faith to make a mark within the art world they denigrated them as "male identified." In the 1980s, so-called academic feminists—heavily influenced by French poststructuralist theory—in turn condemned as "essentialist" activist forerunners who had bled for the cause because they sought to and "empower" women without critiquing deeper forces

at work within society. Yet despite quibbles, together warring factions have created a tidal wave of energy overwhelming the art world, forcing, reshaping,
shaking it through the very force of the collective *weltanschauung* of women—
not that the doors haven't sought to slam shut against it again.

In the 1970s, progress by women was palpable, dizzying. There was activism and collective effort, demonstrations; new genres (e.g., craft-based
art), materials (e.g., the female body itself), and institutions (e.g., the alternative space) were pioneered. Dorothea Rockburne, Jackie Winsor, Mary
Miss, Alice Aycock, and Lynda Benglis rose to career prominence alongside
male colleagues, proving they could create sculpture as hefty, painting as
edgy, and media work as technically advanced. Courageous activists Mary
Beth Edelson, Miriam Schapiro, May Stevens, and Joyce Kozloff formed politically oriented groups agitating for greater gallery representation, redefining plastic creation. A well-educated generation of women was suddenly
muscling into a world where previously less than one in twenty artists in serious galleries were female.

For centuries, society had denigrated women's efforts, dismissed them as
not "good enough." Around 1971, pioneering art historians like Linda
Nochlin, critics like Lucy Lippard, and artists like Faith Ringgold began to
question whether "good enough" wasn't merely an excuse to suppress what
was simply another point of view. Women began not only to claim their own
place but to do the inconceivable—question long-held assumptions within
art. They questioned what "genius" consists of, whether the avant-garde necessarily consists of a single reigning style, which moves to the fore, over-
throwing a previous style. Couldn't several coexist simultaneously?

Some, notably Craig Owens in his noteworthy 1983 essay "The Discourse
of Others," indeed credited women with launching postmodernism itself, the
weltanschauung that has dominated serious culture for the last two decades or
more.[1] He held that this act of questioning sowed the seeds of doubt that
eventually undermined the foundations of modern art (which, in its demise,
was rechristened "modernism"), causing it to topple. Modern art had seen itself as an ever-upward-moving evolution full of aspirations. Impressionism,
cubism, surrealism—each succeeding style moved toward a state of purified
consciousness, feats of transcendence undertaken by geniuses. But, women
asked, couldn't many styles exist simultaneously? And was the "purity" that
modern art seemed to be moving toward necessarily the optimum? What
about autobiography, emotion, old-fashioned representation?

Yet it was precisely at the turn of the decade that the 1970s' triumphal
march and the woman-friendly climate stopped dead. "Feminism panics the
mainstream," art historian Ellen Phelan has observed.[2] In happened almost

precisely at the turn of the decade—Reagan was elected in the United States, Thatcher in England. A "backlash" period arrived, also bringing a new embrace of materialism, cynicism, and a new class striving. An ostensibly enlightened post-Vietnam generation of male artists, many taught in art schools by 1970s feminists, made their mark, with paintings often encoding sexist messages. David Salle, for example, specialized in arch "postmodern" paintings that were a pastiche of images, some troubling: charged images of, say, a naked woman in painful or degraded stance (dressed as a dunce or crouched doggie-style) positioned next to abstract stripes or other patterns. In these works, which sold for high prices, one meaning seemed to be that all imagery is equal. The decade saw dazzling major surveys like London's 1981 A New Spirit in Painting and Berlin's 1982 Zeitgeist. Their rosters included no women, or perhaps one "mascot" (usually, figurative painter Susan Rothenberg, until she began refusing the favor, at which time the designated female became surrealist abstractionist Elizabeth Murray).

Postmodernism customarily is characterized by a use of pastiche, irony, collage, and an antiheroic attitude. The 1980s favored theory over direct political engagement. Many women believed hard-fought political gains over the last decade were permanent and that a new spirit of engagement had been launched; they were profoundly disheartened by how quickly the ERA was abandoned, the degree to which 1970s activism was disowned by young women rejecting what became the dreaded "f" word.

Postmodernism purported to grapple with inequities in a more sophisticated way, deploying a critique of information received, usually subliminally, from institutions of power—the media, corporations, even art itself. Ironically, during this 1980s backlash, when women were shut out from the halls of power, they were among the most celebrated practitioners of what became known as the postmodern critique; not surprisingly, for the techniques of probing behind power had been incubated in the women's movement. For example, Jenny Holzer's *Truisms* (1979–1983) (Abuse of Power Comes As No Surprise, Humanism Is Obsolete) were displayed, as her reputation grew, in LCD lights in Times Square or along the rampways of the Guggenheim Museum. They were phrases mimicking the tone of authority. They were sisters to her *Inflammatory Essays* (1979–1982), phrases on handbills posted on the street, themselves like spears of anger aimed at the patriarchy. (Don't Talk to Me. Don't Be Polite to Me. Don't Try to Make Me Feel Nice. Don't Relax. I'll Cut the Smile off Your Face).

Attacks on 1970s progressivism, and the women who practiced it, came not just from "backlash" sectors of the art community, but from a new generation of feminists. In their 1981 now-classic book *Old Mistresses*,[3] respected

British art historians Rozsika Parker and Griselda Pollock launched a critique of first-generation art feminists, asserting that activists' claims of "progress"— increased gallery representation, women-oriented genres, new art-world clout—were not borne out by the evidence. Yes, they wrote, female students had flooded into universities, but the percentage drifting up into art's upper echelons still amounted to little more than the tokenism of the past.

Instead, they proposed that attention was being directed to the wrong problem. The solution to inequity was not through the acts of morale building that 1970s feminists specialized in. They held that the problem was deeper. In the late eighteenth century, just before the Victorian age, the two wrote, a sentimentalized "ideology of the feminine" developed, involving notions of female delicacy, frailty, and emotionality, distinct from "masculine" qualities. These stereotypes were promoted as "eternal" qualities, imbedded almost structurally in social thinking. By celebrating "womanhood," women's studies programs, female form languages, even when the attempt to identify historical role models were seen as playing into the patriarchy's hands, reinforcing misconceptions about an unchanging female "essence."

"Essentialism" was the unflattering formulation that theoretical feminists began to apply to the approach that they saw consciousness-raising, morale-building precursors adopting in promoting "women's culture." It was applied in particular to pioneer Judy Chicago, notably to her controversial installation *The Dinner Party* (1979), thirty-nine plates on a monumetal banquet table celebrating historic women from Isis to O'Keeffe, each shiny porcelain vessel featuring sculpted "vaginal" imagery rising up relief-like from the surface in an effort to valorize female agency. But "essentialism" was also applied to "goddess" movement searching through mythology, archaeological prehistory for empowering archetypes) and even to art historians looking for forgotten women creators. As a counter example, antiessentialists proposed Mary Kelly's magnum opus *The Post Partum Document* (1976). It was a text-and-photo mixed-media piece, a massive collection of material that documented the first five years of Kelly's son's existence—charts, diary entries, even samples of the baby's stains on diapers. It sought a new mode of portraying female existence, consciously avoided representing the female at all. And it was hailed by "antiessentialists" for its unusual approach to representing female experience, for "refusing to put the mother on view, as object and spectacle."[4] It sought to address an aspect of child development, within a neo-Freudian framework, ignored in psychoanalytic texts, the cathecting, operations of emotional transfer, of the mother psychologically onto the son.

In the ironic mid-1980s, challenging, complex intellectual theories (ironically, all developed in the idealistic 1960s and 1970s) began emigrating from

Paris via London into North American universities. Baudrillard, Derrida, Foucault, Lacan, and Barthes were the hot names of the 1980s, their theories about language, the body, perception, drives, and social and conceptual structuring coming from re-readings of Freud, de Saussure, and Levi-Strauss. Lying at the base were insights developed in the 1950s by structuralists such as Jean Piaget, which held that the mind perceives, and language is structured, according to paired opposites: black/white, rise/fall, heaven/hell. In the pair, one term is favored, good over bad, strong over weak—or male over female. Therefore, that "female" will be the "inferior" part of the pair is built in. According to deconstructionists, it is only by exposing the system's mechanism that one can obtain release, freedom, and equity. Thus, in Barbara Kruger's photo-based work featuring a classical female bust, *Your Gaze Hits the Side of My Face* (1981), the title phrase is applied over this classical rendering of the female. Thus, in a deconstructive act, it decodes, points to, the act as it occurs.

The notion of "the gaze" was to prove pivotal. It was drawn from a construct that in the 1980s had the largest impact of anything that was to hit the art waves that decade—British-bred Laura Mulvey's concept of the "masculine gaze," first proposed in her essay "Visual Pleasure and Narrative Cinema."[5] Mulvey speculated that we experience Hollywood movies (in fact, any visual narratives) identifying with the male point of view, that "woman" is the passive subject of an active male "gaze," and that (adopting a Freudian perspective) pleasure comes from filmic tension stemming from castration anxiety, male potency constantly under threat in subliminal ways, which is relieved by fetishizing female characters.

Thousands of art works, articles, and Ph.D. theses have used the platform of formulation concerning the "gaze" as a springboard for wide-ranging, often enlightening analyses of gender/power relationships beneath visual communication, both in art theory and in artworks themselves. In her celebrated *Untitled Film Stills* (1977–1980), Cindy Sherman famously illustrated gender/power relationships, in black-and-white photos like publicity shots taken from movies showing the sexualization of film melodrama, using elaborately staged self-photographs, fake film scenarios depicting young females in moments of heightened drama. In one, a foreign film-style ingénue stands next to an unlit hearth, crotch level, smoking a cigarette with sultry suggestiveness; in another is a housewife, with tousled hair, whose bag full of groceries has just spilled beside her, as she herself has tumbled on the floor.

Sherman's acts of Hollywood dress-up also exemplified another concept that advanced to the fore in the theory-heavy 1980s—somewhat linked to Pollock and Parker's theories—that "womanhood," rather than a fact of biology, is a construction of society, a kind of masquerade.

Barbara Kruger, "Untitled" (Your gaze hits the side of my face), 1981, 55" x 41". Courtesy Mary Boone Gallery, New York

One theorist who had a huge impact was the controversial neo-Freudian psychoanalyst Jacques Lacan, known not only for a huge following but also for a hermetic writing style whose obtuse language itself seemed to embody his philosophical observations in formulations like "The Law of the Father" and "the Mirror Stage." He developed theories about the intersection of psychology with culture stemming from Freud's ideas about castration anxiety, intertwining this with structuralist theories about language—that the structure of language determines the way we think. For Freud, of course, the penis, the phallus, was supreme; all early child development was seen in relation to this body part, described, of course, from the little boy's point of view. Paradoxically, given the highly phallocentric bias of his thought, a group of French feminists sprang up inspired by his approach—also in opposition to it. In using Lacan's approach, viewing the development of language as interwoven with primitive bodily experience, Luce Irigaray, for one, proposed that "women's desire most likely does not speak the same language as men's desire," that women, with a different genital reality, may have their own distinct way of perceiving. In her landmark "This Sex Which Is Not One,"[7] she observed that women have multiple potential sites of pleasure in the body, in distinction to the male's unitary focus; this leads to a more pluralistic, heterogeneous approach to perception—and to artmaking too, perhaps.

Second wave theoretical feminism penetrated North American campuses around 1985. It rapidly overwhelmed university discourse, dominating it for the next decade, building an exotic vocabulary—differance, jouissance, "writing the body," "gendered space," closure, rupture—an enclosed, self-referencing system defying translation into everyday language. Again, it was believed, it is only through the "critique," the deconstruction, the decoding of the phallocentric moments of language, that energy can be released. But academic feminism always seemed enclosed in aspic of pessimism, an unforgiving prissiness. Purporting to tackle sexism at its root, at times it seemed an excuse for inaction—battling images and sentences rather than the more difficult, threatening events in the world.

In the mid-1980s, however, just when things seemed darkest, the activist generation was to regain its voice. The groundwork was laid by a mysterious event. In 1985, posters began appearing on the streets of Soho, New York's art district: "Women in America Earn Only 2/3 of What Men Do/Women Artists Earn Only 1/3," and "These Galleries Show No More Than 10 Percent Women Artists or None At All." An anonymous group of artists and art professionals, the Guerilla Girls had banded together in response to the Museum of Modern Art's 1984 International Survey of Recent Painting and Sculpture. In that exhibit, of 169 artists only 13 were women; curator Kynaston McShine remarked that any artist not in the show should rethink "his" career. Appearing in public in gorilla masks, the "conscience of the art world" launched a campaign of satirical, accusatory graphism, as well as panel appearances, staged presentations, books, even a movie. Although it wasn't realized at the time, this marked the beginning of a neofeminist movement that was to peak in the mid-1990s.

Even within the reigning conservative climate, issues relating to women's victimization—rape, incest, abuse, eating issues—gained traction, fusing with the sudden rise of twelve-step programs focusing on "recovery." French writer Julia Kristeva's theory of the abject became fashionable, "degraded" aspects of bodily experience—the grotesque, putrid bodily fluids—perceived as a space, as she wrote, where subjectivity dissolves, having to do with the child's differentiation from the mother. Body art, notably Kiki Smith's enigmatic, painful, often life-sized sculptures, resonated with themes of abuse—for example *Tale* (1992), in which a woman is on all fours, a line trailing out of her anus for yards like fecal matter, blood.

And there was Nan Goldin's autobiographical, diaristic slide show, *The Ballad of Sexual Dependency* (1980–1986), which launched her career as a chronicler of the demimonde, and Sue Williams's angry, cartoony paintings wailing out her humiliating experiences as a battered woman. After eight years of the Reagan age, then four of the first Bush presidency, conservatives continually chipping away at abortion rights and affirmative action, finally, art-world women couldn't take it any more. In the spring of 1992, in New York, they gathered en masse to launch WAC (Women's Action Coalition), a lively group that seemed eventually to include every downtown woman from art star to neophyte. Its "WAC Attacks" protested court cases, pornography suits, the Republican convention, an all-male Guggenheim exhibition, and much else.

An early 1990s generation of neofeminists were to turn away from East Village–style angst. Janine Antoni created works of wit and satire, such as *Gnaw* (1992), a huge minimalist cube of chocolate chewed at the edges, making reference to eating disorders. In *Loving Care* (1993) she "painted" the floor in large "Action Painting" swirls with her own hair dipped in dye, works that paid tribute to the political wit in women's body art of the past, while gently mocking the male artistic canon. A sassier, in-your-face "Bad Girl" art arose at the same time, such as Zoe Leonard's 1992 "intervention" at Documenta IX, in which she removed rococo paintings of men and landscapes in a Kassel portrait gallery, replacing them with graphic black-and-white photos of female genitals, views reminiscent of Courbet's *Origin of the World*. WAC died out not long after Bill Clinton was elected president,[6] to be reborn (as described in Edelson's chapter), and so did neofeminism a few years later.

In *The Second Sex*, Simone de Beauvoir undertook a profound inquiry into the implications of women being marginalized as the Other. Once that idea had been digested, it was but a small shift to see how other nondominant groups and races and become the "Other" as well, demonized, stigmatized. "Multicultural-ism" gained currency in the late 1980s. At first it merely involved exhibiting artists of varying ethnic backgrounds together. By the 1990s it had evolved into something more elaborate and focused, "identity politics." Adrian Piper was one of its signal practitioners, starting back in the 1970s, creating performative works examining racial stereotypes. Her video installation *Cornered* (1988), for exam-ple, showed the artist in white pearls sitting at a desk addressing the viewer in a schoolmarmish tone about how African blood runs in the veins of many "white" people, then citing a list of one hundred possible reactions to that statement.

Likewise, in Renée Cox's large-scale Cibachrome *The Yo Mama* (1992–1997), in which she staged herself naked as biblical characters in al-most cinematic tableaux, she satirizes the myth of the black superwoman. (In one Yo Mama photograph (1993), she holds a male baby against her torso, creating the form of a cross.) But just as feminism panics society, the fusion of femaleness and blackness hits society's panic button even more: a self-depiction as Jesus at the Last Supper (1996) almost got a Brooklyn Mu-seum exhibit including the work shut down by then-Mayor Rudolph Giu-liani. Yet in identity politics work by African American women—Lorna Simpson, Lorraine O'Grady, Tracey Rose, and Carrie Mae Weems—feminist concerns take a back seat to race and living as topics of examination.

Meanwhile, even at this late date, feminism remains demonized in most parts of the world, although there are periodic surges of acceptance. As Is-lamic fundamentalism gains a grip in many societies, a few brave women dare to speak out, at risk to their lives. Mexican journalist Cindy Gabriela Flores remarks that in Latin America "very few women are willing to pay the stigma [sic] for being feminists." Even in France, the label is so pejorative, many feminists decline to use it to describe themselves.[7] Nonetheless, starting in the 1990s, art collectives sprang up in Taiwan, India, Poland, Estonia, and Mexico. A sophisticated global feminism has developed as artists trained in North America or Europe began making work exploring Third World issues. In her series *The Women of Allah* (1994), for example, the remarkable Shirin Neshat began exploring the Islamic sect of martyrdom in large-scale photos depicting herself in a chador, brandishing guns. The surface was covered with a scrim of Farsi text. In *Speechless* (1993), what looks like earrings near the face of a veiled woman turn out to be gun barrels aimed at the viewer. The

Renée Cox, The Yo Mama, 1993, 82" x 47". © Renée Cox. Courtesy Robert Miller Gallery, New York

Iranian exile began had developed two-screen, black-and-white video installations with lush musical soundtracks, featuring men and women in traditional, almost medieval, garb in epic short encounters dramatizing the separation of the sexes in Islamic culture—*Turbulent* (1998), *Rapture* (1999), and *Fervor* (2000).

Shirin Neshat, Speechless, *1996, 46 3/4" x 33 7/8". RC print (photo taken by Larry Barns). Courtesy Barbara Gladstone*

From the lowest ebb of the Reagan 1980s to the post-Clinton pinnacle in 2001, women made enormous inroads on a practical level, garnering higher and higher-visibility museum shows, female art professionals rising into increasingly important posts—although none is yet at a top spot, at least as of this writing. Even during the depressing Bush II years, when fears of terrorism have been fanned to create a renewed cult of masculinity, an atmosphere favoring political regression and fostering younger women have vastly more opportunities than did their forerunners. In the 1990s generation, sexual freedom, self-determination, and career opportunities—which include the freedom to choose motherhood as a career—were taken for granted; solidarity with other women was the norm. Nonetheless, women-bashing has seeped back into culture. It may date back to 1993, when the Whitney Museum hosted what was dubbed the "political" biennial. It featured not only many artists doing identity politics (William PopeL. handed out buttons, "I'm Ashamed of Being White"), but also many of the most ardent neofeminist Bad Girls. Nicole Eisenman did a mural commissioned by the museum featuring angry Furies dismantling the building, and Sue Williams did an installation featuring a plastic "pool" of vomit. The exhibit was roundly vilified in the press, women in particular being accused of wallowing in "victim art." Many of those women henceforth began withdrawing from exploring explicit political content.

In place of activism, artists turned to transgression, doing works intending to shock—art featuring dead animal carcasses and strange sexual mutations. Women artists began venturing into dangerous territory, dealing with the eroticized female body—subject matter long a feminist taboo. Painter Lisa Yuskavage, for example, deploys Old Master bravura to paint buxom female nudes. Her pendant painting *Night and Day* (1999–2000) features nubile young women admiring their bodies, teasing the viewer the way a painting seduces, and was inspired by a porno photographer Yuskavage admired. Such works have been castigated as pandering to male lechery, yet her explorations are much more nuanced and even often autobiographical, her big-breasted women seeming uncomfortable in their bodies, trapped in their fleshiness.

At the turn of the millennium, vanguard females seemed to be flirting with and embracing stereotypes once reviled as dangerously degrading: "girly" femininity, dress-up, applied makeup; in short, sexual "display behavior." Vanessa Beecroft was reviled as politically regressive for her performances involving squadrons of whippet-thin naked models in Gucci high heels. Another view might be that postfeminists are involved in an act of recuperation, maintaining their position as autonomous creators while reclaiming "off-limits" imagery, proclaimed taboo by feminist precursors, examining how inherently dangerous it truly is. In an empowered age, women enter male territory as subjects rather

Lisa Yuskavage, Manifest Destiny, 1997–1998, oil on linen, 110" x 55". Courtesy Marianne Boesky Gallery

than objects, as active participants, keeping in control of "the gaze." Pipilotti Rist's video *Pickelporno* (1992), for instance, depicts an erotic encounter between an Asian man and European woman. Played out against a syrupy, pop-music-based soundtrack, lovemaking gains in imagistic fervor—bodies swimming through space amid what seems like lush greenery. Almost imperceptibly, the encounter is seen from the female's point of view; she seems the initiator, the male is the Other, passive and receptive as the female's hand moves over him. Artists like Rist are stealth feminists, making sure that the specter of female power and control remains nonthreatening. She deploys series of sugary female stereotypes–the ocean, flowers, nature, cheerful colors—all the while keeping hold of "the gaze."

Even progressive sectors of society manifest ambivalence about feminism and would rather change the subject completely. One promise of the Internet was its potential to create a neutral space, disembodied, hence beyond race or gender. Performer/activist Coco Fusco has created digital performances such as the twelve-hour Net-broadcast about surveillance, *Dolores from 10 to 10*. As Fusco points out, as the Internet is created by men and dominated by corporate interests, how "neutral is this space truly?"[8] Cyberfeminism, the attempt to see the gender politics within this space, had its official start in 1992, with the Australian collective VNS Matrix. This unruly group, using a vocabulary reminiscent of rowdy early feminists, crafted a raw manifesto proclaiming intent to insert "women, bodily fluids and political consciousness" into "masculinist" electronic spaces. Then in 1997, at the first international cyberfeminist conference in Germany, came the Old Boys Network, an ironic if confusing moniker, which forges links with cells of women around the Internet, drafting its 100 Anti-Theses of Cyberfeminism.

The cybercollective subRosa's cofounder is Faith Wilding. She was a member of Judy Chicago's very first 1971 Cal State Fresno class of young women first exploring agit-prop performance, and thus present at the birth of feminist art itself. Ever since, she has been about the business of raising consciousness on society's margins, now moving into the digital center. SubRosa stages actions concerning digital and reproductive technologies. Its *US Grade AAA Premium Eggs* (2002), at Bowling Green State University, was drawn from actual websites involved in the trade of human gametes, tissues, and organs. Students could "Calculate Net Worth on the Flesh Market," to see how valuable their eggs and other organs were. (Non-Caucasians, artists, or "not a normal woman," although genetically undesirable, can still make money selling their organs, subRosa's site points out.)

Women's studies programs begat "gender studies," which begat gay and lesbian studies, which in turn begat Queer Theory, the academic study of all behaviors perceived to be outside a mainstream norm. Just as the academic "social constructivist" school held that femininity is societal fabrication, queer theory elaborated on Michel Foucault's theoretical insight that gender is at base a kind of performance, that identity is fluid.

In the same spirit, transgender performance seeks to make feminism obsolete. Tobaron Waxman is a transgendered male now engaged in an undercover, and dangerous, effort to train as a Hasidic rabbi. Many younger artists explore the fluidity of identity, such as Korean-born Nikki S. Lee, who uses snapshots to document her life performances in which she integrates herself completely into various groups—sexy Latinas, teenage (male) skateboarders, "flannel" lesbians—in each instance convincingly adopting their dress and personae, blending into each community. Thus, in the last twenty plus years, the notion of what it means to be "female" has been submitted to the most profound examination possible, but the conundrum remains. Ever since its outset, feminism has stirred deeply negative feelings.

Since the 1980s, doors of opportunity have opened, prejudices have been smashed, female art stars' careers have been built, hundreds of books have been written, historical role models have been celebrated, and women's points of view—whether "socially constructed" or feminist-activist—increasingly have been absorbed into culture. In the 2000 to 2001 art season, according to the guide printed in *The New York Times*, remarkably, the number of one-person U.S. museum shows for living artists was for the first time evenly split between males and females, with about a third being for artists "of color"—although that number has fallen back in subsequent years. Spurts of feminist activism over the last decades have allowed women to forge enduring connections with one another. The art world has also become more integrated, more tolerant of multiplicity, more complex, with a more pliant view of identity, more sensitive to how notions of "quality" can be used to buttress an ideological point of view.

A fear of women always lurks below society's surface, as made clear by the virulent hatred that has resurfaced with fundamentalist Islam; one is constantly reminded how fragile progress is. Magazines like *Time, Newsweek,* and *The New York Times Magazine* periodically print articles—in which one discerns a hope—proclaiming that young women are turning away from feminism, repelled—although they never truly do. Certainly, twenty-something artists, with their memories of riot grrrl, "bad girl" feminism from their youth, use feminist themes; issues of the body, repression, relationships, run throughout young women's work. But they seem blurry about what feminism is and are reluctant to identify themselves as such.

Inequities remain. And it remains to be determined whether "femaleness," and indeed whether all identities, are a performance deployed to satisfy society's expectations, or truly a biological state of unchanging difference. Meanwhile, though, small insights have become earthshaking, reverberating into the future, their full impact yet to be fully known.

Biography

Carey Lovelace has written for *Art in America*, *Ms.*, *Newsday*, *Performing Arts Journal*, *Millennium Film Journal*, *ARTnews*, *The New York Times*, the *International Herald Tribute*, and many other publications. She is copresident of the AICA-USA, the U.S. chapter of the International Art Critics Association, and is also an award-winning playwright whose works are frequently produced in New York and elsewhere.

1. "The Discourse of Others: Feminists and Postmodernism," in *The Anti-Aesthetic: Essays on Postmodern Culture*, ed. Hal Foster (Port Townsend, WA: Bay Press, 1983).

2. "Survey," in *Art and Feminism*, 32 (London, Phaidon Press, 2001), 32.

3. *Old Mistresses: Women, Art, and Ideology* (New York: Pantheon Books, 1981).

4. Ibid, 164.

5. In Luce Irigaray, *This Sex Which Is Not One*, trans. Catherine Porter (Ithaca, NY: Cornell University Press, 1985).

6. "Cyberfeminism and Art in Latin America: Pending Fusion," *Cyberfeminism: Special Issue*, at www.artwoman.org 7. Elaine Marks and Isabelle de Courtivron. *The New French Feminisms: An Anthology* (New York: Shocken Books, 1981), x.

7. Cindy Gabriela Flores, July 2002.

8. Coco Fusco, "At Your Service: Latin Women in the Global Information Network," in *The Bodies That Were Not Ours and Other Writing* (London: Routledge, 2001).

~

CHAPTER TWO

Feminist Art:
Interview with Judy Chicago

Gayle Kimball

GK: You've written ten books, including a 1996 update of your life as a woman artist in *Beyond the Flower*, a sequel to *Through the Flower* (1975). Update us again.

JC: A big change in my life and career began with the UCLA Armand Hammer exhibition in 1996—Sexual Politics: Judy Chicago's *Dinner Party* in Feminist Art History—curated by Dr. Amelia Jones, a young art historian who's an expert on feminist art of the 1970s. The show contextualized *The Dinner Party* in twenty years of feminist theory and practice and included the work of fifty-five other feminist artists. In both the exhibition and the accompanying catalog, the international impact of *The Dinner Party* (1979) was examined. The show seemed to usher in a new evaluation of my work; before that it was mostly critical hysteria from both mainstream and feminist critics, probably because when *The Dinner Party* first premiered, there was no real context for it from the perspective of the mainstream art world.

This exhibit was followed by an enormous number of exhibitions of my work—the *Holocaust Project* (1985–1993) was already traveling and continued to do so until the end of 2002. In 1999, a works on paper retrospective was organized by Dr. Viki Thompson Wylder (a scholar on my oeuvre) that traveled for several years to eight museums. My most recent collaborative project, *Resolutions: A Stitch in Time* premiered at the Museum of Art and Design in New York in 2000 and was then toured by them to museums around the United States Also that year, *Judy Chicago: An American Vision* by the internationally known British art writer Edward Lucie-Smith was published. This was the first comprehensive book about my work to appear. In 2002, the National Museum for Women in the Arts (in Washington, D.C.) mounted a career survey show

Judy Chicago, Home Sweet Home. *From* Resolutions: A Stitch in Time, *sprayed acrylic, oil paint and embroidery on linen, 24" x 18". © Judy Chicago, 1999. Needlework by Pamella Nesbit. Photo © Donald Woodman. Collection: The artists.*

almost simultaneously with the Brooklyn Museum's acquisition and exhibition of *The Dinner Party,* which will be followed by its permanent housing in 2007.

These exhibits helped to change the critical climate for my work and, of course, the permanent housing of *The Dinner Party* has been a lifelong goal and will help to accomplish my determination to counter the ongoing and repeated erasure of women's history. Women's achievements have been erased again and again, often within decades of their achievements. At the Brooklyn Museum *The Dinner Party* will be the centerpiece for the Elizabeth A. Sackler Center for Feminist Art, which is now in its planning stages. Elizabeth has been col-lecting my work since 1998 and she acquired, then gifted, *The Dinner Party* to the Brooklyn Museum.

The terms of the acquisition of *The Dinner Party* will provide me a modest income during my lifetime and the bulk of the money will then go to Through the Flower, the small, nonprofit organization that has provided a framework for my participatory projects (I have also often produced individually created works as well as innumerable studies for my major projects). It is primarily be-cause of Through the Flower that *The Dinner Party* toured the world and re-mained safe after more than two decades. Through the Flower, which came into existence in 1978 in order to help me complete *The Dinner Party*, became crucial to its future as well as to my own ongoing artmaking.

GK: In the original chapter, you said, "'The Dinner Party' is either the great-est thing I've ever done or the biggest white elephant." Which is it?

JC: A little of both there for a while. Although *The Dinner Party* is now charac-terized by many art writers as a major monument of twentieth-century art, I of-ten feared that it would be a white elephant because its future was so uncertain. I was desperately afraid that it would end up repeating the story of erasure that it recounts, which might have happened had Elizabeth Sackler not intervened. She not only preserved *The Dinner Party* but also demonstrated the critical im-portance of patronage for feminist art, of which there is still way too little (pa-tronage, that is; there is a lot of feminist art now all over the world). I don't think *The Dinner Party* is necessarily the greatest thing I've ever done, though there are certainly some who would argue with me. In my own view, *The Dinner Party* is only one work in my large and evolving body of art. But it's the work of mine that has most captured the popular imagination. Since then, both my work and I have evolved though I have not swerved from my feminist philosophical base.

GK: How do you define feminist art?

JC: It's women centered or at least sympathetic to women. I say that because it's possible for men to make feminist art in that feminism is a philosophy that challenges the hierarchal system of values that now dominates our planet. Men are at the top of the hierarchy, of course, and white men at its pinnacle. Fem-inist art is oppositional in that it challenges the prevailing values, speaks from other points of view, remakes the world in the image and likeness of those far-ther down the hierarchy (for example, reconfiguring the divine in terms of women or people of color, as done by artists like Monica Sjoo, Yolanda Lopez or Romaire Beardon). Feminist art is content driven, which is one of the rea-sons the art world has had difficulty in defining it. It's not stylistically similar like, for example, abstract expressionism. Also, the art world is uncomfortable with content-based art in general.

Moreover, from the point of view of the mainstream art world, feminist art was something that happened in the United States and maybe Britain in the seventies and now that we live in a "post-feminist world" (an absurdity) is passé. But actually, feminist art of the seventies stimulated a worldwide feminist art movement in all the developed and developing countries of the world. The end of the twentieth century ushered in a momentous change in that, for the first time, women were able to begin to express themselves freely in visual art—and the end is nowhere in sight. But because what women do continues to be devalued, this historic change has not yet been thoroughly acknowledged, understood, or integrated into the ways in which we see and evaluate art.

GK: What are you seeing in young feminist artists?

JC: There are a lot of kickass feminist artists around the world but at the same time, a lot of these young women don't want to call themselves feminists. And of course even while I am saddened by this, I also understand it. When I was a young woman at UCLA, I didn't want to be identified with women, I wanted to be taken seriously and thought that the only way to do that was to hang out with the guys. I didn't want to have anything to do with the two tenured women faculty artists who were there (that was two more than there were to be for many years after they retired). Although I had what could be described as a proto-feminist consciousness, whenever I would protest what was clearly sexist behavior toward me, I would be asked, "Are you some kind of suffragette?" "No, no," I would answer as I certainly didn't want to be identified with those harridans presented by history in such an unattractive way (if even mentioned at all). So I understand young women's reluctance to identify themselves as feminists. Feminism is a no-no, it's been demonized by the media. But this prohibits women from identifying and building on the gains of the past.

GK: What's your current thinking about innate female imagery? Is the difference just socialized or is there something more?

JC: Although there was this ridiculous period in feminist theory in which I was characterized and castigated as an "essentialist," I always knew that the construct of femininity (as it's now called; we used to call it female role) was culturally constructed; I even said that it was hard to know what was nature and what was culture. However, I probably disagree with some of the theorists in that I don't think it really matters; what is important is being able to overcome those aspects of the femininity construct that retard our development as full human beings.

GK: Your art is intended to create social change. What have you heard from people who view your art?

JC: Apparently, it has had an enormous impact; we hear all the time about how seeing my art or reading my books changed people's lives. Although I doubt that there is a direct correlation between art and social change, art can certainly contribute to a transformation of consciousness, to critical thinking, and to challenging widely held assumptions. For example, like me, a lot of women were brought up with the idea that women contributed nothing signif-

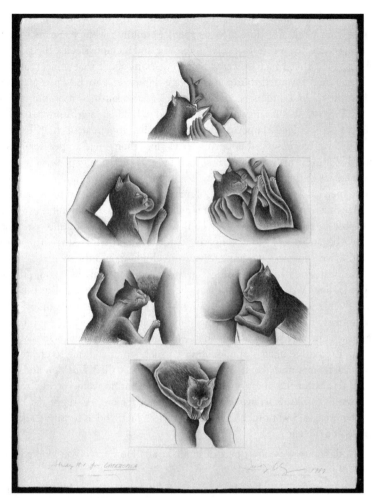

Judy Chicago, Study #1 for Caterotica, *watercolor on arches, 22" x 30".* ©
Judy Chicago, 1999. Photo © Donald Woodman. Collection: the artist

icant to the history of Western civilization. Through visual form, *The Dinner Party* challenges that view, offering an alternative perspective that asserts the many ways women have contributed to history. When viewing *The Dinner Party,* many women awakened to the realization that what they had learned was wrong. Such an insight can lead to further critical thinking, which can lead to freedom. Similarly, in the *Birth Project* (1980–1985), the images challenge the prevailing attitudes that what women do isn't worthy or important in that it celebrates women's generative and creative abilities, which are denigrated in most societies.

GK: In *Powerplay* you explored the subject of masculinity.

JC: *Powerplay* was an investigation of the gender construct of masculinity. I undertook that work after fifteen years spent examining what it means to be a woman, physically, psychologically, spiritually, and metaphysically. By the early eighties, I felt that I had answered many questions about that subject, at least for myself, and I wanted to expand my gaze. However, I found *Powerplay* very frightening to do. I understood that I was going up against a lot of internalized taboos. Virginia Woolf said women are trained to hold up larger mirrors to men. The art historian Paul Harper said that historically, women artists have been far more willing to present themselves as victims than men as perpetrators. I worked alone on this series for many months: I was very angry personally about how men act in the world. It took me a while to get past that and ask what was behind men's rage and emotional dysfunction. Then I realized that men are allowed such a narrow range of emotions and certain areas of vulnerability are entirely prohibited them. I'm sure anybody would get angry if not allowed to cry. I slowly began to feel more sympathetic toward men while still angry about what they've done and are doing to women, children, and the world.

It was just when I was finishing *Powerplay* that I met my husband, photographer Donald Woodman. He's always been a rebel, was a radical in the antiwar movement. Although he is macho in some ways, there are many other ways in which he does not fit into the male role—and he wanted a relationship in which there was room for that. At some point he mentioned that men see few alternative images of masculinity, which stimulated me to create a series in cast-paper and also in bronze. This image is called *WoeMan* and is intended to answer the question posed by Freud, what do women really want? I don't really think it's so mysterious, at least not for me. As suggested by the *WoeMan* images, I want men to be as strong as a man and as sensitive and vulnerable as a woman.

GK: Collaboration is often part of feminist art. How have you worked with groups of people?

JC: As I mentioned earlier, I've gone back and forth between collaboration and individual work. In my group projects, people work on my images, which brought me some measure of criticism in part because we don't have many models that aren't authoritarian. Consequently, many people could not imagine a structure in which I retained aesthetic authority while at the same time providing ample space for collaboration and input. And unlike many other contemporary artists whose work is done collaboratively (much of Warhol's work, Christo's installations, Rauschenberg's prints, or Chilhuly's glass pieces) I scrupulously credit everyone who works with me. Nevertheless, I got criticized and their noncrediting methods are never even questioned. This probably illustrates the old adage; no good deed goes unpunished. Anyway, although there was a lot of misunderstanding about my collaborative methods in the past, some of that misunderstanding has changed—but not all, probably because old canards die hard.

GK: Sometimes in feminist groups anger surfaces at the leaders, because it's a safe place to vent.

JC: Although that happened to me at first, it hasn't happened to me in years. First, in my collaborative projects, I now select people who have worked that out with me already. If they haven't, they don't last long. Also, in my projects, people have to work. Anger can be used to fuel creativity but if it's not, it can become self-destructive and immobilizing. That's why in my projects, we focus on work, not on feelings. Not that we prohibit the expression of feelings, not at all—but it's always in a context of work. Are your feelings getting in the way of your work? If so, why? And how can that be changed?

GK: No feminist art education has filled the void created by the end of the Feminist Studio Workshop and the LA Woman's Building.

JC: That is one of the reasons I returned to teaching in 1999. I teach one semester or quarter a year at different institutions, where I try to introduce feminist art pedagogy, which is aimed at empowering students so that they might flourish as artists in an art world that is tough for everyone and especially for women. I've been giving a lot of thought to the subject of feminist art education and how it can be made more widely available—not only to women but to

"Since 1996 Judy Chicago has been working in watercolors." Looking at the Los Lunas Hill from the North, *watercolor on arches, 22 1/2" x 30". © Judy Chicago, 1996. Photo © Donald Woodman. Collection: the artist*

men as well. In 2001, Donald and I team-taught at Western Kentucky University, where we facilitated a project for both female and male students (men amounted to about one-third of the students, which is as many as can be in a feminist environment before male-dominant tendencies take over). We reexamined the subject of the home thirty years after *Womanhouse* (the first female-centered installation, created in L.A. by my Feminist Art Program at Cal-Arts). Before this project, I worried that men's presence would interfere with the women's freedom of expression, but that proved not to be true. On the contrary, the emotional openness of the women provided an environment in which the men felt safe to be more honest. It was great.

However, I don't want to underestimate the problems in trying to introduce feminist pedagogy into our educational institutions, the same problems I had teaching feminist art at Fresno State and Cal Arts in the 1970s. You're an isolated spot in the mainstream paradigm. How to change this situation seems to be one of the challenges ahead.

Biography

Judy Chicago is an artist, author, educator, and intellectual whose career spans four decades. Her art has been exhibited throughout the United States and Canada, Europe, Asia, Australia, and New Zealand. In addition to a life of prodigious artmaking, Chicago is the author of eight books and the subject of three books, including *Judy Chicago: An American Vision* (2000) by Edward Lucie-Smith. Her most recent book, a suite of prints, *Fragments from Delta of Venus*, is an homage to her mentor, Anais Nin. In 1996, the Library on the History of Women in America at Radcliffe College became the repository for Chicago's papers; she is the first living artist to be included in this major archive. Her major projects include *The Dinner Party*, executed between 1974 and 1979 with the participation of hundreds of volunteers, the *Birth Project*, *Powerplay*, the *Holocaust Project: From Darkness into Light*, and *Resolutions: A Stitch in Time*. Throughout her career, Chicago has remained steadfast in her commitment to the power of art as a vehicle for intellectual transformation and social change and to women's right to engage in the highest level of art production. In 2007, the Brooklyn Museum will become the site of permanent housing for *The Dinner Party* as the centerpiece of the Elizabeth A. Sackler Center for Feminist Art. Judy Chicago lives in New Mexico with her husband, the photographer Donald Woodman, and their beloved cats. Visit the Through the Flower website at www.judychicago.com.

~

CHAPTER THREE

Success Has 1,000 Mothers: Art and Activism from Mary Beth Edelson's Point of View

Mary Beth Edelson

First Coming, 1970s

A woman has no place as an artist unless she proves, over and over again, she won't be eliminated.

—Louise Bourgeois

Dismantling the Master's House with Women's Tools

The 1960s were zero hour before feminism and the 1970s were feminism. Starting from scratch, we sought to formulate the issues to frame the politics of feminism(s). The 1970s were an exceptional time when studio practice, community activism, art history, and criticism momentarily converged. Women came together, giving their time and energy to a revolution that permeated every aspect of our daily lives, providing a future for women artists that could previously only have been imagined.

In my case, as an artist and activist deeply implicated in all of this, two recurring themes were my body and creating the politics of feminist spirituality. I referred to my body as a "found art object" with the intention of morphing it into "the subject" that I could then use as a "starter" to set in motion building feminist issues as I saw them. In the past thirty years my work has focused on visual presentation of women with power, including addressing cultural assumptions about bodies, agency, sexuality, the sacred, and human liberation on all counts.

Much of Edelson's early work found roots in the dialogue she was instrumental in developing on the subject of the Goddess that concerns the implications of organized religion for women at the same time it invites direct female access to the divine. By not separating the politics of human rights from the spiritual or from contemporary creative ritual. Edelson presents both an offer and a challenge. . . . Indeed, a critique of women's subordinate status in the history and structure of religions and a concern for women's spirituality constitutes one of her main contributions to feminist aesthetics.[1]

Notes on This Goddess Thing

I used the construct of Goddess as a blank slate that could be written on, and this platform offered a framework for dismantling the master's house with women's tools. Within this context emerged a playful, irreverent muse, who had many names, for presenting a strategic women's spirituality while challenging the dogma of organized religion. If She were there at all, She would emerge as we constructed our ever-changing sense of ourselves.

Mary Sabbintino, director of Galerie Lelong, recently asked me if I would like to be in an exhibition titled *Goddess at Galerie Lelong*. I didn't know whether to laugh or cry, so charged was her suggestion that it was time to bring back the Goddess. But she was correct that the cycle had come around again. I have been asked to define Goddess on various occasions—a dicey

Mary Beth Edelson, Body Performance, ed of 15, Grapceva Cave, *1977. Hvar Is., Former Yugoslavia*

project at best. In 1989 I offered this groping personal definition that I continue to alter:

> SHE is, for me, an internalized sacred metaphor for an expanded and generous wisdom that respects all peoples. SHE is alive and evolving in contemporary psyches as well as being an ancient, primal, creative energy in both women and men that embodies the balance of intellect-body-spirit. SHE sees clearly unacknowledged radical truths in accepting both the dark and light sides of the way it is and yet SHE does not forget to be playful. Dogma is an anathema to HER. HER presence is inconstant when SHE is scorned, but when embraced SHE manifests in dynamic, nonhierarchical networks of cooperative relationships that include actively working for human liberation.

How many twists and turns this Goddess odyssey has taken over the years—and how utterly unforeseeable were the punishing and ecstatic events that knowing Her brought my way. Had enough time lapsed for an objective critical reconsideration of this Hot Mother, who scares the living hell out of those who see her as a Monster and has such power that, in the words of writers J. C. Smith and Carla J. Ferstman, "If SHE appeared what you felt about HER reflects who you are"[2]? Suppositions about Goddess can be equivocated with attitudes in many cultures about women as unclean, unholy, and uncontrollable. Such assumptions are embedded in all patriarchal religions and in the contemporary psyche of those who have not confronted them.

A Fast-Forward Evolution

What unfolded in a short period of time in the early 1970s was a fast-forward evolutionary process that facilitated the feminist movement becoming an experimental laboratory. One of the enterprises was producing spirituality invented by women who fully understood the political implications of this proposal and then communicated it to others. This project was prompted at first by individual women already on this track with years of research behind them (e.g., Merlin Stone's *When God Was a Woman*, 1976) and who were also active in their local feminist communities. It is generally agreed that this investigation into the sacred grew out of the feminist movement and began synchronistically on both the East and West Coasts in the United States around 1970, and by the mid-1970s, was recognized as a movement. Important collective events and publications in the early years included the first national women's spirituality conference organized by Pomegranate Productions, a collaborative group in Boston, attended by 1,800 women from around the country. It was at this first spirituality conference that we realized, for the first time, how many of us there were, and that we already occupied some common ground. Where else would you find women spontaneously stripping to the waist and dancing on a cathedral altar while the other women formed a bare-breasted snake dance up and down the aisles? We already shared a tolerance for diverse points of view, so the plan was not to make one. We felt free to reference other religious practices if it suited us as well as Jung, Graves, Gimbutus, and at least the books listed in the bibliography. Our common practice was ever-changing ritual. Three other conferences followed: Staten Island, New York; Santa Cruz, California; and the conference organized by Gayle Kimball titled "Feminist Visions of the Future" in Chico, California.

The early core Goddess Group in New York that regularly met during this formative period were architect and professor Mimi Lobel, artist and writer Buffie Johnson, writer Merlin Stone, teacher Rosemary Dudly, folklorist Kay Turner, and Mary Beth Edelson. This group instigated producing the influential *Great Goddess* issue of *Heresies* magazine, with each woman contributing an article to the issue. (Some of their other publications on goddess/spirituality related topics are in the bibliography.) By the time we moved into the 1980s, bookstore shelves were stocked with volumes on the topic as it went mainstream.

During workshops and conferences in the 1970s, spirituality feminists who were also activists discussed the need for a less contentious and more self-analytical way of interacting while mobilizing for political action. The importance of good working relationships was obvious when we became bogged down in miscommunications that consumed both energy and time and therefore interfered with getting on with the task at hand. The sustained models to evolve from experimental spiritual processes included performative creative ritual, going around the circle sharing feelings, and multistage consciousness that also provided a broader, more inclusive view of the world and its diverse cultures. These models were integrated into general feminist practices of nonhierarchical leadership, rotation, consciousness raising, and regular critical analysis of group functions.

Workshops and retreats in particular offered the opportunity to engineer and practice these models. The hypothesis put to the test was: Might it be possible to construct a culture that included a feminist spiritual practice, that could produce a more harmonious working process that could then be applied to activism? Placing a bet on a feminist utopianlike aspiration was conceivable because we periodically experienced a cooperative community that was so intellectually vibrant, spontaneous, and magically ecstatic that it left us longing for it again.

By using experiments like tapping into the unconscious, dreams, and psychodrama, plus academic research, it was possible to produce a functioning culture in a short period of time. As Carey Lovelace, playwright and art author, noted, "that particular mix of psychological inquiry, politics and art is only one of the gifts that first-generation feminism has left behind."[3] Even as the cultural, political, and social circumstances converged for a rapid evolution of female spirituality, never in our wildest dreams in those early years did we expect this investigation to go beyond its underground roots.

This feminist practice wasn't at ease above ground, where it might be susceptible to a stable, repeatable, canonized format that could take itself too seriously. We weren't interested in becoming a dogma that comes to believe it is the one and only true religion, starting wars, crusades, and goddess knows what else. What we were proposing was not another organized religion but a participatory paradigmatic sweep that would affect our collective vision(s) for women's rights and human liberation. For example, we challenged assumptions held across the globe within organized religions that place women in inferior service-oriented positions without control over their own lives, status, or bodies and without the agency to fulfill their potential. Their situation, especially in the Middle East, has become all the more painfully clear in recent years. Religious assumptions and traditions about women spill over into legal systems in all countries and become the law of the land, providing official sanction for discrimination.

Part of the mix was to teach ourselves how to recognize the early warning signs of efforts to control women, for example by limiting their social contacts, and to identify propaganda whether in advertising, film, TV, printed media, or by church or state. The strategy of control was aimed at instructing women on how they should and should not behave, to the benefit of patriarchy. My research on domestic violence and organized religion's chronic subordination of women, often based on patriarchal rule books, was accompanied by a clear-eyed understanding of our just cause, power, and historical circumstances, as well as that our future prospects are inextricably intertwined with feminist and human rights movements.

To conceive of a practiced spirituality grounded in sacred femaleness without the baggage of centuries of sexist and fossilized theology was electrifying. We were making it up as we went along, experimenting with direct access to the sacred, while applying research and inspiration on everything from ancient goddesses, to film and folklore studies, to psychoanalytical feminist interpretations of culture and mythology. We posed questions the patriarchy could not remedy without ceasing to be, such as, "Why are there no female priests?" This project was as liberating as rejecting organized religion's excessive fascination with romantic mythical beliefs in a single mystical male, who imparted infallible fixed wisdom direct from God, to a chosen people, for all time. When exposed to a wider population, the chutzpah to present homemade spiritual practice by females was threatening and disquieting. The enterprising heretic was at best viewed as inhabiting the twilight zone.

Second Coming: Backlash Nation, 1980s

The 1980s were a difficult decade for the feminist pioneers. The Reagan backlash permeated the culture, art world prices for a few spiraled out of control and them plummeted, and art galleries closed and exhibition opportunities were few. Feminist art theory flourished, but here too was a backlash that affected many of the feminist pioneers. It would seem that feminist theorists had zero tolerance for the complexities and context of the 1970s and the debt they owed to their groundbreaking activist mothers.

Holland Cotter observed in the *New York Times* (October 11, 2002):

> Most of the interesting America artists of the last 30 years are as interesting as they are in part because of the feminist art movement of the early 1970s. It changed everything. It gave a new content to painting, sculpture and photography. It pushed performance, video and installation art to the fore. It smashed the barrier between high art and low art, and it put folk art, outsider art, non-Western art, not to mention so-called women's art (sewing, quilting, crafts of all kinds) center stage. What art in the next 30 years will look like I don't know, but feminist influences will be at its source. All this should be obvious, but it needs to keep being re-said. Of the liberation movements for which the late 20th century will be remembered, few have been as disparaged as feminism, and that scorn extends to the women's art movement. Even presumably well-intentioned art-worldlings seem incapable of talking about it without condescension, as if it were some indiscreet adolescent episode best forgotten.

I retreated from the explicit subject of Goddess in the beginning of the 1980s because the project became codified, imitative, and trivial. I was flattered to influence other artists, but I was annoyed by second-rate knock-off art that cheapened the project. The lack of innovation and community in the 1980s flattened the project, as marketing and promotion supplanted it in the art world. The processes of continuously examining priorities and issues that are the hallmark for being relevant vanished into individual projects on career tracks, along with the community that sustained the movement.

The decade of greed and meanspiritedness seemed to overwhelm the times in much the same way as the current even more cynical zeitgeist.

Strategic Essentialism (Risky Business)

The either/or choices offered by feminist academics divided artists into camps of essentialists, those judged to be constantly using biological givens as their reference, and constructionist, judged to be employing constructed social meanings for making art. Furthermore, the labels were applied to women artists without their voices and intentions having a part in formulating these disturbingly pervasive theories, which spread from academia to art criticism. Artists who explored the female body and experience were labeled "essentialist," although we never saw ourselves this way or denied the influence of social construction on gender roles. It's ironic that feminist theory was used to attack feminist artists.

If one accepts the application of the definition of essentialism, then it could be claimed that women were not capable of change and therefore not responsible if they were naturally emotional creatures closer to nature. It would then follow that they could not, for example, be trusted with being heads of state, CEOs, or in any position other than the primal state as baby-producing nurturers.

Censorship and exclusion of many artists followed in the wake of the antiessentialist massacres of the 1980s. As it was applied in the art field by many academics, essentialism was extended beyond the classic interpretations of being the true essence of things (and therefore fixed and unchangeable) to a wider range of theorizing and surgical deployment. For example, as I wrote in 1989, "This construct [anti-essentialism] advanced the idea that women artists working with nature accepted their bodies and intuition at the expense of their cognitive minds, and that constructualist artists accepted their intellects at the expense of their sensual bodies."[4] These additions or subtends stretched thin their suppositions and resulted in a hierarchy of inclusion and exclusion of what was judged as allowed or disallowed. "The reasons for the development of anti-essentialist positions in feminist theory become clear because if women are thought of as culturally influenced, then change is possible, and therefore strategies for progressive or revolutionary political change can be developed, implemented and tested."[5]

When applied to women artists, however, this theory of essentialism reinstated an obsolete, masculinist dichotomy of prioritizing culture over nature that was both forced and removed from the reality of the studio. Theorists ignored the real-life circumstances of the creative process in which working artists slide between, under, and around formulaic models, to avoid strictures that negatively encourage self-censorship, staleness, or shutting down creative juices.

In the art world the purveyors of antiessentialism avoided matters of race and difference by simply not linking women of color to their analysis, despite often providing the best examples of their definition of an essentialist. Were these women judged too inessential for consideration or perhaps too untouchable when positioned in the context of their desire to aggressively preserve essence within a black analysis? Some people of color were intentionally exploring and defining their identity as people of color, and this would, according to antiessentialist analysis, be an essentialist position. Men were also exempt from being labeled as essentialist, as were dead artists. It may be more interesting to note who was not included in this essentialist roundup and why, than who was.

Essentialism also did not work to the advantage of women artists when we were merged as a group under the rubric of Judy Chicago's *The Dinner Party*. Chicago's interpretation of how to visualize feminism and interpret womanliness and her hierarchical working processes were problematic for many practicing woman artists. For a time, her positions were assumed by the general public to be one and the same with all feminist artists and this contributed to some artists wishing not to be identified as feminist. All this provided yet another example of a cultural view of women, and especially feminists, as interchangeable with one another, not as separate, distinct individuals but as a category.

That some of this binary reasoning and its conclusions left no room for a continuum or balance and seemed outside the realm of "common sense"—with neither data to back it up nor sustained dialogues with the accused—did not seem, to the anti-essentialists, to be a cause for alarm. But logic tells us that "[e]ssentialism and constructivism are interdependent . . . [and] essence itself can be seen as constructed; and the constructivists, in their efforts to identify different factors, in fact build webs of essences."[6]

Essentialism was a pervasive, polarizing construct that pronounced a lesser status on women critics pronounced to be essentialist. By the early 1990s antiessentialism had been reevaluated and found wanting, but not before doing considerable damage to some women artists. "It is important in looking at the history of Western philosophy to ask whether women had any part in the formulation of accounts of women's nature" or of "human nature"[7] and to compare that history with feminist academics who formulated antiessentialism without those so labeled having any part in that formulation. I know no woman artist who claimed to be an essentialist.

Visceral Disgust
A sizable number of men and women who reacted with visceral disgust toward Goddess and body artists dished out heavy-handed, condescending, trivializing and blaming as their rallying cry for identification in the inner circle of antiessentialism in the art world. This disgust was akin to the repulsion expressed by some people today for women body builders who have "bodies like men" and are "going against the grain of nature." These rejections, in my view, are fueled by a bias against the female and her body and are embedded in all patriarchal religions, as well as in the contemporary psyches of those who have not confronted them. This is especially so if a woman

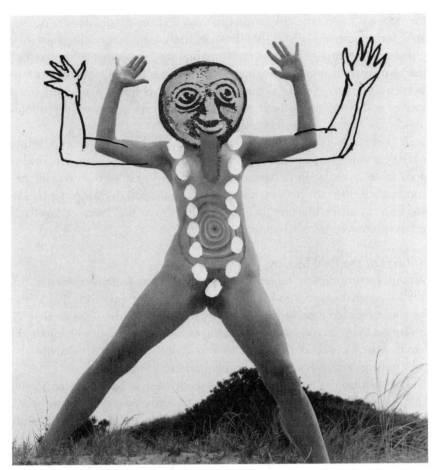

Mary Beth Edelson, Body Performance, Shella: Slick Tongue Plays Kali, *1973, photo, paint, ink, collage*

breaks out of the patriarchal essentialist mold of what is traditionally acceptable for women, that is, she should be giving, cheerful, clean in body and mind, and above all controllable.

Two-Nail Coffin
Writer Whitney Chadwick, noting the absurd polarizing groups in feminism in the arts, pointed out the following examples: feminism/postfeminism, essentialism/constructivism, and feminist practice/poststructural theory and the political divide between theory and practice. As a method, poststructuralism is used to confirm or disrupt visual images and unravel meaning even as it often prioritizes text over image and theory over practice. It opens

the door to "taking the risk of essentialism" and the possibility of a negotiated "strategic essentialism" that does not fear contradictory outcomes (like visual artists writing theory). "Poststructuralism [also] remains centered in the university, answerable neither to the realities of studio practice nor to women's need to transform patriarchy through political action [is] often viewed as denying the authenticity of individual experience, while reinforcing the goals of academic feminist intellectuals."[8]

To date no dialogue or comprehensive theoretical renovation of the artists who were felled by this false essentialist construct has been carried out. Indeed, even as essentialism has been deconstructed, rather than moving beyond an unrealistic orthodoxy, it seems to keep the ball in play. As writer Diana Fuss noted, it still exists "in an increasingly more sophisticated level and yet ever removed from actual studio practice."

Killing Off the Real McCoy

Whether intentional or an unforeseen consequence, feminist theory in the 1980s appeared to serve to kill off the Founding Mothers of the 1970s, the very source material on which this theory was based. Without the mothers of invention there was no model, no paradigm, no pipeline from which to build feminist theory, and yet the focus, for a time, appeared to be on denying the debt to their source by discrediting the pioneering feminists.

The political voices of activists in the movement, as well as the critiquing of art production, were subordinated under the orthodoxy of feminist theory. It was wielded like a weapon for establishing pecking order within the ranks of feminism. You could count on one hand the number of women artists selected for approval by the theorists, whose elitism supported yet another star system. It should be noted that these selected artists were not involved in feminist activist groups and were mostly from the generation after the 1970s, when theory came in vogue. The double whammy of the Reagan backlash against feminism and the theoretical antiessentialism proselytizing undermined a number of feminist artists.

Realities of Studio Practice

Several realities of studio practice to take into consideration are the following:

- Creativity flows from a quasi-magical state of mind that might come in a flash, be nonlogical, out-of-the-box thoughts that are eccentric, obsessional, and personal.
- Thinking in the box can veto the creative process while being at cross-purposes with accessing it.

- Artwork may not reveal all it has to say at any given time to the viewer or the creating artist.
- The urgency of artmaking drives artists to say "they produce art because they must."
- Artmaking is a risk-taking and subversive activity that presents the as-yet-underrepresented of our culture, when it goes beyond just tinkering with the same ideas.

When critiqued and translated into text, visual work becomes something else altogether. The critique may fall more into the category of being the writer's own creation than a desire to understand the artwork being critiqued. The writing, then, crosses over and displaces the visual artwork with itself. Is it possible that, in the 1980s, this cross-over occurred in theoretical writing, that is, the writer privileged her critique over the artwork by twisting it into a reconstructed creation of her theoretical project?

Binary, Balance, and Beyond
Moving beyond binarisms by rethinking both positions and taking what you need and leaving the rest might lead to an intervention in which essentialists and antiessentialists negotiate their way to a *strategic essentialism* that both positions would agree is worth the risk. Feminist theorists and writers Diana Fuss,[9] Hillary Robinson,[10] Belinda Edmonson,[11] and Edelson provide some workable suggestions.

The possibility of a balanced critique that deconstructs both essentialism and antiessentialism without privileging one over the other is suggested by Diana Fuss, who emphasizes avoiding solidification while facilitating fluidity during the process. Occupying a position of continuation between essentialism and antiessentialism also provides a more realistic critique for studio practice.

The key, according to Hilary Robinson, is "privileging 'positionality' that is, whose voice is using the tool of 'strategic essentialism' determines whether or not it is 'strategic' or regressive essentialism." For example, a feminist might call another feminist a crone, cunt, or babe as a term of endearment, but for a man to address a woman accordingly would be retrograde. Robinson explains, "If patriarchy—and modernism—marginalizes women, *as women*, then one of the starting points for countering this has to be *as women*, while at the same time working to undo that particular category. This is a complex position to adopt, both intellectually and emotionally. One of the main debates in feminist theory has concerned how this can be achieved, how feminism can identify the category 'woman,' work to undo it, maintain difference from men, and inhabit a female body all at once, without revalidating notions that women will behave a certain way, make particular art, because it is biologically inevitable."[12] As noted by Belinda Edmondson, all sides of the debate make the same mistake of treating "essentialism" as if it has "essence" in and of itself, when the only real essence of feminism is politics.[13]

The Artwork Itself, 1970s to 2000s

I'll look next at specific themes in my artworks that give examples of issues presented here, prefaced by a comment on humor and how it is used in my art production. Basic themes in my work are the status of women, participation, and tricksterishness. The most current projects include the recently published book *The Art of Mary Beth Edelson* and installations on the subject of forgiving as it relates not only to individuals but also to armed global conflicts.

Humor is a mode of speech that is indirect and ambiguous and therefore can have multiple interpretations. It can potentially disrupt dominant meanings and the social order while protecting the joker from consequences that might occur if the same message were delivered in a serious mode. Humor sabotages critics, for unlike language, laughter does not belong to the patriarchy and therefore has the possibility of breaking that hold while taking advantage of humor's natural attraction. After all, humor gives the pleasure of laughter as well as being in an inner circle of "getting it," and therefore people are more apt to accept what you have to say—or at least go along with it—if you give them a good laugh. My attraction to making use of humor in my artworks began in junior high school. Political humor came later and was

Mary Beth Edelson, Some Living American Women Artists/Last Supper, *32" x 46" poster, 1972*

put to use in drawings, photographic body works, installations, and story boxes, but most obviously in my posters.

Posters

In 1971, I began collecting headshot photos of women for the poster *Some Living American Women Artists/Last Supper*, and then collaging these heads over the disciples in a reproduction of Leonardo da Vinci's *Last Supper*. This poster, printed in 1972, embodied the inclusive spirit of 1970s feminism and was widely reproduced in underground feminist publications as well as the mainstream press, as the iconic image of that period. (Recently shown at the Tate, London, in the exhibition *Century City: Art and Culture in the Modern Metropolis, 1905–2001*.)

The *Last Supper* poster presumes to present women in positions of power that were not in reality available to them, as well as to challenge organized religion's historical oppression of women. Those who judged this artwork as an affront sought to censor the poster, and while they failed to appreciate the humor, they did grasp the paradigmatic implications of hijacking sacred power for the purpose of placing it in female hands. The intention of the poster was to identify and commemorate women artists who had received little recognition, as well as to tweak the nose of patriarchal religion for cutting women out of positions of power and authority.

The poster raises multiple issues and challenges the consequential ways in which men and women are symbolized and controlled in patriarchal religions, from the story of Eve to withholding ordination of women as priests, ministers, rabbis, and mullahs. Denying property rights and women's civil rights, reproductive choice, access to education, enforced veiling, and even a driver's license are all perpetuated on women in some cultures—in the name of religion. Even though the *Last Supper* is a Christian image, the point is to challenge organized religions across the board.

Celebrated in the *Death of the Patriarchy* poster series are both Heresies, a feminist collective that published *Heresies* magazine on art and politics, and A.I.R., the first feminist art gallery in New York City (still operating in a prime location in Chelsea). The posters pay tribute to the women who took the initial power, agency, and action necessary to provide sustainable community groups that were the backbone for building the feminist movement in the art world.

Photographic Body Works

The pioneer performance artists used their bodies as construction sites, experimenting with them in advance of feminist theoretical writings on the subject, and this meant that we were both uninformed and unrestrained by those theories. Consequently, these artists were in the unique position of creating a new genre while being at once vulnerable, unpretentiously direct, and speculative. I used my body with tongue in cheek as a "found object." My photographic performance works provided an inventory of self-constructed and ever-evolving issues as well as portraits of noninterchangeable women. While the moment has passed when women's bodies can be viewed as "found objects" with the intention of setting in motion unexplored "female subjects," at last this groundbreaking process can be pronounced as "strategical" and not just labeled with the dismissive "essentialist!" Once theoretical writings were digested, the dialogue and artworks shifted away from invention to

Mary Beth Edelson, Body Performance, Trickster's Body, 1973, collage, watercolor

evaluation and ironic commentary as this unique creative moment passed away, along with the acute vulnerability.

Specifically, the way I produced my body works included concentrating on a particular intention by drawing scriptlike storyboards and then going out into the field or studio, setting up the camera on a tripod, and photographing. A proviso I gave myself limited each photographic piece to a single roll of twelve shots, which enhanced my focus and the incisiveness of the end product. It also removed the hit-and-miss aspect of taking a number of photo shots and hoping something will come of it.

Because the first nude series of photographs taken in the summer of 1973 at Outer Banks, North Carolina, lent themselves to multiple readings, I decided to print editions of each photograph for the purpose of drawing or collaging different images or configurations on each print. This process presented not only diverse artworks but also a challenge, for how far I could extend the specificity of the same photograph without becoming repetitive?

Photographic works from my early body performance series employ collage and handwork using oil paint, ink, gouging tools, and china marker. For example, *Nobody Messes with Her* (1973, oil, ink) suggests the abyss of rage that resides in the depths of the unconscious that is a portal for releasing female potency and agency. She is a female who is nude, but there is no mistaking her for one who excites male desire.

Baubo and Sheela-Na-Gig and Kali

The ancient figures Baubo and Sheela-na-gig first captured my imagination in the early 1970s and have been a continuous subject of my artworks in a variety of media and installations throughout the years. Baubo is a pre-Greco consort of the Goddess Demeter whose body is presented as a sexual riddle. Is she all head or headless, and what is the nature of her puzzling sexuality? "Baubo's exhibitionism is interpreted as a potential alternative to the castrating display of the Medusa: Her display is to another woman and its effect is to provoke laughter and to end grief and morning."[14]

The Irish Sheel-na-gigs were carved into stone blocks and found around Irish church sites. Sheela makes a bizarre display of her genitalia that appears irreverent and comically "in your face." I have used both of these figures to bypass the "morality of patriarchy that robs the female of her will to power."[15]

These two figures were also intriguing because they are so out of their original context as to be unknowable. They fall outside of contemporary sexual categories and are therefore unverifiable on both accounts. The two suggest irreverent, playful, trickster antics, and their "truth is not shameful, but just a joke. . . . The laugh, [exists] outside the semantic and 'on the edge of language,'

[and] breaks the hold of a phallocentric grammar. . . . Baubo [is] a figure who resides outside the regime of [this] phallocentrism, undermining its logic, including the inscription of Dionysus's face on Baubo's body."[16] My interpretation of both Baubo and Sheela-na-gig in artworks uses humor to reinforce independence and uncontrollability.

Kali/Bobbitt, 1994–2001, is an installation consisting of a full-sized mannequin wearing a black wig, girdle of knives, and kitsch phallic jewelry. She is a contemporary Kali, the Goddess who transforms life with her dance of death, merged with Lorna Bobbitt of the sensational castration court case. I wrote the following immediately after 9/11 about the essence of *Kali/Bobbitt*:

> Her nature is liberation; She dances mad with freedom's joy. Sometimes She is the "Smokey One" who reduces the universe to ashes. She manifests Herself for the annihilation of demonic power, to restore peace and to make visible the unacknowledged radical truth revealed in the smoking ashes. This warrior woman is one-in-herself and She can move around with the flexibility of a Bandit Queen. The vulnerable and the abused look to her for protection, She

Mary Beth Edelson, installation, Kali/Bobbitt, 1994, 8′ x 10′ mannequin with wig and girdle of knives

raises their spirits and money while She organizes and lobbies for change. No one assumes that they are superior to Her.[17]

The Story Gathering Boxes

When I began collecting personal stories in the *Story Gathering Boxes* from gallery-goers in 1972 I was interested in breaking down traditional barriers set up between the public and artworks. "The problem with the 'story of man' was that women could not recognize themselves in it. So those who produce

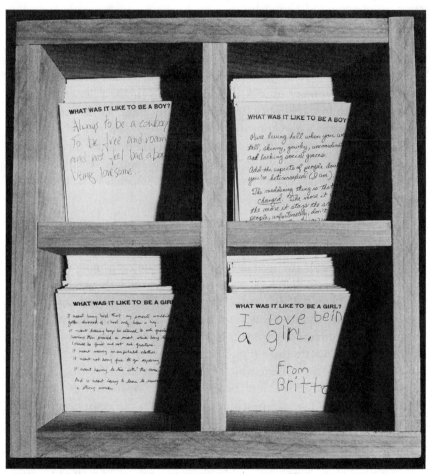

Mary Beth Edelson, Story Gathering Box: Childhood, *1972 ongoing. Wooden box with paper tablets for viewer to write their own stories. Displayed on tables with two stools, size of table 38" x 24" x 31"; Each box is 16" x 17" x 8". Childhood, 1995 ongoing. Box contains the following questions: "What was it like to be a girl? What was it like to be a boy?"*

the 'story of women' want to make sure they appear in it. The best way to ensure that is to be the storyteller.".[18]

Sacred ancient Egyptian canopic chests that held the organs of the pharaoh inspired the configuration of the wood boxes that house the stories. Divided into four equal sections, the boxes contain jute paper tablets with ever-changing topics rubber-stamped at the top of the cards. The public is invited to write stories about these topics and then replace them in the box for others to read. Selected stories from the boxes have been reprinted in women's studies and psychology books and have been of special interest as fresh raw material to fiction writers.

By inviting viewers to actively participate, their position changed from passive viewer to producer. The boxes were presented on a table with stools, which provides a place within the gallery to sit and resonate with the art or have a conversation. It was a small "rebellion against the implied message of art galleries that you are to look but not touch, you are welcome to breeze through the exhibition but not linger, you are to stand but not sit, and that the exhibiting artist is the know-it-all and you are the know-nothing."[19]

The accumulation over thirty-five years of stories includes topics ranging from gender-related issues like, "What did your mother teach you about men?" to more political questions about domestic violence, warring, and forgiveness.

Rescripting Hollywood

I began investigating how women had been treated over the years in the cinema when they took the ultimate symbol of privileged male power—the gun—into their own hands. I researched Hollywood shooters, especially femmes fatales, from the 1920s silent films to current films, to assess changes over time. I found that the gun was a readable barometer in each decade of the propaganda directed at women by a male-dominated film industry. My intention was to isolate these filmic images from their original context and project my own story on them, which I then portrayed on drawings, collages, books, aprons, pillowcases, and bedspreads, but especially on large-scale transparent chiffon fabric. The chiffon hangs from the ceiling to the floor and varies in width from 45 inches to 40 feet long. The scale of artwork articulated and defined space without obstructing the view. Angelica Huston, Gena Rowlands, Sharon Stone, Marlene Dietrich, Susan Sarandon, and even Marilyn Monroe are depicted in these artworks as self-defining agents who ultimately defied Hollywood stereotyping.

Film theorist E. Ann Kaplan said that the femme fatale figure "is ripe for reinterpretation."[20] Traditionally not associated with feminism, the femme

Mary Beth Edelson, installation, Already Marked, 1995–2000, chiffon panels, 12' x 4', Grenoble, France

Mary Beth Edelson, sculptural work, Get It?, *1992, silk screened, comforter and pillow-cases with sheets, bed frame, pillows, and mattress*

fatale was represented as irresistibly attractive and dangerous to men, especially in noir films from the 1940s to 1970s; however, she was a woman with a plan. Even if she was cut down by the end of the film, not very nice to her sisters, and far too obsessed with the male in her life, the femme fatale presented the possibility of a woman having agency and her own strategies, and it did not hurt that she looked good doing it.

The Hollywood film series also includes issues about domestic violence. For example, *Get It?* (1992) is a full-sized double bed with sheets and pillowcases silk-screened with the image of Gena Rowlands, from the film *Gloria*, pointing a gun directly at the viewer. By representing this female shooter on domestic sheets and pillowcases, a threat is implied to anyone who would abuse this bed, while removing the woman from the realm of victimization.

The Book: *The Art of Mary Beth Edelson*
I dedicated myself for four years to producing *The Art of Mary Beth Edelson* (2002), an ambitious 200-page, full-color book. It surveys thirty years of my work, examines major issues in the feminist art movement, and includes con-

versations with other artists.[21] The personal gifts of such an undertaking are not only the end product of the book but the time spent to step back and reflect, which then provides a clearer focus for future projects. One focus that emerged was the current lack of community and physical eye-to-eye contact between friends, as well as the shrinking public space, especially in my city, New York. Future plans include living to be ninety-three in good health, producing more interactive grassroots projects, continuing exhibitions and residencies, and spending time in Egypt producing four *Story Gathering Boxes* carved from Egyptian translucent alabaster. I'll continue with activism, as that's who I am.

Constructing Public Social Space: Five Projects, 1979 to 2006

The following art projects all respond in part to the disappearance of allocated indoor and outdoor public space in many parts of the globe and within our individual communities.

Because each project takes on an unpredictable life of its own—due in part to the collaborative nature—the most comprehensible way to communicate their reality is to tell the story of each project. The following projects are discussed: *Beauborg Habitat* proposal presented by IFCG (International Feminist Colaborative) in 1997 to the Beauborg, with documentation exhibited in 2003 at Mumok Museum in Vienna; *NamNam/Eye Contact* in conjunction with both the Lofoten International Art Festival (LIAF) and Nordland Art and Film School, Kablevåg; *Forgiving* project produced in both Zurich, Switzerland, and Norway in 2003 and 2004; and *Utopians 2005*, New Harmony, Indiana, 2005–2006. Also included are brief descriptions of five projects by other artists.

Vienna Project: *Interactive Performative Habitat* and Beaubourg, Paris 1979–2003: (IFCG) International Collaborative Feminist Group (Nil Yalter, Paris; Miriam Sharon, Tel Aviv; Mary Beth Edelson, New York City; Suzanne Lacy, Los Angeles; Ulrike Rosenback, Köln)

A group of five artists from four different countries and three different religious backgrounds proposed an installation and performance for the Centre Georges Pompidou, Beauborg, Paris, during the summer of 1979. The group viewed themselves as a metaphor for the nomadic experience, given that feminist artists travel within the community of feminist artists from one city or country to another in a "tribal-like" feminist network. What we had in mind for this project was to create a discrete area within the museum that was set aside, but exposed to public view, in which museum-goers might observe the processes that evolve from our physical and social presence in the Beauborg. The project was designed so that each artist created and installed her own habitat, while living continuously in the museum with the other artists and presenting daily performances that are either preplanned or spontaneous group collaborations.

"Social interactions are of interest to us, and will be considered as our primary art form. The habitats installed by each artist provoke differing forms of communication through their individual designs, and test the receptivity of each habitat to this social experiment. The traces left behind of our movements and communications with each other are diaristic residue of our temporary community, along with our photographic and video documentation. However, our behavior, social patterns and interactions with the public and each other are the primary art form" (IFCG collaborative proposal). The proposal was not accepted in 1979.

Twenty-five years later in 2003–2004 Austrian feminist artists Carola Dertnig and Stefanie Seibold curated an exhibition at the Mumok Museum of Modern Art, Vienna, that exhibited the correspondence, photographs, and proposal from the project. Perhaps one day we will have the opportunity to give new meaning to "long live the feminist revolution" by actually producing *Interactive Performative Habitat*, IFCG, and its temporary community and dwellings in some satisfying form.

A Sampling of Public Site Projects by Four International Artists, 1999–2003, who also reclaim public space. For example, Lara Almarcegui, from the Netherlands, builds structures in community gardens that are functional, for the gardeners, and a meeting place for conversation. Lyn Lowenstein, London, constructs tentlike structures from recycled materials including protest posters and banners that celebrates activists. Sabine Hornig, Berlin, produces thick-walled concrete structures with a strong presence that you cannot quite enter to inhabit, but that inspire interjection. For the past three years, a Williamsburg artist has provided a "freeshop" in Brooklyn. All items in the storefront are free for the taking. Her space is also used for community meetings, renting studios to artists in the back room pays for expenses.

Eye Contact. The *NamNam* restaurant project and the *Forgiving* project, presented in collaboration with Norlund Film and Art School, Kablevåg and LIAF (Lofoten Internation Art Festival), located within the Arctic Circle during the time of the midnight sun, Norway, in 2004

Two end products were produced in Lofoten. The first was *NamNam* (Norwegian for yum yum), the restaurant project, a workshop with the Kablevåg students, Liv Brita Malnes, the rector, and a restaurateur. The second was *Forgiving*, a participatory and architecturally referenced installation with the curator, Tor Inge Kveum, for the L.I.A.F. exhibition on the theme of forgiving. The two phases of the project, one performative and the other creating public space, enriched the context of both.

The collaborative model that I have developed to realize these public projects begins with a workshop of students and branches out to include local artists and community people who relate to the focus of the project. The collaborative workshop serves to structure the project but ultimately dissolves into working teams for the production phase. The end products may be arrived at by using mixed art media that include performance, video, photography, installation, architecture, graphic design, websites, sculpture, painting, collage, and publication. Also considered are working through interdisciplinary conceptualization, including coalitions with other groups and various academic departments; philosophy, sociopolitical, psychology, feminist, writing, and of course all the various aspects of cultural production in university art departments. Being media savvy is also part of the mix. A publication that enables us to share the outcomes is always desirable.

NamNam restaurant project. My broad assignment to the workshop group was to produce a grassroots community project within the conditions of an existing but redefined social space. The four-month project focused on building community in the village of Kablevåg and was contingent on the community's needs and for their benefit.

The first days of conceptualizing the project reached a consensus around three issues: the elderly and teenagers, with the sharpest focus on immigrants/refugees, as well as how to bring these groups together under the same umbrella. Working with these dissimilar groups coalesced around the concept of using a restaurant as a unifying platform, realized through cooperating with Rashad Akhtar, a charismatic immigrant Pakistani restaurant owner.

Rashad was worried about supporting his family because his fast-food restaurant was failing. When we approached him, he was willing to take the chance of working with us to create a new restaurant concept. Rashad let us 1) take over his restaurant for four days; 2) change the name of the restaurant (we renamed it NamNam); and 3) redesign the signage, menu, and décor. We asked in exchange that he present healthy Indian (his choice) food at an affordable price. The food available in the small town of

Kablevåg was either unhealthy fast food or very expensive cuisine, and there was no variety.

The students were highly motivated once they realized that we were affecting real people's lives. Our productions for NamNam included redesigning the restaurant as well as a publicity campaign resulting in coverage and crowds for the restaurant's unveiling. A lively native and contemporary music program plus art performances were also launched on opening night.

Special emphasis was placed on the immigrants/refugees because their needs were the most pressing. Due to the homogeneity of the local (as well as general Scandinavian) population, experience communicating with people different from themselves is not often part of daily life. We began with the elementary gesture of just making eye contact; it is such a simple idea, but amazingly difficult to begin. The students teased, "Have you made eye contact with a refugee today?" Never mind, it worked, and the jokes made it easier for them to bridge the gap on the street. Going beyond looking at each other at arm's length to having dinner and conversations also brought an awareness of their conditions. Some of the hurdles discussed in the workshop were risking the embarrassment of not being politically correct, as well as seeing themselves differently by recognizing that *not* making the effort to reach out is not an innocent act but maintains the status quo. The immigrants responded quickly because they were eager to meet the Norwegians and to feel welcomed into the community, which in turn facilitated inviting their participation in the *NamNam* project.

The refugee community, located in the same neighborhood as the restaurant, enjoys the spicy food and a hospitable meeting place. A ramp was built to facilitate entrance of the elderly into the restaurant. Teenagers living in Kablevåg without their parents now have an alternative to fast food and a place to hang out. Rashad has offered the always hungry and broke students who worked on the project a discounted price for their meals at NamNam.

We coordinated the four days that we ran the restaurant with the L.I.A.F. festival, in particular with the seminar and opening night exhibition. The seminar focused on critical issues encased in the title of the exhibition *Humans Fucking Humans* and the artworks produced for the festival. As the final seminar speaker I presented a wrap-up discourse by using the *NamNam* project as an example, through praxis, of the theoretical papers presented by previous speakers. After the seminar adjourned we were bused to the NamNam restaurant where we all ate dinner together.

The mood of the diners was joyful, both about the success of the workshop participants, who were clearly pleased with being able to produce

Mary Beth Edelson, installation, Forgiving, *2003, 9′ (w) x 8′ (l) x 8′ (h). Wood, muslin, fluorescent tubes, altar, pillows and rocks installed at Shedhalle, Zurich, Switzerland*

this ambitious project, and because they delighted in actualizing a hypothetical proposition that had been discussed at the seminar that afternoon. Witnessing the project unfold and taking effect in the community seemed to thrill us all.

The results so far are beyond our dreams. The reconceptualized restaurant continues and is a community meeting place for a cross-section of people who would not normally make eye contact.

The *Forgiving* installation. The architectural installation titled *Forgiving* at L.I.A.F. invited viewers to contemplate forgiveness as it relates to entrenched civil wars like those between Palestine and Israel, Protestants and Catholics in Northern Ireland, or the Arabs and non-Arabs currently unfolding in Sudan. I calculated, keeping in mind the African reconciliation model, that after all the rights and wrongs are added in, forgiving may be a constructive course to embark on to arrive at civility. Adding to the appeal of forgiving is its connectivity to global but also local and individual interactions.

Forgiving was originally created in Zurich at the Shedhalle space, with curator Frederikke Hansen, within an exhibition whose central theme was "Making Peace." In Zurich participants were invited to write on the strips of paper after they contemplated forgiveness. Many then rolled up the paper and stuck it between a pile of rocks inside the *Forgiving* installation. During the opening I also presented the "Scream Out" performance in Zurich, described later under WAC.

The structure of the *Forgiving* installation in Lofoten is made of wood with a skin of luminescent orange nylon, pulled tightly over the surface. A thin fluorescent tubing runs around the lower perimeter of the exterior installation, which appears to levitate the structure. The interior is designed with signifiers of comfort and reassurance that are at the polar end of power-based behavior. Once the person is prepared, the metaphorical and dazzling properties of light in the interior space aspire to open the participant to contemplate the sublime act of forgiving.

The time in the Kablevåg workshop and the production of *NamNam* served to decode issues and bring them to life, while the architectural installation provided physical meditative space, but both are embedded in real-life experiences.

Utopiana **2005-2006 on Location in New Harmony, Indiana.** The historic New Harmony Utopian Community of the early 1800s is referenced in relationship to how that might manifest itself in 2005, within my *Utopiana* 2005–2006 project for New Harmony. The workshop format described under "Constructing Social Space" is used to realize *Utopiana*.

Before I arrive to begin the workshop we circulate through the press, schools, and coffee shops the question, "What in our contemporary culture is utopian that we do not recognize as such?"

During my two-month residency we review utopia in New Harmony, using that history record as a staging arena to evaluate the common ground that we share with that time while contrasting it with our own contemporary culture. Given the rich history of New Harmony as one of the most prominent experimental utopian sites in the United States, the very land itself presents an inspirational challenge for extracting utopian impulses in our own culture. The processes of approaching contemporary New Harmony, its history, and its relationship to *Utopiana* is basically a dynamic experiment in community. Revealing contemporary undercurrents of utopian enterprises, from the Internet to global travel to the desire to reclaim community, delight, and social space in today's world is a main focus of this experimental project.

The Here and Now of It: Today's Goddess Girls Rule. Like Sigourney Weaver in *Aliens*, the Goddess has been napping for awhile, or in exile, or just inconstant, and she awakes to a radically transformed world in which goddesses are everywhere, but she hardly recognizes herself in 2005. In this new psychological landscape she is a teenager again taking on the demons of the underworld in TV's *Buffy the Vampire Slayer* or *Xena*, riding her horse through the forest. She is a staple in every mythological, sci-fi, fantasy film, dressed in phantasmagoric outfits that outshine the hapless mortals. Shelves of books full of scholarly research include recent archaeological evidence of the meaning of women's altars, the Goddess and Her beasts, and the psychoanalytic meaning of Goddess (see the bibliography). Drugstore books, like *How to Be a Goddess* by Valerie Khoo, advise listening to your inner goddess, with inspirational messages from Artemis, Athena, Demeter, etc., depicted as peppy young blondes. Farther afield, Bollywood films with contemporary Indian goddesses are popular manifestations in India, and Hong Kong films' whirling females of supernatural power and strength are always ready for action. So there it is, She has awakened into being a really cool international pop culture icon, an undeniable symbol of accepted female power.

Meanwhile, in the everyday world, following the Goddess exhibition at Galerie LeLong (New York City, 2002), a symposium on "Goddesses, Wonder Women and Riot Girls"[22] was held at the School of Visual Arts with an international panel of artists, writers, and a girl rapper in a packed auditorium with standing room only.

In the planning stages is an international exhibition to be held in Brazil, curated by writer and entrepreneur Shelley Rice. Her intention is to reexamine essentialism and antiessentialism. She explains:

My idea for this project grew out of the multiple perspectives provided by globalization, which have made it imperative that we take another look at the lessons inherent in work like Maya Deren's and Ana Mendieta's. The Goddess quest, which grew out of American feminists' need to provide "divine" role models for women in the 1970s might now provide us with an inroad to profoundly explore the many different cultural traditions impacting on our collective lives today. Whereas Edelson and [Carolee]) Scheenmann were profoundly aware that their goddess was an alternative view of spirituality, a subjective bolster to women denied power in a man's world, the contemporary scene is filled with images of powerful women: in body art by the ex-super model Veruschka and the French artists Orlan and Annette Messager; in ritual icons by the African-American Renée Cox, the Australian aborigine Tracy Moffat, the Japanese Mariko Mori, the Iranian Shirin Neshat and the Brazilian Janaina Tschape: animated cartoons from

WAC at post office in New York City on April 15, tax day, protesting tax dollars for the military while domestic programs are being cut, 2003. Photo by Mary Beth Edelson

Japan and Hollywood like Powerpuff Girls, have influenced youth cultures all over the world. In other words, the landscape has radically changed since the 1970s. The Goddess "rules" these days, as kids would say, and this project will attempt to examine, in a large and global way, her hegemony, influences and impact.

Contemporary Feminist Groups WAC (Women's Action Coalition), New York City. WAC is committed to direct action on issues affecting the rights of women. Formed in 1991 and recently reactivated, WAC is known as a lively, smart, irreverent, and risk-taking group of activists. In the early 1990s it wasn't uncommon to have 500 people attending meetings. WAC went into hiatus until 2003, but then as a result of the Iraq war, the economy, and the presidential election it was reactivated. One action was handing out copies of U.S. tax forms on April 15 at the main post office in New York City, filled out with the actual amount of money that goes to the military versus the amount that goes for domestic programs. Another WAC action (conceived by Karen Finley in collaboration with WAC and presented in New York City and Zurich in 2003) demonstrates the frustrations Americans feel because their voices are not being heard. "Scream Out" consists of reading forty statements by forty women about topics such as the USA Patriot Act, manipulation of direct democracy and the public interest, and the Iraqi war. Forty women individually scream out after each reading, and then a collective scream from performers and audience ends the action. (See www.wacnyc.net for the script of the performance, as well as visuals and sound presentation from other actions.)

Campaign Headquarters against Domestic Violence (PostWAC, 1994). I began focusing on domestic violence, and with the help of the nonprofit organization Creative Time and artist Janet Henry, produced a three-month storefront project. Our most far-reaching contribution was the introduction of self-defense workshops, tailored for women in shelters. This precedent-setting, experimental self-defense project for abused women was then picked up and repeated by domestic violence agencies around the country.

Guerrilla Girls were known originally for their provocative posters plastered on the streets of Soho in New York City attacking sexism in the art world. They then branched out to publications, exhibitions, and touring. The Guerrilla Girls are recognizable by their trademark—a gorilla mask that they wear to conceal their identities.

> In 1985, a band of feminist artists founded the Guerrilla Girls in the wake of Kynaston McShine's remark that any artist who wasn't in his International Survey show at the Museum of Modern Art should "rethink HIS career." Dubbing ourselves "The Conscience of the Artworld," we began making posters that bluntly stated the facts of discrimination, and used humor to convey information, provoke discussion and to show that feminists can be funny . . . . In the ensuing 15 years, we produced over 80 posters, billboards, postcards, books, and magazine projects, examining discrimination in the art world and our culture at large. We travel the world over, daring to speak out against discrimination and inequity wherever it rears its ugly head. . . . In 1995 we published our first book, "Confessions of the Guerrilla Girls," and our second book, "The Guerrilla Girl's Bedside Companion to the History of Western Art," was published in 1998.
>
> Toward the end of the 20th century, the Guerrilla Girls sought out new frontiers in their fight for truth, justice and the feminist way, forming three wings to accommodate their broadening interests.[23]

Political grassroots groups of women and men are well structured with the help of the Internet to be mobilized for unfettered direct democracy, pro-environmental initiatives, reclaiming and designing urban public space, re-productive choice, freedom to exercise our constitutional right to free speech and free assembly, and political dissent. Here are a few grassroots websites:

MoveOn.org, moveon-help@list.moveon.org
The Not In Our Name, www.nion.us/NION.HTM.
(A.N.S.W.E.R.), NYAnswer@action-mail.org
CODE PINK, codepink@codepinkalert.org
Operation Homeland Resistance, www.homelandresistance.org, info@
   homelandresistance.org

Third Coming in the Twenty-First Century: Success Has 1,000 Mothers

The First Coming the international 1970s Goddess girls, were the test pilots who took the heat and presented a hypothetical framework and practice and began that cultural movement. The Second Coming in the 1980s were the marketers trafficking in the Goddess. I don't think I can give the Third Coming of this culture a name as it is too pivotal a moment to call, but here is how I would like it to play out for all the talented women artists who created a transformed world and still have not received the credit they deserve.

The First Coming pioneers of the feminist movement are promoted to historical status, with all that implies. Archives in universities, libraries, and colleges across the country now compete for our personal archives, and this competition is in full swing at New York University, Rutgers University, and several Midwest colleges, with Brooklyn Museum getting geared up to begin. WAC archives from 1993 are at the New York Public Library on 42nd Street, and A.I.R. archives are in that gallery in New York City. *Heresies* magazine existed from 1977 until 1996, an amazing feat for an all-volunteer collective publishing project. The *Goddess Issue* of *Heresies* immediately sold out, was reissued, and is now a collector's item fetching high prices on the Internet, when you can find it at all. Heresies collective needs an archivist; any volunteers? (A.I.R. gallery info@airnyc.org.)

Unfinished business includes major group and individual exhibitions in museums of women artists and appropriate gallery representation. Recently a committee of three (Debra Wacks, Kathleen Wentrack, and Edelson) wrote a proposal for a major survey exhibition of feminist art; the letter was signed by twenty-five actively working feminist artists and submitted to the Brooklyn Museum. The museum proposal presents a radical departure from business as usual exhibitions by taking a cue, and applying it to our proposal, from the brilliantly curated Picasso/Matisse exhibition in 2002, in which similar works by these two giants were placed in proximity to each other and in the chronological time frame that they created. Their mutual dependence was highlighted as well as the ongoing dialogue that takes place in their work. It is clear to viewers of this exhibition that acknowledging these exchanges takes nothing away from either artist, but rather makes visible the lively working processes of engaged artists.

By not revealing these natural exchanges, as is commonplace in many museum exhibitions, they remain hidden from the viewer, who is manipulated in favor of building the illusion of a lone star genius who has not been placed in context. These promotional dressings can also create competition between artists when none previously existed.

We decided to highlight the natural exchanges that have occurred in the feminist movement, as well as the chronology of the work produced, in our proposal to the museum for a major feminist survey. Also included in the proposal are lively feminist community projects as well as a shop within the museum of vintage and current feminist paraphernalia that would be for sale. See www.home.earthlink.net/~yourstory for the full proposal. The Brooklyn Museum has hired a full-time *feminist* curator, Maura Reilley—the first ever!

Today I view myself as an active participant in international groups of artists who travel and carry the spirit of that nomadic community with them. We communicate through the Internet and participate in individual and collaborative projects around the globe that are interdisciplinary and fluid by nature. These communications include symposia and workshops, as well as casual conversations with friends that articulate and give shape to a vision that has no name but longs for a vital progressive community and is cross-cultural to the core.

Notes

1. Griselda Steiner, "Book Profile: The Art of Mary Beth Edelson," *Organica* (Winter, 2003).

2. J.C. Smith and Carla J. Ferstman, *The Castration of Oedipus: Feminism, Psychoanalysis, and the Will to Power* (New York University Press, 1996), 27.

3. *Heresies* Magazine Working Collective members for the *Great Goddess* Issue were as follows: Mary Albanese, Martha Alsup, Tracy Boyd, Janet Culbertson, Rosemary Dudley, Mary Beth Edelson, Gail Feinstein, Deborah Freedman, Gina Foglia,

Donna Henes, Anne Healy, Buffie Johnson, Diane Levin, Grace Shinell, Merlin Stone, Carolee Thea, Mierle Laderman Ukeles.

4. Carey Lovelace, "Art and Politics: Feminism at 40," *Art in America* (May 2003): 73.

5. Mary Beth Edelson, "Male Grazing: Open Letter to Thomas McEvilley," (1989), in *Feminism-Art-Theory*, ed. Hilary Robinson (Blackwell Pub, 2001).

6. Hilary Robinson, "Reframing Women" (1995), in *Feminism-Art-Theory*, ed. Hilary Robinson (Blackwell Publishers, 2001), 535–536.

7. Ibid, 443–444.

8. Elizabeth V. Spellman, *Inessential Women: Problems of Exclusion in Feminist Thought* (Boston: Beacon Press, 1988).

9.

10. Whitney Chadwick, "Negotiating the Feminist Divide" (1989), in *Feminism-Art-Theory*, ed. Hilary Robinson (Blackwell Publishers, 2001), 526.

11. Diana Fuss, *Essentially Speaking* (Routledge, 1989), 118.

12. Hilary Robinson, "Reframing Women" (1995), in *Feminism-Art-Theory*, ed. Hilary Robinson (Blackwell Publishers, 2001), 536.

13. Belinda Edmondson, "Black Aesthetics, Feminist Aesthetics, and the Problems of Oppositional Discourse," (1992), in *Feminism-Art-Theory*, op.cit.

14. Hilary Robinson, "Theorizing Representation," in *Feminism-Art-Theory* op.cit, 443.

15. Belinda Edmondson, "Black Aesthetics, Feminist Aesthetics, and the Problems of Oppositional Discourse," (1992), in *Feminism-Art-Theory*, op.cit., 337.

16. Mary Beth Edelson, *The Art of Mary Beth Edelson* (Seven Cycles/Peter Wollen, 2002), 73.

17. J.C. Smith and Carla J. Ferstman, *The Castration of Oedipus: Feminism, Psychoanalysis, and the Will to Power* (New York University Press, 1996), 40.

18. Mary Ann Doane, "Femme Fatales," Sarah Kofman quote (Routledge, 1991), 66.

19. Mary Beth Edelson, *The Art of Mary Beth Edelson*, op.cit., 4–5.

20. Elizabeth V. Spellman, *Inessential Women: Problems of Exclusion in Feminist Thought* (Beacon Press, 1988), 159.

21. Mary Beth Edelson, *The Art of Mary Beth Edelson*, op.cit., 82.

22. E. Ann Kaplan in a conversation with Edelson " the *femmes fatale* figure ". . . is ripe for reinterpretation" Also see: Mary Beth Edelson, "Trickster and Gunslinger, " in *The Art of Mary Beth Edelson*, op.cit., 120–123.

23. See www.home.earthlink.net/~yourstory for more on the book *The Art of Mary Beth Edelson* as well as information on ordering the book. Funders for the book include: Andy Warhol Foundation, Pollack-Krasner Foundation, National Endowment for the Arts. Conversations are with artists Nancy Spero, Miriam Schapiro, Yvette Brachman, Janet Henry and Carolee Schneemann.

24. Panelist Kathleen Hanna, Caroleee Scheemann, Janaina Tschapre, Deb Willis, Edelson, and moderator Shelley Rice.
25. Committee members are Debra Wacks, Kathleen Wentrack, and Edelson, 24.

Bibliography

Feminist Spirituality/ Body Performance/ Related Publications
Mary Daly, Gyn/Ecology (Beacon Press, 1978).
Elizabeth Gould Davis, The First Sex (Penguin, 1971).
Simone De Beauvior, The Second Sex (Knopf, 1953).
Riane Eisler, the Chalice and The Blade (Harper and Row, 1987).
Marija Gimbutas, The Goddesses and Gods of Old Europe (University of California Press, 1982).
Robert Graves, The White Goddess (Farrar, Straus and Giroux, 1948).
"The Great Goddess," Heresies: A Feminist Publication on Art and Politics (Heresies Collective, 1982).
Susan Griffen, Woman and Nature (Harper and Row, 1978).
Joan Halifax, Shamanic Voices (E.P. Dutten, 1979).
Gayle Kimball, Women's Culture (Scarecrow Press, 1981).
Lucy R. Lippard, Overlay: Contemporary Art and the Art of Prehistory (Pantheon Books, 1983).
Erich Neumann, The Great Mother (Princeton University Press, 1955).
Elaine Pagels, Adam, Eve, and The Serpent (Random House, 1988).
Elaine Pagels, The Gnostic Gospels (Random House, 1979).
Moira Roth, The Amazing Decade (Astro Artz, 1983).
Charlene Spretnak, The Politics of Women's Spirituality (Anchor Press, 1982).
Merlin Stone, When God Was A Woman (Dial Press, 1976).
Edward Whitmont, C., Return of the Goddess (Crossroad, 1982).

Biography

Mary Beth Edelson is featured in over 30 books, and her artwork was widely exhibited and critiqued in the US and abroad and collected by major museums. In addition to international recognition, she was an early member of the AIR gallery, NYC, and founding member of Heresies magazine collective, and on-going participant in WAC, NYC. A 30-year survey of Edelson's work toured seven exhibition sites in the U.S. 2000 to 2002, and continues in Europe through 2006.

Her production consists of a hybrid of diverse mediums, including photo-based work, painting, sculpture, drawing, performance, silkscreen, artists' books, posters, fabric works, installation, collages, story-gathering boxes, and video. The artwork is rooted in feminism, political activism, community, ritual performance, and feminist film theory. She has written four books; the most recent is *The Art of Mary Beth Edelson*, which surveys 30 years of her artwork, providing a sense of the circumstances of feminist art production, while interlacing her communities, a history of feminism, and other artists. Edelson's current work centers on producing structures that can be entered and provide social space for contemplation, planning actions, performance, forums, etc. Some of these structures are collaborative and encourage the use of recyclable materials. The latest structure focused on forgiveness. She lives and works in New York City.

CHAPTER FOUR

Galloping in Slow Motion: Women's Influence on Film and Television

Mollie Gregory

Gender, being a woman, affects everything. It's universal. It's like the color of one's skin. Gender . . . even involves the way people speak to you. It isn't negative all the time, it's just that . . . you're a woman.

—Martha Coolidge, film director

Everything I learned in life I learned from the movies: how to walk and talk and dress and smoke.

—Brianne Murphy, cinematographer

Can there be any question about movies teaching the ways men and women deal with each other—what a husband is, a wife, a woman, a man, what violence is, what a victim is?

—Lynne Littman, film director

What women write, produce, edit, or direct, and how they define their own experiences, will influence women and men everywhere because movies are our culture's tutor and our mythmaker.

Before the 1970s, in the art and business of American entertainment, most women worked as publicists, casting agents, costume designers, and script supervisors (once called "script girls"). You could count the number of female film producers on one hand and executives on the other. By 2000, there were hundreds. That social upheaval began to alter the culture of exclusion not only in film and television but in other arenas all over the country.[1]

The change came from a combination of forces: the influence of the women's movement in the late 1960s, which united women in a deep, mutual awareness of their isolated second-class status; the fierce struggle in the 1970s to enact the Equal Rights Amendment to the U.S. Constitution, and its failure; the action of the federal equal employment laws and the establishment of the EEOC (Equal Employment Opportunities Commission); and two Supreme Court decisions in 1973, one, *Roe v. Wade,* which made early term abortions legal, the other declaring that job advertisements could not specify gender. Most important was the dogged determination of women who wanted to work and wouldn't take "no" for an answer.

In this turbulent period from 1970 to 2000, more women made films, realizing their different approaches to the work and their need to continue to develop their own ideas *as women* for film or television. Many also felt the need to know our own history in all the arts, not as a representation of a few star personalities but as a group influence, the pressure of many that can transform the social bargain, the very content and context of the way we live.

The force of change stemming from that period has slowed to a glacial pace, but it seems unlikely to go into total relapse, even though statistics of women's actual participation in film and television are disgracefully, surprisingly low. For instance, of the top-selling, widely distributed 250 films in 2004, 19 percent of executive producers were women; producers, 24 percent; directors, 5 percent; writers, 12 percent; editors, 16 percent; and cinematographers, 3 percent.[2] Statistics gathered by the writers, directors, or screen actors guilds are somewhat higher because they include shorts, documentaries, and all independent films.

These low numbers seem to contradict the broad changes that have taken place, but considering how few women worked at all in these positions before 1970, they indicate many deep changes. To hear their stories, I interviewed 125 women "behind the camera" about their firsthand experiences as women at work in movies and in television; as independent filmmakers, writers, directors, or executives; on the back lot; and in new media. They came from New York and Oregon, Louisiana and Minnesota, England, Cuba, and China. A few even came from California. I interviewed performers only when they had also written, directed, or produced, such as Jane Alexander, Barbra Streisand, Lily Tomlin, and Liv Ullmann. Most of the women interviewed were not independent filmmakers, though many started out that way. To a greater or lesser degree, everyone works hard to navigate the tension between art and commerce, but women have additional conflicts at work—discrimination, sexual harassment, and major family responsibilities. I reported the results in my book *Women Who Run the Show: How a Brilliant and Creative New Generation of Women Stormed Hollywood.*

Many women—filmmakers, production designers, directors—working in film or television in the 1970s said it was like a war. "Women working today have never been in battle, *but we were*," said an entertainment attorney. "I deserve war pay." I extended the metaphor, dividing the book into decades. I called the 1970s "Beachhead." In that decade, a few women directed television shows, a few wrote and produced or became production designers like Polly Platt (*The Last Picture Show, What's Up Doc?*), and a few women were promoted to vice presidents of production. The 1980s, "Securing the Perimeter," saw even more gains when Sherry Lansing became the first woman to head production at a studio and Dawn Steel became the first president of a studio. Many more women were working as writers and producers, or they created their own TV shows, like Susan Harris (*The Golden Girls*). In the 1990s, "Breakthrough," despite evidence of retrenchment more women worked on many levels and three women headed studios (Amy Pascal at Columbia, Stacey Snider at Universal, and Sherry Lansing at Paramount).

Women battled for their voices, story ideas, opinions, aesthetics, and just for jobs. By 2002, the Writers Guild (WGA), Directors Guild (DGA), Screen Actors Guild (SAG), Producers Guild, Editors Guild, and ASCAP (the American Society of Composers, Authors and Publishers) were all headed by women. At no other period in our history did women *in numbers* not only go to work but also have realistic hopes of competing on new levels to achieve their aspirations.

The giant contradictory enterprise called entertainment is made up of big and small movies, documentaries, experimental shorts, video games, music, animation, and television shows of all kinds. Women's presence *in numbers* can potentially change the stories, interpretations, and points of view in this enterprise, which has so much influence and so few principles, save profit.

"Look at the long reach of television," said Marcy Carsey, a television producer and a founder of the Oxygen Channel. "Television is the single most powerful medium in the history of the world. It's in people's living rooms, it's part of their lives, and it's worldwide. It couldn't be more intimate and it couldn't be more powerful."[3] "Television, movies and music shape children's views of the world, what's right and wrong," said entertainment attorney Melanie Cook. "They drive our culture; drive the world's culture."[4]

If You Don't Know Where You've Been, You Don't Know Where You Are

We forget history so fast in this country. "Like water on a hot sidewalk," said television writer Dianne Dixon. "It evaporates before it's recorded."[5] The absence of women from the historical record, as historian Rosalind Miles has written, makes it even more urgent to record their firsthand experiences.[6] Moreover, "learning about the past of women," Gerda Lerner writes, "[helps] contemporary women evaluate their own position in society and aspire to higher goals."[7] Knowing the challenges and solutions other women found fuels social change.

Until the 1970s, men had almost no experience working with women producers or directors or even writers. A whole new view of the collaboration called film began. In my interviews, women of all ages and experience spoke about the ways they worked that differed from the ways men worked. Younger women interviewed, who began working in the 1990s, knew only vaguely what women had endured in the 1970s or 1980s, and seemed optimistic about their own possibilities, expected to direct or produce, and crowed, in effect, "We're girls!"

Though they are buoyant, it is clear that young women still do not have the chances or choices enjoyed by men. "Certainly there are more women in the room now and outwardly the attitude about them changed," says Barbara Corday, cocreator of *Cagney & Lacey*. "Women in those jobs became much more accepted [in the 1990s]. . . . What did not change was the back room politics."[8]

Buried in the turmoil of thirty years is the almost unchanged social structure of art and business, still run along models built by men. Looking back on recorded experiences of women in the 1970s and 1980s, we know that much has changed, but without a sense of history it is hard to measure what has occurred and what has not. Culturally and creatively, women's impact on the stories, styles, and culture of filmmaking is still not a widespread reality.

Whose Story Are We Telling?

Women's creative work, ranging from experimental shorts or episodes on prime-time television, is crucial to the culture because the experiences of women and men are different. Anne Kenney, an executive producer of *Family Law*, said, "women writers have to contend not only with men's individual perceptions of women but with this huge body of existing work that depicts women. Women are like this and not like this. But who wrote those things?"[9]

Mainly men, and they still do. In a speech, Meryl Streep (*Out of Africa*, *The Hours*) noted that on the American Film Institute's list of the one hundred best movies of the twentieth century, "all but four are driven by male protagonists: *Snow White, The Wizard of Oz, All About Eve, The Sound of Music.*"[10] We've gone a distance from Dorothy in Kansas to Ridley in outer space. It is common now to hear producers like Gale Anne Hurd (*Aliens, The Terminator*) say, "In my films, I prefer to have the female characters be more than just girlfriends or victims."[11]

Lindsay Law, executive producer of many films including *I Shot Andy Warhol* and *The Thin Blue Line*, commented on the intrinsic differences between women's and men's stories. "[Women] dig deeper into themselves, both in what they bring to the project and the subject matter. Women seem to make things they care about as opposed to 'I can sell this.'"[12] In 1999, he noted the difficult time he'd had convincing networks and studios to hire women. Selling an inexperienced female director to management was much harder than selling an inexperienced male."[13]

"If anyone had said to me, 'You can't write a man because you are not a man,'" producer-writer Fay Kanin stated, "I would have said, 'I write a man in a way a woman writes a man.' That's very important. Just as a man writes a woman in a way he sees her, a woman writes a man the way she sees him. I don't think we should just have men write men."[14]

Every woman knows the frustration of explaining to men what seems obvious to them, and which the women in the room instantly know—why a scene or female character will work as written or played.[15] Women have closely observed men for centuries—because they have to. Men have not spent centuries analyzing why women do one thing instead of another—because they don't have to. "A linguistic study around 1996 examined the way men and women talk—different languages," says film director Lynne Littman, referring to the work of Dr. Deborah Tannen (e.g., in her book *You Just Don't Understand*). "If guys are hiring a director and have a choice of going with someone who speaks their language or with someone who makes them ask, 'What *is* she talking about? What's she *doing?*' Which director would you go with?"[16]

"The worst experience I ever had as a writer was when nothing I was trying to communicate was understood," says television comedy writer Treva Silverman (*The Mary Tyler Moore Show*):

> I was working with an executive producer on another show and I'd love to say he wasn't talented and smart and therefore he didn't understand me. He was very talented and very smart, but just in a different way. It was awful because he just didn't know what the hell I was writing . . . or talking about. And I couldn't make it better because if you don't like asparagus, you don't like it— good or mediocre, you just don't like it.[17]

"Women are more invested in the nuances of relationships. They like to know all the shades of feeling. What grabs them is different," said television writer Ann Beckett. In *First Do No Harm*, Meryl Streep (also one of the producers), plays a woman who has become a learned advocate in seeking treatment for her epileptic son while her truckdriver husband has hung back, feeling inadequate because he doesn't earn enough and doesn't know how to talk to doctors.

> At the start of rehearsals, Streep turned to Beckett and asked: "Where do you think she is with him at this point?" Beckett answered, "Knows the truth that's emerged and plays wife looking to husband here to soften it." Streep nodded and proceeded to play the scene perfectly. Afterward, producer Jim Abrams asked Beckett, "What were you talking about? It was like you were talking in code. . . ." Beckett tried to explain. Finally, she just said, "I think it's a woman thing."[18]

Women have different stories to tell. Writer Gail Parent said she could pinpoint the moment women were incorporated into the comedy sitcom world:

> I was at the MTM production offices when a woman, maybe Charlotte Brown, suggested a story about how much it cost to be a bridesmaid. The producers, Allan Burns and Jim Brooks, and the rest of the staff looked at each other and realized they would never have come up with that story. That moment is still so vivid in my mind. . . . I give those guys real credit, too, for realizing that comedy could also come from experiences only women have.[19]

The importance of women in various roles behind the camera cannot be overstated. The annual studies by Dr. Martha Lauzen, San Diego State University, on the participation of women in both film and television, point out that when one woman is in a position of power, as a producer, director, or writer on a film or a television show, the number of females in other positions increases. Lauzen also found that shows with a female producer or writer present more female characters on the screen. In television, more females in those positions also tend to show female characters with different language behavior, as in advice giving or interruptions. The female writers empower their female characters. Women in power roles behind the scenes produce in those shows a more equal behavior on screen between men and women: insults decrease, compliments increase. When women write shows, their dialogue reflects more appearance comments about other characters, a reflection of women's real-life experiences.[20]

In 1993, producer Lynda Obst (*Sleepless in Seattle, The Fisher King*) said, "We need strong stories, the way boy movies have. I'd love to find a film with a strong premise that isn't as sexist as *Fatal Attraction* but one that taps into a girl myth as powerfully as that movie tapped into a boy myth."[21]

Ten years later, more women are making independent films (Karyn Kusama's *Girlfight*, Jessica Sharzer's *The Wormhole*, Deborah Hoffman and Frances Reid's *Long Night's Journey into Day*, Sarba Das's *Come On*), network shows (*Family Law* and *Judging Amy*), and cable shows (*If These Walls Could Talk, Sex in the City*).[22]

The variety of women's work as writers, directors, and producers is stupendous: Penelope Spheeris, Barbara Kopple, Kimberly Peirce, Rachel Talalay, Kathryn Bigelow, Mary Harron, Christine Vauchon, Pamela Koffler, Stacey Sher, Stephanie Austin, Janet Yang, Maggie Renzi, Ruth Caleb, Jane Rosenthal, Lisa Henson, Julie Lynn, Jada Pinkett Smith, Dorothy Berwin, Caroline Kaplan, to name a few. Often, their ideas and approaches are different. Like many performers, Liv Ullmann is directing (*Private Confessions, Faithless*). She believes women directors change the atmosphere on a set. "We are less controlling. We know what we want but we're not afraid to listen to others with different opinions." In my interview with her, she spoke of director Martha Coolidge's *Rambling Rose:* "the details and . . . that wonderfully slow pace as if we had time to explore what was happening in this family." Having just interviewed Barbra Streisand, I asked her about Streisand's film, *Yentl*. She praised it, saying, "That film could not have been made by a man. [If it had] people would have said, 'Oh, my God, look what we have found! Look at this new director!' They would have held that director in high regard."[23] Reviewer Pauline Kael wrote that the movies seemed "distinctively feminine," citing scenes that "are simply different from scenes conceived and directed by men."[24]

Moreover, women are making films with other women, and not always by design. For example, Marian Rees said about her 1998 production of *Ruby Bridges*, "It was not an intentional gathering of all these women—the director, the producer, the executive producer, the writer, the composer, the associate editor, and the executives at Disney. I was standing on the set one day and thought, 'This is as good as it gets.'"[25]

Judith James and Camille Cosby produced *Having Our Say: The Delany Sisters' First 100 Years* (1999), a two-hour television movie for CBS. It starred Diahann Carroll, Ruby Dee, and Amy Madigan. Lynne Littman directed, and Emily Mann wrote both the play and the film script, based on the book by Sarah and A. Elizabeth Delany with Amy Hill Hearth. They had a set full of women.

"It was wonderful," says James. "Men were working with us but it was nice to have a group of women in those positions on that show. We had a comfort level with each other where no one said, 'Oh, there she goes being touchy-feely,' or any of the statements that often come up with men." On the set, James felt the women didn't have to couch judiciously a demand or a thought. "We just had a different management style." Part of the joy was the shorthand. "It's just easier when you're talking to a woman. Men have shorthand, too, which makes it easier for them to work together. Having a lot of women on the set in control of the work made communication faster for us. In a way, I guess it's the numbers. Guys have controlled their sets for decades . . . . People have a good time when they share the same language."

In any career over the years, one works in certain expected ways and then suddenly a new way appears. For instance, on James's production of *Mr. Holland's Opus* (1996), the crew was mainly men, but the subject matter, about the human heart and human interactions, spoke to everyone on the film. She thinks it is the kind of film women often create.

"Opus is about music and art and loving our children," says James, "and about a deaf child. That's not the movie's log line, but those issues lodge deep inside the movie. It was the first movie I've been on where the whole crew read the script, right down to the second and third grips. Several crew members had a deaf person in the family. They brought them to the set . . . [and] the signers we had for the deaf actors translated for kids. No one felt they were imposing by bringing a child to the set. It had nothing to do with male-female. It was human."[26] On the set of *Having Our Say*, Lynne Littman, the director, said that

> Judy and Camille, the producers, were like the mama lions . . . they allowed the creative process to keep on going. That production was a different experience. It was not mysterious, it was thrilling! Every woman should have some taste of this, and it had nothing to do with not adoring men. I got a glimpse of the kind of entitlement that's been a male experience [as they make films] throughout the world. Experiencing that, it's heady stuff. . . . Sexism resides on an unconscious level in us. But on that set . . . we knew that we had made another country. We were not explaining ourselves. We didn't have to translate. It was ours.[27]

A few prominent women, who started as assistants in the 1980s, are mining ore in the formerly all-male preserve of action adventure: Laura Ziskin produced *Spider-Man 1 & 2*, Lauren Shuler Donner *X-Men 1 & 2*, Gale Anne Hurd *Hulk*, and Laurie MacDonald *Men in Black I* and *II*.

What hasn't changed is that even though women produced these action films, none were directed, written, or shot by a woman. However, consider other recent films that women produced but wrote or directed: *Monsoon Wedding*, directed by Mira Nair, written by Sabrina Dhawan; *Double Happiness*, written and directed by Mina Shum; *The Rosa Parks Story*, directed by Julie Dash, who also wrote and directed *Daughters of the Dust*; *Things Behind the Sun* and *Gas, Food, Lodging* by writer-director Alison Anders; *My Big Fat Greek Wedding* written and coproduced by Nia Vardalos, *Thirteen*, cowritten and directed by Catherine Hardwicke; or the long careers of producer Sarah Radclyffe (*Free Jimmy, A World Apart*), writer-producer-director Nora Ephron (*You've Got Mail*), or performer, now director, Diane Keaton (*Unstrung Heroes*).

Films like these show the range of what women create now compared to the extremely narrow possibilities open to them just a few years ago. From my own experience as a filmmaker and writer, the social change is striking. No woman today will be told, as Martha Coolidge and I were told, separately, that women could not be directing majors at New York University's Cinema School in the 1960s because "there are no women directors." There were no role models for what Martha, for example, or any number of other women, wanted to do. Martha stormed ahead, writing and directing *Not a Pretty Picture* in 1975, a film dealing with date rape. In the 1960s, very few women were admitted to NYU's film department; the only female instructor I had was Shirley Clarke, writer-director-editor (*The Cool World, Portrait of Jason*). Screenwriter Diana Gould said, "At film school all the boys were going to be directors and I was supposed to be Hedda Hopper."

Women are seen as understanding emotional nuances, or perhaps different nuances that they allow to emerge. As a reviewer said of Sophia Coppola's *Lost in Translation*, "Coppola has an eye for the quiet, surprising details that build character and mood."[28] But individual women are as varied in their instincts and interests as men. Documentaries about mothers, children, gardening, or anything male producers once thought that I, as a woman, was suited to write never interested me much. I wanted broader issues—racism, women's rights, urban pollution, and urban poverty. I simply went on making the films that interested *me*. I was not aware of it then, but like all the women I interviewed, I found that if I worked twice as hard for less money, I could get films made. In the 1980s, women were being promoted or we saw them producing and directing; we felt that through the power of films attitudes about women would shift in elemental ways. Some of that happened, but the revolution we saw as certain was deferred—particularly for minority voices in film about the complex lives women really lead, from their points of view, on all levels of society.

Director Neema Barnette, for example, grew up in Harlem and came to Hollywood in the early 1980s. Executive producers Gloria Steinem and Rosilyn Heller (one of the first women to be a studio vice president in 1974) hired Barnette to direct *Better Off Dead*, a Viacom and Lifetime production. The film dealt with big issues framed by the relationship of two women, one black, one white, one in prison, one a district attorney. Mare Winningham played the white woman on death row; Tyra Ferrell played the African American D.A. who tries to save her. Barnette relates, "I began getting calls from executives at Lifetime about the black female character, the district attorney. They wanted her to be more animated. 'What do you want,' I asked, 'more like Mrs. Jefferson?'" Barnette saw again the powerful mythic image of black women in America. "The television execs were perpetuating the image that they, in television, had created," she said. "I am a black woman and I was trying to create a real image. The executive kept wanting Tyra's character to be happier. I didn't want her, the black character, to be accommodating. . . . I'm everybody's mammy. I wanted the two women to become friends through their emotional experiences, because to Tyra, Mare Winningham's character [in prison] was dirty white trash. To Mare, Tyra was just a nigger. When you bond through that kind of relationship, the bond can't be broken. In terms of these characters I knew what I was talking about but no one believed me. And we are dealing with the myth of a black woman versus reality. Many white executives don't think that we're capable of directing our own stories, or they don't want to deal with the changes that need to be made in those stories to develop true images. I don't know any black female director who isn't image conscious. We have so much to change in terms of black female images, just like the changes of white female images that began in the 1980s. Different people tell the story they know because they live it."[29]

"What really happens is the influence of one person and the influence of numbers," says producer Marcia Nasatir (*The Big Chill*, *Ironweed*). "It's the reason women had no influence and now have some."[30] That is what women have accomplished in film and television in the last thirty years: Women had no influence and now have some. Whoever is in the room, male or female, black or white, will contribute to decisions about the kinds of movies that will be made—what the world will see. It is a profoundly important process that is often dealt with in a bewildering or expedient way.

Producer Paula Weinstein (*Iron-Jawed Angels*, *Analyze This*) knows this terrain. "Being a woman has influenced my career in terms of storytelling," she says.

Part of this is trusting one's instincts, that emotional and instinctual intelligence, which, once accepted and appreciated and allowed to flourish, is great. I've learned how to trust that and not go to the more male head side, particularly in making movies and telling stories. Does my instinct tell me this is true, do I believe it, and is it something I want to see?[31]

"But do women support women-made movies?" wonders Phylis Geller, former Sr. VP, Cultural Programming and New Media, Washington DC Educational Television Association (WETA).

We must address the political imperative of promotion. I spoke once to a national women's leadership group, women in business, education, government. They admitted they were not aware when a film is directed or written by a woman but if they knew, they'd make the effort to see it. We all got excited about a potentially huge network of women's groups who would spread the word, so much simpler now with the Internet, that such and such a film deserved the support of women.[32]

Her point is important. All filmmakers, no matter what kind of film they produce, face the difficulties of the market. In the 1990s, the traditional market, friendly to stories about and for men and boys, began to expand. Today, young females are the second most reliable movie audience. Amy Pascal, vice chair of Sony Pictures Entertainment, has long supported the idea that teenage girls formed a large untapped movie market.

"Unfortunately, it's still true that both boys and girls will go to movies about boys," said Pascal in 1999, "but boys will not go to movies about girls. So before those movies could be really successful, we had to wait until there was a large enough female audience who go to the movies by themselves. More girls have earning power today and more girls assert their interest in what they want to see."

Pascal worked on the 1994 version of *Little Women*. It was produced by Denise DiNovi, written by Robin Swicord, and directed by Gillian Armstrong. "Robin Swicord and I dreamed of doing it years before," says Pascal. "I sensed [the story] would connect with a contemporary audience of primarily women in the way it always had. But [at the studio] many did not."[33]

"Even though the studio viewed *Little Women* as a movie that wouldn't cross over to other markets," screenwriter Robin Swicord said, "we felt the existing [female] market was big enough in 1994 to warrant their investment. It took a lot of convincing . . . and a lot of people, Amy Pascal, Lisa Henson and others, to get it going. There were many obstacles; they even took the money away from us while we were shooting. And yet we prevailed. After that, people stopped talking so much about movies aimed at female audiences being flukes, which is what they always said if you mentioned *Steel Magnolias*. *Little Women* broke down a barrier."[34]

The movie was a worldwide hit and earned three Oscar nominations.

"Women are half the population!" Sara Risher, chair of New Line Cinema Production, said. "I feel that if [the marketing people] can't make a success out of that kind of movie, then someone's marketing it wrong. They often said, 'I can't sell those movies.' Well, learn. We've got to reach women, they're out there, and they watch movies." Risher started the ChickFlicks division of New Line in 1999.[35]

Whose story is being told, who is telling it, and how to get it seen are the real challenges for women in the next decades. The political, economic, and creative dimensions have stepped into the sunlight only because many women now work in film and television.

Which Battles Do I Fight Today?

Even though much has changed for women, much remains the same, for reasons that have to do with women as well as men. "A couple years ago," says producer Judith James, "TNT wanted to do a two-hour special about women in power in Hollywood. I wanted to do a segment with women's faces darkened out and their voices altered telling how they got through the day. One woman in a high position might get through with 'Daddy may I . . .?' Others might use sexual innuendo. I thought we'd also do interviews on the street, asking other women how they get through their day, and we could be funny and sophisticated about it. I wanted to do that special because we should grow up—these things are in our world and we have to deal with them. It scared the shit out of TNT. 'That's not appropriate, we're in responsible positions, we don't think like that.' Even friends told me, 'I've never found that [in my work].' It may not be a male world now, but it is a male-constructed world, and I think some women still get scared. They are protecting their image and their hard-won gains."[36]

No matter how long a woman has worked, it still comes down to choosing the battle. It comes down to speaking up. "I'm sitting in a screening," Donna Smith said, "and a male executive said, 'Not enough titties.' I looked at him, and said, 'You are out of line.' 'Oh, c'mon, Donna, you know . . .' 'Yes, I know and I'm calling you out on that comment.'"[37]

Speaking up can be costly. Smith was in no danger of losing her job, but if there is only one other woman in the room and five guys who can fire you

in a heartbeat, you think twice. Some women admit that ten years ago in certain situations they didn't say anything. Today, they feel they've changed but
men have not.

"It is important go on the record," says producer Ilene Kahn Power (*Elvis*).
Only a few years ago women were often patronized, and depending on their
age or number of credits, still are. To them, men said, in effect, 'We're so glad
you're so creative and got this project going, now we'll take over.' When
women made an issue of it, the guys quickly admitted, 'Yes, you're so right,'
but they often started doing it all over again. "It's like, respect, guys, a little
respect," says Power. "We all hoped that each time a woman spoke up it
raised their consciousness for the next time. I think it has. But you have to
speak up. You have to nip it in the bud." [38]

"I was on a plane recently, another producer told me, when I heard the
CEO of *my* media production company say about me to the president, 'Now,
is she coming to this?' Not only am I the executive vice president of the company, but I put all the elements together . . . to create the program we were
flying in to finalize. . . . When a little misspeak like that occurs, your eyes sort
of roll back, and it's like, 'Yeahhhh.' It doesn't stop me or any other woman,
but you know oppression in a subtle quiet way, and you wince. That's what
girls and women go through all our lives. This little wincing. It's a reminder,
keep your guard up, keep being out there, stay in their face, claim your credits, or you will sink." [39]

Younger Women, an Entirely Different View

Culture is not a slab of concrete. It responds to pressure.

"A friend of mine graduated from [UC] Berkeley," said film producer Debra
Hill, "worked her way through KNXT and on and on, became a major news
producer and won a lot of awards. Her daughter went to Brown and then to
journalism school. My friend, her mother, said to her, 'Why do you want a masters in journalism?' Her daughter said, 'I can always be a news producer. It's a
good fallback position.' In one generation, an entirely different perspective." [40]

Women beginning to work today did not experience the struggles of the
1970s or 1980s. They have grown up seeing women working as writers, producers, or filmmakers. They don't think of themselves as part of the women's
movement, they admit they work mostly with men, but they're making their
films, and being a woman isn't much of an issue because no one has seemed
to hold them back. And yet . . .

"Young women are rarely aggressive," says Sheila Nevins, executive vice
president of Original Programming, HBO.

I've pushed them ahead but they are not self-motivated. Men always ask me for more . . . [but] women are still intimidated. For all the changes that have occurred, there's a distinct difference still and it's mainly in expectation. Oddly, women can be competitive, aggressive and ambitious, but they feel less entitlement than men. I prefer working with women. I feel a sisterhood with the struggles of women. I like working with men, too, but there's a distinct difference. There is a difference.[41]

A few young women I interviewed said that their peers unknowingly allow the problems women have always faced at work to continue.

"Sexism persists; we have to contend with it on a daily basis," says Alyss Dixson, who, at thirty, is starting her own production company. "It is heartbreaking that women help perpetuate it by not speaking up. . . . Women are part of a code of silence. Guys have a vested interest in making an old boy network, and when their assistants, young guys, hear them call women bimbos or whores, and they see me accepting that, he thinks it is okay. That's how the stuff gets perpetuated."[42]

Most of the women I spoke with felt that women in their twenties today have great opportunities that were not available even ten years ago, but that their chances are still not the same ones that men enjoy.

The Next Frontier, and the Next, and the Next

In the early 1980s, many women in film and television believed that "the battles" would be over by 2000. But women's history shows us that it takes years to change social attitudes and put the results into practice.

"We can observe," writes historian Gerda Lerner, "that it took the organized women's movement of the 19th century 72 years of ceaseless activity to win the right to vote. We can also notice that it took more than 100 years to accomplish a basic reform, the outlawing of child labor. . . . Reforms in a democracy are not made within a few years of effort; they take decades."[43]

It is the "essentially repetitive nature" of the struggle, writes historian Rosalind Miles.[44] In addition, compared to the 1970s, it is clear now that there are various forms of oppression, that "not all women are equally oppressed."[45] Race, gender, and class mix in an uneasy stew of conflict and with the individual's need for self-expression, which differs depending on that person's cultural heritage. Miles blames Hollywood for much of the mythology once and still perpetuated about women and men. Film, television, and commercials, "pseudomodern industries, the mass media, lead us firmly by the genitals backward into the future," she writes, and now "we can recognize the new arena in which the next stage for freedom and equality of women will be fought out."[46] What women write, produce, edit, or direct, and how they define their own experiences, will influence women and men everywhere because movies are our culture's tutor and our mythmaker.

Clusters of huge changes have won and then lost ground under withering backlashes and antifeminist campaigns. Yet women, while caring for their families, keep pouring into work. "Now, no one notices a woman film producer because there are so many," says Alexandra Rose, coproducer of *Norma Rae* in 1979 with Tamara Asseyev.

Betty Friedan said to me, speaking of those women who began working in the late 1970s or early 1980s, "Your generation was the only one that had any fun. My generation got so beaten up in the trenches of feminism that we're exhausted and angry. You're the first telephone line person, the first film producer, first commercial air lines pilot, first firefighter, first policewoman. Every other woman that comes after you will be like the men, one of the crowd." And she was right, I enjoyed everything I did. Then she said, "You are lucky." They were warriors; they never got what they fought for. They fought for us but didn't themselves receive the benefits. They took all the slings and arrows for us. [47]

There is a line in 1970s low budget film, *Summer School Teachers:* "I don't want to watch. I want to play."[48] It describes perfectly what drove women into film and television. Storytelling is a human need. The stories women tell in films or on television bring women into what I call the "global cultural conversation." Make a film, talk to the world. Those are the stakes today. We're either in the conversation or we are on the sidelines, watching.

"Movies are the people's art form,"[49] said writer-producer Fay Kanin, the first woman to be president of the Motion Picture Academy. For decades, movies have been one-half the people's art form.

As limited as many opportunities still are for most women, the outline of their influence in the art and enterprise of global entertainment can now be seen, because for thirty years women have persistently and optimistically made themselves part of the picture.

"Women have an extraordinarily unique opportunity," says producer Laura Ziskin. "Men have built the cities, made and defined the culture, interpreted the world. Movies are arguably the most influential medium in the world. They have a tremendous cultural impact. Because women are now making movies, then women's ideas, philosophy, point of view will seep into that culture. And that's never happened in history. We can't even see the impact of that yet."[50]

Biography

Mollie Gregory is the author of *Women Who Run the Show: How a Brilliant and Creative New Generation of Women Stormed Hollywood*, the dramatic story of women in the entertainment industry from 1970 to 2000. Her earlier nonfiction book was *Making Films Your Business*, a survival guide for independent filmmakers. She also writes novels, including *Equal to Princes, Triplets, Privileged Lies*. She began her career writing documentary films (*Off the Edge, Songs from the Fourth World*), and produced others (*Welfare: Exploding the Myths, E. R. A and the American Way*). She is a past president of PEN USA West and of Women in Film, and a former chair of the Writers Guild Women's Committee. She lives in Los Angeles.

1. Mollie Gregory, *Women Who Run the Show* (New York.: St. Martin's Press, 2002). All quotes in this essay are taken from the author's book, except where otherwise noted.

2. Martha M. Lauzen, "The Celluloid Ceiling: Behind-the-Scenes Employment in the Top 250 Films of 2004, unpublished report," Department of Communications, San Diego State University (June 2005). See also Lauzen, "Boxed In: Women On-Screen and Behind-the-Scenes in the 2002–2003 Prime-Time Season" (September 2003). See also www.nywiftv.org, New York Women in Film and TV.

3. Marcy Carsey, Carsey-Werner Co., producer of *Third Rock from the Sun, Cosby*, and *Roseanne*, interview by Mollie Gregory.

4. Melanie Cook, attorney, Ziffren, Brinttenham, Branca, Fischer, Gilbert-Lurie and Stiffelman, LLP, interview by Mollie Gregory.

5. Dianne Dixon, writer of animation, children's programming, and television programs (*Designing Women, Nurses*), interview by Mollie Gregory.

6. See Rosalind Miles, *Who Cooked the Last Supper: A Women's History of the World* (New York: Three Rivers Press, 1988).

7. Gerda Lerner, "What We Can Learn from Women's History Month," *The Progressive Media Project*, March 10, 2003, at www.progressive.org/mediaproject03/mplrn1003.html (accessed August 8, 2003).

8. Barbara Corday, co-creator, *Cagney & Lacey*; former president/COO, Columbia Pictures Television; former chair, Motion Picture/TV Production, University of Southern California, interview by Mollie Gregory.

9. Susan Littwin, "What Do Women Writers Want?" *Written By* 6, no. 4 (April 2002).

10. Meryl Streep, acceptance speech, 23rd Annual Women in Film Crystal Awards, June 19, 1998.

11. Gale Anne Hurd, producer, *The Waterdance, Alien Nation, Switchback, The Ghost and the Darkness, Armageddon*, interview by Mollie Gregory..

12. Nancy Mills, "Women Directors: Doors Open," *Los Angeles Times*, November 19, 1986, 1 CA.

13. Phylis Geller, writer/producer/director, *Cosmic Journey*, A&E; executive producer, *Korean War Stories*, PBS, interview by Mollie Gregory.

14. Fay Kanin, writer-producer, *Tell Me Where It Hurts, Friendly Fire*; interview by Mollie Gregory.

15. Regarding Barbara Hall, executive producer/head writer of *Judging Amy*, see Susan Littwin, "A Show of Her Own," no. 4 (April 2000).

16. Lynne Littman, director, *Number Our Days, Testament, In Her Own Time*, interview by Mollie Gregory. See also Debra Tannen, *Talking from 9 to 5, Gender and Discourse, The Argument Culture: Stopping America's War of Words*.

17. Treva Silverman, TV writer, *The Monkees, Room 222, Taxi*; first woman executive on *The Mary Tyler Moore Show* (Emmy), interview by Mollie Gregory.

18. Littwin, "A Show of Her Own," 13. Ann Beckett, writer-producer, *The Broken Cord, First Do No Harm.*

19. Gail Parent, co-executive producer, *The Golden Girls*; producer, *Tracy Takes On*. interview by Mollie Gregory. Charlotte Brown, writer-producer-director, *Rhoda, The Good News.*

20. Excerpted from Lauzen, "The Celluloid Ceiling" and "Boxed-In."

21. Suzanna Andrews, "The Great Divide: The Sexes and the Box Office," *New York Times*, May 23, 1993, (H15), 2.

22. Directors on *Sex in the City*: Allison Anders, Victoria Hochberg, Susan Seidelman. It is produced by Suzanne and Jennifer Todd. *Judging Amy* is executive-produced by Barbara Hall, who is also the head writer. Ann Kenney is the executive producer of *Family Law.*

23. Liv Ullmann, performer, *Cries and Whispers, Scenes from A Marriage, Face to Face*; screenwriter/director, *Sofie*; director, *Private Confessions, Faithless*; author, *Changing*, editor of *Letter to My Grandchild*. interview by Mollie Gregory.

24. Pauline Kael, "The Current Cinema," *New Yorker*, November 28, 1983.

25. Marian Rees, producer of *Miss Rose White, Love Is Never Silent, In Pursuit of Honor, Decoration Day*; ALT Films for PBS, *Cora Unashamed, Song of the Lark, Almost a Woman*, interview by Mollie Gregory.

26. Judith James, producer, *Mr. Holland's Opus, Kissinger and Nixon, Brotherhood of Justice, Quiz Show, Prisoner of Honor, Having Our Say: The Delaney Sisters First 100 Years*, interview by Mollie Gregory.

27. Littman, interview.

28. Edward Guthmann, "Lost in Translation," *San Francisco Chronicle*, September 12, 2003, ll.

29. Neema Barnette, TV, *Cosby, Hooperman, A Different World, China Beach, Zora Is My Name*; film, *Sybil Brand, Close to Danger, The Silent Crime*, interview by Mollie Gregory.

30. Marcia Nasatir, producer *The Big Chill, Ironweed, Hamburger Hill, A Match Made in Heaven, Vertical Limit*; first woman VP, United Artists, 1974 (*Rocky, One Flew Over the Cuckoo's Nest*), interview by Mollie Gregory.

31. Paula Weinstein, president, Spring Creek Pictures, copresident with Barry Levinson, Baltimore Springcreek Pictures: *Fearless, Truman, The Cherokee Kid, Analyze This, The Perfect Storm, The House of the Spirits*, interview by Mollie Gregory.

32. Geller, interview.

33. Amy Pascal, vice chair, Sony Pictures Entertainment; chair, Columbia Pictures (*Spider-Man, Men in Black I and II, Awakenings, A League of their Own, Hanging Up, The End of the Affair*), interview by Mollie Gregory.

34. Robin Swicord, *Shag, You Ruined My Life*; writer-producer, *Little Women, Matilda, The Perez Family, Practical Magic*, interview by Mollie Gregory.

35. Sara Risher, chair, New Line Productions, interview by Mollie Gregory.

36. James, interview.

37. Donna Smith, as president/CEO, Cinema Completions International, quoting her remarks, Arbus-Perlman monthly lunch, April 2000.

38. Ilene Kahn Power, producer, *Gia, Stalin, Fatherland, White Mile*. Interview by Mollie Gregory.

39. Anonymous, interview by Mollie Gregory.

40. Debra Hill, writer/producer, *Halloween, Escape from L.A.*; producer, *The Fisher King, Crazy in Alabama, Attack of the 50-foot Woman, The Dead Zone*; television director, *Dream On, Monsters*, interview by Mollie Gregory.

41. Sheila Nevins, executive vice president, Original Programming, HBO, *I Am a Promise, Educating Peter, Family Bonds, Jockey, Looking for Fidel, Common Threads: Stories from the Quilt, You Don't Have to Die*, interview by Mollie Gregory.

42. Alyss Dixson, former vice president production, Paramount Pictures, interview by Mollie Gregory.

43. Lerner, "What We Can Learn from Women's History Month," 2.

44. Miles, *Who Cooked the Last Supper*, 277.

45. Miles, *Who Cooked the Last Supper*, 282.

46. Miles, *Who Cooked the Last Supper*, 284–86.

47. Alexandra Rose, producer, *I Wanna Hold Your Hand, Nothing in Common, Quigley Down Under*; with Tamara Asseyev, *Norma Rae*, interview by Mollie Gregory.

48. Julie Corman, producer, *The Lady in Red, Boxcar Bertha, Summer School Teachers* (written by Barbara Peters), interview by Mollie Gregory.

49. Kanin, interview.

50. Laura Ziskin, former president, Fox 2000 (*Courage Under Fire, Soul Food, The Thin Red Line*); producer, *Pretty Woman, No Way Out, What About Bob?*; executive producer, *As Good As It Gets, Dinner with Friends, Fail Safe*; producer, 74th Academy Awards, 2002, interview by Mollie Gregory.

CHAPTER FIVE

~

Women's Theatre: Transforming Dreams

Susan Suntree

When I wrote my original essay, "Women's Theatre: Creating our Dream Now," nearly a quarter of a century ago, I was flush with the joy of self-discovery and the newly found resources of creative freedom and challenge presented by making women's theatre. At the same time, I was unaware of how many women across the country were creating women's theatres and performances and passionately theorizing about what we were doing. Reviewing women's work during the past three decades, and reflecting on the questions and necessities that have prompted my own performances, I am awed by the insurgent vitality and by the breadth and depth of our influences.

Our work continues to be staged in a culture that is emotionally and financially drained by wars and commercialism, with scant common space, where obvious common tasks like education, health care, art, and protection of water, air, and public land are not priorities. Because it is largely situated outside institutional walls, our work wields the power to create public space, shout headlines, tell secrets, name names. And as we perform, we nourish our mutual fascination with the work of renewal in a riven, unsettling world. It is an endeavor of which I am immensely proud to be a part.

Reclaiming Our History and Reshaping the Theatre

When I began, I didn't realize how indebted we all were to the vision of early twentieth-century women theatre artists, founders of many regional and Off-Broadway theatres, who "freed themselves from being 'commodities' in the hands of producers to head their own companies or join institutional theatres or even just tour an individual production that would allow them to perform personally and culturally meaningful plays."[1] These women, whose contributions to American theatre were just being rediscovered and recorded by feminist historians, seemed to speak through us as we determined to carry on their legacy of working from the wild heart of our inspirations and actual lives.

Since the 1970s, when dozens of women's theatre troupes and individual women's performance projects sprang up across the country,[2] the work of women's theatre has evolved, expanded, and cross-pollinated, keeping the promise of its historic roots. While the number of groups that might specifically designate themselves "women's theatre," typically because they produce plays by, for, and about women, appears to have declined, women performers have multiplied as we create works inspired by the situations and issues that control and influence our lives.

Today our plays and performances may frame events from a woman's point of view, or present women as central to the story, or portray us as having the power to struggle for our own liberation from degrading conditions, or restore women once lost in the annals of historical events. And sometimes we are self-performers working seams of autobiography. Of necessity, because new ideas require new forms of expression, and because the traditional theatre arts institutions have continued to block most women from artistic and decision-making roles, women and minority artists are freed to discover new dimensions of theatre and performance. This outsider status continues into the present with dispiriting and exhilarating results.

Definitions and Theories

During the past couple of decades, the development of women's theatre has been accompanied by significant theoretical work by scholars such as Peggy Phelan, Jill Dolan, Sue-Ellen Case, Linda Walsh Jenkins, and Helen Krich Chinoy. And there continues to be intense debate about definitions. Shall we use *woman* or *feminist, theatre* or *performance?* Janet Brown, in *Feminist Drama: Definition and Critical Analysis,* defines a feminist play as one in which "the agent is a woman, her purpose is autonomy, and her scene a society in which women are powerless."[3] W. B. Worthen, in *Modern Drama,* states, "Performance art is distinguished from drama in that there is no fictive 'play' being performed: the performance itself is the work of art."[4] The problem with this definition is that many performance artworks are scripted and include stories.

Theatre critic Elinor Fuchs acknowledges the complex and multiple ways these terms are currently used. She writes that "in the past twenty-five years the term 'theatre,' floating far from its old associate 'drama,' has itself become a proliferating source of meanings. . . . Performance, performance art, art performance, solo performance, the 'performance piece,' even performance theatre have arisen, all with different shades of meaning."[5] My focus in this essay is on practice rather than theory; I am going to use "woman" as a term that includes "feminist" in my meaning, and I'll do my best to dance with the terms "theatre" and "performance."

In the 1970s, the work of composing definitions of women's theatre was carried out largely in the action of performances. For example, "[A]t a Lesbian Art Project held in May 1979 in downtown Los Angeles, [Terry] Wolverton and a dozen collaborators presented *An Oral Herstory of Lesbianism* with storytelling, magic, and theatre. A journey into lesbian consciousness, the women sought to answer theatre-related questions such as: Is it performance? Is it art? Is it therapy?"[6] These questions were debated by performers as well as by scholars who were struggling for recognition of women's theatre as a field of study.

Today, women's theatre and performance art scholars, who were once marginalized in their institutions, ironically play the role of centralizing authorities. Feminist scholars tend to value work that does not represent a singular point of view, nor that represents a norm by which all other works should be judged, nor that intends to represent all people and situations (like the word "man" does when it is used to represent humanity). Similarly, what constitutes femaleness is debated on personal, political, spiritual, sociological, and biological grounds.

This way of looking at things, characterized as postmodern, emphasizes that reality and society are best understood as fragmented and centerless, which is partly liberating because it releases us from stifling, even dishonest, social and artistic codes. But this viewpoint can also be debilitating, even paralyzing, because there is no definite meaning to refer to. Even language itself becomes so slippery that communication can seem impossible and political action pointless. The margins have become the center, or, more specifically, there is no center and no margin; ours is a multicentered world, where many voices speak their truths.

Worldwide, since the 1970s the people who live at the cultural margins have been constantly and dramatically migrating. War, famine, and the cultural upheavals created by the economic policies of such international institutions as the World Monetary Fund have displaced massive numbers so that immigration is recasting populations on every continent. Simultaneously, fast-evolving, mass-produced technologies accelerate the travel of bodies, ideas, and images.

Film, television, websites, and cell phones, to name only a few of these tools, have made a kaleidoscope out of what were once thought of as centrally organized or master images, cultures, ideas, identities, narratives, and, therefore, performance strategies. I watched performers at large demonstrations outside the 1990 Democratic convention in Los Angeles use cell phones to coordinate street theatre events in a decentralized fashion never before possible. Nowadays, multiplied and broadcast images and speech, like seeds, generate imagined or actual moments of public power and make everyone, at one time or another, a performer.

No wonder there are so many different women's theatres and performance ideologies—there are so many arenas of female/human identity and so many communities who, for once and then all over again, need to speak out and be seen. Criticism of women's theatre as a homogeneous provenance of white, middle-class women, whether heterosexual or lesbian, is irrevocably changed. Ethnic, gender, sexual preference, class, age, and environmental politics in varying measures mix it up on a regular basis.

Confronting Women's Oppression, Telling Women's Stories

There has been noticeable progress, legally and personally, in the status of women since the 1970s, yet women's theatre work continues to confront entrenched oppressions of women. Though it shares roots with avant-garde theatre movements, its political heart makes women's theatre close kin with the community-based theatre movement that has burgeoned during the past two decades.[7] Even when community-based theatre projects are not solely focused on women's experiences, they are frequently led by women and often foreground women's lives and women players in the productions.[8]

Utilizing a variety of production models, including instruction or direction from professional or visiting artists to communal and collaborative creation and presentation, women's theatres share a range of methods with community-based performers. Each group redefines traditional attitudes toward the director's authority and the influence of the playwright's text, if there is one. Women's theatres, like community-based groups, present works that muster an intimacy and immediacy with their audiences, who shift from expecting entertainment to feeling essentially engaged.

As has been demonstrated by South Africa's Truth and Reconciliation Commission, telling one's story in public—about state violence, incest, damaged body image, the economic control of bread—asserts power that fractures taboos and shuffles the social order. The ongoing necessity of speaking in public about experiences and feelings women have long kept secret and of presenting stories risen from actual women's lives allows women to control how they are seen and understood. A moving example is *My Hips and Thighs Speak Rapture*, produced at the University of Louisville, Kentucky, in 2001. Written by Elizabeth Spreen, the script is based on true stories told in a workshop led by the project's director, Rinda Frye.

Frye gathered a multigenerational, multiethnic group of students to explore, through physical and written improvisations and ritual exercises, how women think about their bodies after one of the graduates of her department revealed that, "she and several classmates had been anorexic during their graduate courses some fifteen years ago due in part to comments by professors about their need to lose weight in order to 'get work.'" [9] In the course of their workshop, "students talked about their own experiences, their secret memories. One by one, more than 60 percent of the class admitted to experiencing some form of childhood sexual abuse—a third had survived incest."[10]

Frye observed that the process of creating the play changed her students' lives, and its performance deeply affected its audiences, who reacted by "alternately laughing and gasping in all the right places" and who then "rose to their feet and cheered."[11] Someone in her department announced that it was the worst theatre ever and another said it was the kind of work that saved academic theatre from artistic death. Bold audience reaction has long been a hallmark of women's theatre productions.

Internationally, women create theatre to help themselves and their communities examine and cope with gender conflicts and local political and economic struggles. For example, in Chiapas, Mexico, where the indigenous people have led an insurrection against the Mexican government protesting their terrible poverty and exclusion from the government, Isabel Juarez Espinos and Petrona de la Cruz, acknowledged to be their country's first female Indian playwrights, founded Fortaleza de la Mujer Maya (Empowerment of Mayan Women), a theatre group composed of Mayan women and children who are credited with creating a theatrical revolution.

In rural Kenya, Africa, the Kawuonda Women's Group collaboratively support one another in creating income-generating projects like a bakery and in creating plays, woven from song, dance, traditional stories, and improvisation, presented outdoors for their communities. Their work "is a sanctuary where the women can nurture their creativity, express their frustrations and jubilations, and explore strategies of domestic survival and communal development. And as public performance, their community theatre functions as a cultural binding force. It takes over the grandmother's traditional storytelling role by replaying scenes from the past lest the children forget. But at the same time, the Kawuonda plays also build bridges to those men who care to listen."[12]

Women's theatre has become a potent form of local action as women around the world act to support their personal, creative, and economic lives, often despite harrowing and dangerous circumstances.

Performance Art Contributions

Interest in politics and concern for community problems have also inspired what is now called performance art. Beginning with the visual art-based Happenings of the 1950s, painters and sculptors took to the streets and other non-gallery locations to physically enact abstract, unexpected, sometimes shocking events. But by the 1970s, performance-based art was a signature form created by women, infused by ritual, goddess imagery, visual art materials and methods, autobiography, dreamscapes, communal creation, and political heat. The epithets, "It's therapy" and "It's political," once wielded with devastating scorn, have paled as the connection between the personal and the political, a hallmark feminist concern, has permeated American culture. Women performance artists also evolved the site-specific production, meaning they created their work outside the theatre hall, from which they were largely excluded.

In my own work, though I began working outdoors and in nontheatre locations because, among other reasons, these sites didn't cost money, I have come to prefer creating this way because the site will push my thinking and creative awareness. In my experience it's wonderfully true that necessity breeds invention. My work "out-of-doors" teaches me to co-create with the ground and its flora and fauna, the street and its traffic and pedestrians, the weather, light and shade, patterns of ambient sounds and silences. Similarly, works created for indoor locations—laundromats, bars, planetariums, hallways, cafeterias—you name it, and women have performed there—demand the same rigorous attention, which stimulates new and previously unimagined ideas and choices.

For practical as well as creative reasons, another hallmark of women's performance art has been the one-person show in which a performer might play only herself or an entire cast of characters. British performance artist Bobby Baker creates one-woman, site-specific shows that are simultaneously mundane, sacred, ritualized, comedic, and highly visual. She plays herself living her everyday roles as, among others, mother and shopper at such sites as her personal kitchen, grocery stores, and in churches.

In *The Kitchen Show*, she invited an audience to her home where, in her actual kitchen, she performed variations on twelve gestures of cooking such as stirring, throwing, peeling, eating, praying, dancing, tidying, resting, and roaming around. As the performance continued, critic Grisela Pollack writes, "There are actions like offering a cup of tea or coffee which are both simple tasks and dense social rituals. . . . Bobby Baker focuses attention on the gesture of stirring by fixing her hand into that pose with lengths of adhesive bandage. Suddenly the hand that stirs the coffee in this sunny and plant-filled kitchen becomes a kind of bondage, an injury on a body marked and incapacitated like the bound foot of old China in its submission to the invisible bonds of hospitable service patriarchal cultures call femininity. . . . The Kitchen is a theatre for many emotions. But *Kitchen Show* makes us see the actions without an overdressing of drama. They are performed, not acted."[13]

Creating a one-woman show not only encourages an artist to freely experiment, since it's up to the performer and not a board of directors to decide what she wants to create, it also allows women to choose difficult, challenging, unexpected topics.

Laurie Anderson and Anna Devere Smith examine our culture, from literary tropes such as *Moby Dick* to urban uprisings, using their singular bodies as mediums for investigation. In Allaire Koslo's *Purple Breasts*, cowritten with Daryle Lindstrom while she was dying of breast cancer, Koslo plays the many characters that shaped Lindstom's experiences in and out of hospitals as well as her emotional journey from hope to fury to her own kind of peace. In their one-person shows, women artists celebrate the female body as it shape-shifts genders, ethnicities, ages, and sometimes time and space.

The creative current of performance art has been so strong that it has influenced the definition of theatre and greatly expanded the range of its sites and subjects as well as reorganizing the relationship of performers to their audiences, directors to actors, and playwrights and scripts to the whole enterprise. Theatre studies in universities, for example, is now often accompanied by, and in some cases supplanted by, performance studies, and *Theatre Journal,* the international publication of American Theatre In Higher Education, renamed its "Theatre Reviews" section "Performance Reviews."

Ritual, Nature, and Healing

Many women performing artists, along with minority artists and others impelled by a need for new forms of expression and new lineages with which to identify, have traveled outside Western, urban literate cultural forms. "Non-literate and traditional non-Western theatre, accessed through travel, research, archaeology, anthropology, and other physical and social sciences, became teachers, providing new ways of examining and experiencing the-atre's purpose and practice."[14] For example, in my solo piece, *Origins of Praise*, about the death of my grandmother and suburbanization of the desert where I grew up, I was schooled and inspired by a mourning ritual of the area's indigenous people, the Paiute.[15] In *Sacred Sites/Los Angeles*, I perform the story of how the Los Angeles landscape has come to be the way it is, weaving indigenous myth, masks, and music with contemporary science. Playing a woman who creates the world as she examines it, I tell its creation from multiple perspectives, including a raven's.

Feminist art critic Lucy Lippard feels that this kind of exploration outside urban societies is best when it, "looks to the past for formal and emotive models, to the future for social models related to those of the past, and re-mains firmly rooted in the present," even as she warns against romanticizing the past or some exotic "other" that might soothe our sense of being rootless or perpetual outsiders.[16]

Similarly, the accustomed polarities, like personal-public, art-life, high art-low art, spirit-body, art-science, no longer, if they ever did, fit actual women's experiences, and women have sought performance models formu-lated without these binaries. Barbara T. Smith, who began her performance work in the 1960s with her study of ritual, reflects that, "It is no accident that there is a widespread interest in remembering our ancient tribal past and

Susan Suntree as Raven in "Sacred Sites/Los Angeles." Photo by Eugene van Erven

connections to sacred ways long lost. Anthropologists used to call 'quaint' and 'superstitious' such beliefs that, without prayers and certain ritual practices, the sun might not come up. Now we see that we have for so long treated the earth as an inert thing to use and exploit, that she may in fact be dying and the sun might not come up for us."[17] Smith's performances characterize a major theme of women's performance, which is to connect the urgent need for healing the environment with healing women's bodies and the larger body of our communities and cultures.

Performing Women's Bodies

An axiom of the women's movement that bears repeating is that the personal is political and vice versa. Women's bodies bear not only personal histories, but also the burden of male-dominated culture that has plenty of opinions about the proper management and usage of the female body. In styles and methods ranging from Carol Schneeman's influential performance, *Eye Body*, in the 1960s, when she created a piece that include her painted, nude presence lying among snakes, which Fuchs characterizes as "beautiful . . . celebratory . . . sacral, " to the coarse and confrontational rants and anti-erotic messes of Karen Finley in the 1980s, women's theatre and performance have taken on their own naked bodies as subjects and objects, especially in the 1980s.[18] By 1990, when the National Endowment for the Arts excluded from funding Karen Finely, lesbian performer Holly Hughes, and gay performers Tim Miller and John Fleck, the body politic was thrust fully center stage.

At the beginning of the 1980s, a scene in the Mabou Mines play, *Dead End Kids: A History of Nuclear Power*, directed by JoAnne Akalatis, was heatedly debated. In it a male character, intended to ironically portray America's degrading and dangerous nuclear ambitions, viciously harangues a young, sympathetic, but visibly powerless female character, demanding that she perform the sexual act of giving "head" to the headless neck of a dead, plucked chicken drawn from his pants. While many defended it, many others were seriously offended and felt that no matter what ironies the players intended, the scene was degrading to women.[19]

In contrast to performances presenting despoiled female bodies during the 1980s, some performances celebrated female sexuality, though the imagery may have been considered by some to be shocking. Porn star Annie Sprinkle began her career as a performance artist by welcoming audiences, in one of her shows, to examine her cervix while she held open her vagina with a speculum. Lesbian performance artist Holly Hughes created performances filled with "raunchy tales, spicy asides, and sometimes painful personal sagas"

and "proclaimed herself the 'preeminent lesbian playwright of my generation.'"[20] Hughes continues in the present decade to vamp, revamp, and re-
constitute sexual politics in homoerotic performances doubly charged by her
writing's poetic and political force.

In 1985, I created and directed *Skins: A Woman's Mystery Play*, which was
performed in the store windows of a lingerie shop, Playmates, on a seedy section of Hollywood Boulevard. Women dressed in costumes composed from
the store's lingerie portrayed various female mythic characters confronting
Changing Woman, who escapes the paralysis imposed by the costume and
posture imposed on her by the Businessman.

On her journey through the windows, she interacts with a series of goddesses
who attend to her body from head to toe as she strips and redresses as a self-
adorned beauty. After the Businessman climbs out of his glass display box, where
he found himself slowly tortured by his own toys and the cramped dimensions
of his seeming empire, he returns to claim Changing Woman, who captures,
strips, and redresses him in the celebrational finale. In these works, obscenity
does a striptease, unveiling the multicentered eroticism of the female body.

Performances of female sexuality and the naked female body generate
heated debates. Can women perform their own unclothed bodies in any way
they like and claim that they are redefining their cultural presence and blast-
ing holes in the constructs that separate good girls from bad girls? Can images of female degradation really critique female degradation? Or is what we
see really what we get, with the clever gymnastics of the theorizing mind providing rationalizing and distracting cover, for example, for the controversial
scene in *Dead End Kids*?

When men from the porn shop around the corner ogled the *Skins* performers in the store windows, obviously ignoring the actions of the performance and its multivalent cues and reformation of the female protagonist and
her consort, did the performance, in fact, shore up male sexist fires or douse
them and light female-sourced erotic flames? Must a performance aim to
serve or challenge everyone in its audience? Is it legitimate to aim a performance at some people and not others? These questions, among others, and
performed experiments are on going.

In her essay "Les Demoiselles d/L.A.: Sacred Naked Nature Girls' *Untitled
Flesh*," about the women's ensemble Sacred Naked Nature Girls, who performed as a troupe from 1994 to 1997, Meiling Cheng notes how the group
was determinedly heterogeneous in sexual identities and ethnicities. They
used their differences in some performances to highlight women's common
experiences of sexual victimization, while in others they emphasized their
conflicting attitudes, including ambivalences, about wielding sexual power.

By using improvisation and group composition, by interacting with their audiences, and by evoking ritualized goddess imagery, the Girls harkened to their women's theatre and performance predecessors. Their ethnic, ideological, and gender differences, their willingness to perform as themselves, female and naked, without sensationalizing degradation or required redemption, mark new ways of thinking about the female body. Shifting focus, "from the ordeal of bearing physical and emotional distress to the possibilities of healing," as they portray the "multiplicities of female desire," their work emphasizes women's evolving attitudes toward their bodies and declares new freedoms for women's performance.[21]

Plays and Playwrights

In the early twentieth century Gertrude Stein wrote plays that bypassed character development in favor of experiments with language, perception, and influential circumstances. Though her works are often judged abstruse, they provide historical context for women playwrights like Megan Terry, Caryl Churchill, and Maria Irene Fornas, among others, who have reformulated the role of character in their plays. Theatre critic Elinor Fuchs observes, "The question is not whether there are living creatures on the stage, but what it is we are following when we engage them."[22] She observes that in much contemporary playwriting and performance, the focus shifts away from the development and examination of characters toward the exploration of multiple subjects or of processes and conditions in which subjects/characters find themselves.

Women playwrights have contributed to the evolution of play structure partly from necessity as they seek to portray the world from new angles and partly to portray forces that propel and define situations rather than continue the modernist focus on the psychology of the individual, usually male, suffering in gender-conditioned isolation. Once when I took over a course in American Post–World War II Theatre, I realized that all of the plays listed on the syllabus, which were well-known works by famous playwrights, concluded with murder or suicide, except one. The exception was a play written by a woman, Marsha Norman's *Getting Out*, in which the female protagonist considers mayhem but turns, instead, to other women for solace and survival.

The textbook introduction to this script reported a (male) critic's concern that this ending was "too romantic."[23] Though Norman's play is a traditionally structured, realistic drama, nevertheless it shifts emphasis from the individual to the community even as it celebrates the protagonist's transformation. According to theatre scholar Helene Keyssar, "In feminist drama . . . the

impulse is not towards self-recognition and revelation of a 'true' self but towards recognition of others and a concomitant transformation of the self and
the world."[24] When a play centers on the volition of an individual protagonist, it's easy to overlook the social structures, events, and situations that
limit or mold behavior. This time-honored individual orientation portrays
our isolated plight as hopelessly, inescapably ours alone. No wonder so many
characters want to die!

Challenging Theatre Institutions

After decades of founding, supporting, and artistically influencing theatre institutions, women playwrights and most women performing artists, especially
in the larger theatres, continue to find themselves shut out of decision-making
roles. Recent statistics undeniably describe a scene in which women are side-
lined. But first the good news. According to the *New York Council on the Arts
Theatre Program Report on the Status of Women: A Limited Engagement?* published in 2002, a "new generation of women artists, nurtured and developed in
the non-profit , is achieving impressive prominence."[25]

Their list includes the first women in theatre history to be awarded Tonys
for Best Director (Garry Hines) and Best Director of a Musical (Julie Tay-
mor), in 1998. In the 1998–1999 season, Paula Vogel's *How I Learned to Drive*
was the most produced play nationwide by TCG (Theatre Communications
Group) members. Five women playwrights saw their works listed for the
2000–2001 season as among the ten most produced plays nationally, with
Yasmina Reza's *Art* tied for first place. The others are Rebecca Gilman's *Spinning into Butter*, Becky Mode's *Fully Committed*, Margaret Edson's *Wit*, and
Claudia Shear's *Dirty Blonde*. Eve Ensler's *Vagina Monologues* is being produced nationally and internationally, while Tina Landau and Susan Stroman
are busy directing hits on Broadway.

Now the bad news. The 1999 Tony Awards issue of *Theatre* magazine
sported a full-page ad placed by The Guerrilla Girls, an anonymous group of
visual artists and performers who protest the exclusion or underrepresenta-
tion of women from visual and performing arts institutions. Its headline read:
"There's a tragedy on Broadway and it isn't *Electra*."[26] Their proclamation
highlights the fact that in the theatre, when women chase after money, it's
nickels and dimes, and they're all rolling downhill.

In 1999, women wrote 8 percent of all Broadway plays and only 1 percent
of musicals. In theatres with budgets of less than $500,000, of all plays pro-
duced, women playwrights contributed 30 percent, and over 40 percent of all
plays had women directors. According to *American Theatre* magazine, the

2001–2002 season for Off-Broadway and regional theatres lists women directors at 16 percent and women playwrights at 17 percent, a notable decline from the heights of the 2000–2001 season, for which *American Theatre* magazine lists women directors at 23 percent and women playwrights at 20 percent. Note, however, that even these figures are compiled from total productions and don't account for the fact that there were multiple productions of Reza's *Art* and Edison's *Wit* that year. In the years from 1969 to 1975, women playwrights and directors hired by regional and Off-Broadway companies barely reached 7 percent.

Given the fact that since 1969 women "trained in equal numbers with men at the most prestigious theatre training programs, and though they received a majority of honors as emerging artists," women's lack of advancement in the theatre raises many questions about entrenched cultural attitudes and problems with the theatre as an institution.[27]

A panel that evaluated the statistics cited in the *New York State Council on the Arts Report on the Status of Women* discussed multiple causes for this trying situation. According to theatre researcher Virginia Valan, "Success is largely the accumulation of advantage."[28]

Among the many ways cited in the *Report* that women theatre artists are disadvantaged is the fact that mainstream reviewers are almost exclusively male; that research indicates women and men "share the same consistent subconscious over-valuation of the work of men and under-valuation of the work of women"; and that women are educated to identify with male protagonists, while men identify only with male protagonists.[29]

Consequently, plays by or about women are not perceived as universal but unconventional, and women playwrights are often encouraged to write plays with male leads if they want to see their work produced. Finally, in a climate of minimal funding for the arts, even theatres that will often produce women writers tend, for financial safety, to return to producing more well-known or mainstream plays, which are mostly written by white men.

In her contribution to *A Sourcebook of Feminist Theatre and Performance*, "Women at the Helm: In Leadership Posts Once Reserved for Men, They're Challenging Our Assumptions About Sex and Power," Misha Berson sees "[t]remors of change stirred in the late 1980s."[30] She goes on to write about and interview women artists who lead some of the largest and most influential nonprofit theatres in the country. As decision makers, these women may or may not change women's status in the theatrical landscape. It's too soon to tell, but Berson is optimistic despite noting, "The women I canvassed declared without apology that they feel no special obligation to produce women writers."[31] Jan Lewis, artistic director of the Jewish Women's Theatre Project in Los Angeles, is less sanguine. In fiscally challenging times like the present, she notes from experience, entry positions for women, like literary managers and dramaturges, are usually the first to be cut.[32]

Like many women working in small theatres, she finds that their social and artistic vision fuels their staying power. This is well illustrated by the decades-long careers of Joan Schirle, co-artistic director of the Dell'Arte Company, and Joan Holden, for over three decades the principle playwright at the San Francisco Mime Troupe, who have felt the rewards of working in a small company to be powerful enough to hold them for many years.

Choosing the Streets

In recent years, many women theatre and performance artists have discovered street theatre to be a worthy creative challenge. In 1996, I saw how I could apply my interests in community-based theatre to a local environmental crisis with international implications and founded FrogWorks with a small group of women. Our mission was to save the Ballona Wetlands, the last coastal wetland in Los Angeles, from developers who intend to cover it over with the largest development in the history of Los Angeles.

This presented us with an environmental issue that constellated many social concerns, including the link between social and environmental justice. Our troupe, composed of five women and one a man, works collaboratively, women play men's roles, and we foreground the crisis at the wetlands by focusing our plays on the predicaments faced by female protagonists.[33]

Other women-led troupes focus on national issues. Former actress Jodie Evans founded Code Pink to protest the war in Iraq and other social and political injustices. Using street theatre and other performance strategies, the women of Code Pink deliver memorable visual scenes for the public and for the media. For example, they delivered a "pink slip," literally the full-length pink slip Evans was wearing before she tore it off, to Senator Hillary Rodham Clinton to protest her support of the war in Iraq. They have succeeded in drawing public attention because their work is bold and entertainingly whimsical. Obviously, they invert the gendered sweetness of pink, turning it into a sign of courageous resistance. As White House political strategist Karl Rove is reported to have said, "You pink ladies are everywhere."[34]

During the planning and art-making workshops for demonstrations at the Democratic Convention in Los Angeles in 2000, I was amazed by the numbers of young women who were creating and performing dynamic, adventurous street theatre that utilized and expanded upon performance strategies

Private Betty Lou Pickle Plant (Susan Suntree), Betty the Light-footed Clapper Rail (Allaire Koslo), and Coyote (David Koff) in FrogWorks' "Saving Private Pickle Plant." Photo by Zoey Zimmerman

and troupe organization drawn from women's theatre. Twenty-seven-year-old Malaika Edwards is a cofounder of the *Art in Action Southwest Road Show: Another World Is Possible*, a performance about environmental justice and immigration issues that she collectively created and performed with a troupe composed of six women and one man.

Sounding like young women in the 1970s, she says that in her experience, "Women's thinking tends to steer more in the direction of collectivism and is more holistic, stewarding rather than conquering." Edwards observes that among her peers, women generally want to work with women because many men find it hard accept women's leadership: "We want to create a space that is different from our patriarchal world. Activism has shifted from being top-down, white male lead, and hierarchical to being grassroots, regional, and inclusive of various struggles."[35]

Signaling how a new generation of women is evolving women's theatre, she emphasizes that, "Things are different now. We don't single out women's issues. Now we are integrating issues—with more focus on racism—and seeing women's issues as part of a larger context."[36] A new generation of performing women, self-confident and willing to lead, are redefining and reshaping our cultural landscape.

Redefining Theatre

Perhaps the problem of women's advancement in the theatre is the problem of theatre itself. Historically identified with set scripts, specific buildings, and the support systems required to maintain them, boards of directors demand commercialization so that the bills are paid and the lights stay on. Theatre's institutional demeanor and high ticket prices also shape audience expectations of what will happen when they enter the building. Whatever is presented, it is made safer by the construct of the theatre itself.

Even the most revolutionary play, for example, loses at least some of its bite when the audience is composed of only those who can afford to be revolutionized. Nevertheless, commercial concerns don't fully explain the lack of women represented in theatre institutions. In Holland, for example, where theatre is heavily subsidized, women are still marginalized.

Theorist Baz Kershaw suggests an approach to this problem when he asserts that, "the place of *theatre* in post-industrial societies seems increasingly compromised" because "the performative quality of power is shaping the global future as it never has before." Consequently, "the processes of *performance* have become ever more crucial in the great cultural, social and political changes of our times."[37] Theatre, which he defines as buildings and their institutions, is too inflexible to face the demands of a society that mostly knows itself through media performances.

Since women's theatre and performance is by its nature a redefining cultural force, it is no wonder women find themselves out-of-doors, and, often lately, on the streets. Virginia Valin cautions that, "because women operate outside of the mainstream, they tend to 'reform' it less quickly than they could from within."[38] But perhaps outside is where our work best serves our truest aspirations for ourselves and our communities in these disordered times.

Notes

1. Helen Krich Chinoy, "Art Versus Business: The Role of Women in American Theatre," *The Drama Review* 24. no. 2 (1980): 7.

2. See Helen Krich Chinoy and Linda Jenkins, *Women in the American Theatre* (New York: Theatre Communications Group, 1987) and Dinah Luise Leavitt, *Feminist Theatre Groups* (NC: McFarland and Company, Inc., 1980).

3. Janet Brown, *Feminist Drama: Definitions and Critical Analysis* (Metuchen, N.J.: Scarecrow Press, 1979), 15.

4. W. B. Worthen, *Modern Drama* (Fort Worth: Harcourt Brace, 1995), 1190.

5. Elinor Fuchs, *The Death of Character: Perspectives on Theatre After Modernism* (Bloomington: Indiana University Press, 1996), 7.

6. Carol Martin, ed., *A Sourcebook of Feminist Theatre and Performance* (London and New York: Routledge, 1996), 60.

7. *See* Susan C. Haedicke and Tobin Nellhouse, eds., *Performing Democracy: International Perspectives on Urban Community-Based Performance* (Ann Arbor: University of Michigan Press, 2001).

8. *See* Eugene van Erven, *Community Theatre: Global Perspectives* (London and New York: Routledge, 2001).

9. Rinda Frye, "My Hips and Thighs Speak Rapture" (Essay provided by the author), 1.

10. Frye, "My Hips and Thighs Speak Rapture," 12.

11. Frye, "My Hips and Thighs Speak Rapture," 23.

12. van Erven, *Community Theatre: Global Perspectives*, 201.

13. Grisela Pollack, *"The Kitchen Show: Bobby Baker"* (London: Artsadmin, 1991). See www.bobbybakersdailylife.com.

14. Susan Suntree, "Dynamic Exhibition: Making Theatre in Museums," in *Redefining Archaeology: Feminist Perspectives*, eds. Mary Casey et al., (Canberra: ANA Publications, RSPAS, Australian National University, 1998), 216.

15. *See* Susan Suntree, "Origins of Praise," in *The House of Women: Women's Art and Culture in the Eighties*, ed. Sondra Hale (Long Beach: California State University at Long Beach, 1986).

16. Lucy Lippard, *Overlay: Contemporary Art and the Art of Prehistory* (New York: Pantheon, 1983). Cited in Suntree, "Dynamic Exhibition: Making Theatre in Museums," 217.

17. Barbara T. Smith, "Art and Ceremony," *High Performance* 1987, www.communityarts.net (15 Aug. 2003).

18. Fuchs, *The Death of Character: Perspectives on Theatre After Modernism*, 109.

19. Fuchs, *The Death of Character: Perspectives on Theatre After Modernism*, 111–112.

20. Rebecca Schneider, "Holly Hughes: Polymorphous Perversity and the Lesbian Scientist," in *A Sourcebook of Feminist Theatre and Performance*, ed. Carol Martin, (London and New York: Routledge, 1996) 239.

21. Meiling Cheng, "Les Demoiselles d/L.A.: Sacred Naked Nature Girls' *Untitled Flesh*," *The Drama Review* 42, no. 2 (Summer 1998): 91.

22. Fuchs, *The Death of Character: Perspectives on Theatre After Modernism*, 49.

23. Stephen Watt and Gary A. Richardson, eds., *American Drama: Colonial to Contemporary* (Fort Worth: Harcourt Brace College Publishers: 1995), 854.

24. Helene Keyssar, *Feminist Theatre: An Introduction to Plays of Contemporary British and American Women* (New York: Grove Press: 1985), xiv.

25. Susan Jonas and Susan Bennett, *"New York State Council On The Arts Theatre Program Report on the Status of Women: A Limited Engagement? Executive Summary."* New York Council on the Arts (January 2002), 1. All statistics in this section are taken from this report.

26. *See* The Guerrilla Girls website (www.guerrillagirls.com).

27. Jonas and Bennett, "*New York State Council on the Arts Theatre Program Report on the Status of Women: A Limited Engagement? Executive Summary*," 5.

28. Jonas and Bennett, "*New York State Council on the Arts Theatre Program Report on the Status of Women: A Limited Engagement? Executive Summary*," 5.

29. Jonas and Bennett, "*New York State Council on the Arts Theatre Program Report on the Status of Women: A Limited Engagement? Executive Summary*," 4.

30. Misha Berson, "Women at the Helm: In Leadership Posts Once Reserved for Men, They're Challenging Our Assumptions About Sex and Power," in Martin, ed., *A Sourcebook of Feminist Theatre and Performance*, 61.

31. Berson, "Women at the Helm: In Leadership Posts Once Reserved for Men, They're Challenging Our Assumptions About Sex and Power," 74.

32. Jan Lewis, personal interview. 9 September 2003.

33. *See* Susan Suntree. "FrogWorks in Los Angeles," in *Performing Democracy: International Perspectives on Urban Community-Based Performance*, eds. Susan C. Haedicke and Tobin Nellhouse (Ann Arbor: University of Michigan Press, 2001).

34. Quoted in Anne-Marie O'Conner, "Women Take a Leading Role in Protesting against the War with Iraq," *Los Angeles Times*, 15 March 2003, B1,12.

35. Malaika Edwards, personal interview (12 August 2002).

36. Malaika Edwards, personal interview (12 August 2002).

37. Baz Kershaw, *The Radical in Performance: Between Brecht and Baudrillard* (London and New York, Routledge: 1999), 5.

38. Quoted in Jonas and Bennett, "*New York State Council on the Arts Theatre Program Report on the Status of Women: A Limited Engagement? Executive Summary*," 5.

Biography

Susan Suntree is a theatre artist and poet whose work investigates the dynamics of myth, science, and nature as they engage contemporary life. Her performances and poetry have been presented nationally and internationally, and her publications include essays, books of poetry, biography, and translation, as well as reviews for *Theatre Journal*. Some of her plays are the four-part cycle, *Seed to Snow: Plays for the Seasons*; a one woman piece, *Origins of Praise*; *SKINS: A Women's Mystery Play; Talking to the Sun*; and *The Symphony of Giordano Bruno*. *Sacred Sites/Los Angeles*, her recent one-woman performance, explores the prehistory and sacred geography of Los Angeles where she lives and is the subject of her forthcoming book. She is a founding member of FrogWorks, an eco-political street theater troupe. She was, also, the founder and co-director of *Earth Water Air Los Angeles*, a giant puppet pageant and performance trek across Los Angeles connecting endangered open spaces. She was born in Los Angeles, lives in Santa Monica, and currently teaches private workshops and at East Los Angeles College.

PART TWO

MUSIC

~

CHAPTER SIX

Women's Music:
Passing the Legacy

Boden Sandstrom

Introduction

For those of us who lived and breathed women's music for the past three decades, the last few years have been marked by major milestones, as well as mourning for the loss of several founding mothers, among them Ginni Clemmens (singer, songwriter, and producer), Mary Spottswood Pou (producer and publisher), and Kay Gardner. Gardner was not only a musician, choir director, conductor, composer, and priestess but a theorist of feminine aesthetics in music and the use of sound in healing. She eloquently discusses her ideas on women's music in both editions of *Women's Culture*. These foremothers of women's music all made valuable contributions to its birth and are greatly missed.

One notable accomplishment in portraying the rich history of women's music has been the completion and screening of the documentary, *Radical Harmonies*, directed by Dee Mosbacher, which contextualizes the roots of women's music and documents the growth of the cultural network that has been its sustaining force.[1] It also tackles some of the difficult issues that have emerged within women's music such as racism, accessibility, and separatism.

However, the impact of these cultural phenomena remains unrecognized not only by mainstream media but also by many academic historians and educators. This frustrating fact was driven home at the most recent GRAMMY Awards ceremonies, during which the passing of those who have contributed to the music industry was commemorated. Not one of the women mentioned above was honored, though their combined artistic legacy includes production companies, recordings, books, academic achievement, and many memorable performances. (Journalists started using the term "women's music" to refer to the current proliferation of women in popular music.)

According to the media, women's music sprang onto the scene with two groundbreaking moments in music history. The first occurred in 1996, when Alanis Morissette swept the GRAMMY Awards. This was the first year in which a majority of women dominated the *Billboard* charts, inspiring the media to dub it "The Year of the Woman."[2] The second was in 1997, when Sarah McLachlan took women pop and rock musicians on the road to perform in a traveling festival known as Lilith Fair. Seldom does McLachlan publicly acknowledge the annual women's music festivals that inspired Lilith Fair, most prominent among them the National Women's Music Festival (founded in 1974) and the Michigan Womyn's Music Festival (founded in 1976). However, in the introduction to the book *From Lilith to Lilith Fair*, she recognizes their impact: "The fact that there have been women's festivals happening all over North America for years . . . helped to create a space where my idea could be heard, accepted and brought into the mainstream."[3] The sheer diversity of performers and genres staged at these festivals, and the fact that women, rather than men, execute the entire range of technical and production work, clearly distinguish the "grandmothers of all festivals" from their somewhat upstart prodigy.

What Is Women's Music?

In the first edition of this book, Ruth Scovill stated in the chapter "Women's Music,": "There is no simple definition of Women's Music, and to create unnecessary boundaries by defining it would only restrict its natural growth."[4] Scovill understood that music carries meaning but that this meaning can be interpreted differently depending on its community. Scovill also understood that women's music would evolve. Just as women's music and its performance helped negotiate the identity of women yesterday, the women's music of today is a locus for identity negotiation among young women, particularly lesbians.

According to Scovill, the primary feature that distinguishes women's music from the popular music of the time (1970s) is that it "holds the feminist and humanist ideals of self-affirmation and mutual support."[5] She makes a case for this by examining three basic components of women's music: lyrics, production, and musical structure.

The lyrics demonstrate contrasting values of self-affirmation in the areas of sexuality and relationships, and empowerment of woman versus degradation and stereotyping in most popular music. Artists mentioned by Scovill whose lyrics illustrate these points are Holly Near, Carly Simon, Beverly Grant, Cris Williamson, and Meg Christian.

Production of women's music is typically accomplished through a reciprocal and responsible relationship between audience and performer and a collaborative relationship between the technical production and concert production to ensure accountability to the women's community.[6]

Scovill also raises the possibility of a distinct musical structure in compositions by women. She cites theories of Kay Gardner (circular form or structure related to "divine proportion," or "golden section" by mathematicians, also known as the Fibonacci series) and Margie Adam (rhythmic complexity of women's composition and different use of tonal space) and speculates on the possibility of "a different musical form."[7] There is much work that needs to be done in applying these theories to the body of work of women's music.

Women's music is a genre of music, within a particular historical context. Elements that distinguish musical genres can be complex and difficult to define. Criteria can include economics (music as a commodity), social context including the audience, and content (lyrics, musical structure, and instrumentation). It can also include the aesthetics of the music and its efficacy—that is, whom does the music serve and resonate with. Scovill defines women's music as primarily the music of feminists whose overarching political objectives were to redefine the role of women in society; therefore it included political feminists who were not necessarily writing or singing what became known as "women-identified music" (music specifically written by, for, and about women). Women-identified music became known as women's music, and one of its defining elements is the cultural network that developed to support the music.

The uniqueness of women's music is that it evolved as the expression of a distinctly lesbian cultural ethos in that it has been primarily lesbians who have written, performed, and distributed the music, and who continue to shape its contemporary expressions. The aesthetics of this genre include the celebration of women's lives, feminist politics, spirituality, accountability, lesbian relationships, the empowerment of women, and feminine composition. Women's music and the resultant women's music network were spearheaded by lesbians because in large part the performance of women-identified music was, and is, specifically an artistic emotional expression of lesbian feminists, although also relevant to nonlesbian women. Laura Post, in *Backstage Pass: Interviews with Women in Music*, defines it as, "a cultural construct, encompassing music and other arts, built upon the foundation of world music, and ultimately connected to the gay and feminist movements."[8]

The vitality and richness of the genre is manifest in the cultural network that supports it, culled from the fertile soil of women's music traditions throughout the world that span centuries.[9] Within the United States, diverse communities including Native American, African American, Latin American, and Jewish and European immigrants contributed oral traditions, country, bluegrass, spirituals, and labor and civil rights protest songs, whose intersections at the crossroads of political and social upheaval throughout the twentieth century created the context for women's music.

Women scholars have grappled with definitions of women's music. According to Cynthia Lont in her dissertation on women's music:

> This alternative music industry was originally called "lesbian music" because many felt the music was started by lesbians for lesbians. Others believed the music was started by heterosexual feminists and taken over by lesbian-feminists when they broke away from the women's liberation movement in the early 1970s. The term "women's music" stuck because it was less threatening, both to the dominant social order and to women's music performers and audiences.[10]

Victoria Louise Nagle, in her dissertation on women's music and the lesbian-feminist movement, placed the emphasis on the women-identified aspects of the music. She maintained that women's music is interchangeable with lesbian-feminist music, in that its content most typically embodies the lesbian-feminist resistance to patriarchy. Women's music can also be considered as commodity. Bonnie Morris, in *Eden Built by Eves*, maintains that the audience defines women's music by attending events or through purchasing albums. "The festival audience is looking for an extension of its collective self-image on that stage."[11]

Women's Music Network[12]

The emergence of women's music coincided with one of the most dynamic periods of the women's rights movement in the United States—often referred to as the "second wave" of feminism.[13] Alongside feminist political activity, an ideology of "cultural feminism,"[14] developed which Kimball referred to as a "third wave" of feminism.[15] During this period, a body of women's music evolved, creating an underground performance circuit and an infrastructure of related businesses.

Just as the politics of feminism had catalyzed the women's movement, this crystallization of the norms and values of cultural feminism found expression in the artistry of women—working as artists, technicians, producers, and writers. Within this culture, an intricate network of festivals, record companies, and radio programs, channeling the collective efforts of female producers, distributors and technicians, formed the infrastructure of the women's music circuit. This circuit is the primary factor that distinguishes women's music. According to Toni Armstrong Jr., the editor of *Hot Wire* (one of the most influential women's music journals): "[T]his is a crucial point; 'women's music' is more than any individual concert, festival set, or recording project. Women's music is a national network/movement involving thousands of women."[16]

The ideological foundation of the women's music industry was grounded in the discourse of radical feminism and lesbian separatism. The separatist movement provided the political ideology for the creation of their own music industry; that is, to create a musical culture and aspire toward creative autonomy in technical positions as well as production. Training of women for nontraditional jobs was a top priority for the women-owned businesses that emerged through the creation of this music. The exclusion of women in the existing music industry is well documented in Gillian G. Gaar's *She's a Rebel.*[17] Women had been largely excluded from every facet of the music industry since the inception of rock and roll. Women's recording and production companies, sound and lighting businesses, distribution companies, coffeehouses, radio shows, and a myriad of other related commercial entities developed rapidly and spread throughout the country.

Within the women's music circuit the majority of performers were lesbian. Those remembered as concert favorites at the early music festivals include Meg Christian, Casse Culver, Willie Tyson, Alix Dobkin, Kay Gardner, Linda Tillery, Teresa Trull, Rhiannon, Mary Watkins, Margie Adam, Maxine Feldman, Gwen Avery, and Ferron. However, many key performers and organizers were not lesbians, and performing groups often consisted of mixed sexual identities. Kristen Lems, a self-defined heterosexual woman, started the National Women's Music Festival—the first such festival. She was also a favorite singer at many feminist political rallies and conferences. Grammy Award-winning Sweet Honey in the Rock, which is not lesbian-identified, is one of the most popular and inspirational performing groups on the women's music circuit. It is an African American woman a cappella group founded by Bernice Johnson Reagon in 1973. Reagon was active in the civil rights movement and performed with the Freedom Singers.

Lesbian Separatism

The question of what constitutes the essence of women's music is complex because its context and meaning are multifaceted. Lont's definition of women's music focused on its uniqueness. The women who write, produce, and perform it aspired for economic control of the music and means of its production.[18] Olivia Records was one of the first commercial recording companies to model itself on the ethos of woman-identification. It began producing women's music in 1975. A collective of women whose twin objectives were to record women-identified artists and become economically independent founded Olivia. Many of Olivia's members hailed from some of the most politically dynamic college campuses of the 1960s and 1970s, such as the University of Michigan in Ann Arbor and Mount Holyoke in Massachusetts, and were thus also schooled in neo-Marxist ideologies and organizations that comprised the New Left.

However, their experiences of oppression in the male-dominated Left mirrored those of the women within the larger society, and in 1972, having gravitated to Washington, D.C., from various parts of the country, they began publishing *The Furies: Lesbian/Feminist Monthly*. All collective members were lesbians who helped to articulate a working strategy of lesbian separatism. Charlotte Bunch, a preeminent feminist theorist throughout this period and beyond, explained the early history of the lesbian separatist movement:

> Women turned to separatist groups apart first from men, and then from others within the women's movement for several important reasons: to escape the debilitating effects of being with one's oppressor; to develop an analysis of one's particular oppression and force its recognition by others . . . to create strength and unity of the oppressed as a base for survival and power within the whole society, and to build a political ideology and strategy more quickly with those who share certain oppression and/or ideological positions.[19]

Cris Williamson, who wrote some of the most eloquent early songs celebrating lesbian relationships, met with the Furies's collective during one of her Washington, D.C., concerts. Her suggestion to start a woman-owned and managed recording company was well received. The editors of *The Furies* had been searching for a viable business that would enable them and other women to become politically and economically independent. One of the collective members, Ginny Berson, stated their motives:

> We thought the way for women to get power was through economics, by controlling our economic situations. We wanted to set up some sort of alternative economic institution which would both produce a product that women wanted to buy and also employ women in a non-oppressive situation—to get them out of regular jobs. Second, we wanted to be in a position to affect large numbers of women and that had to be through the media. The something out to large numbers of women was music. So we put the two together and got a women's recording company.[20]

Olivia Records went on to become one of the most successful independent record companies of its time. The recording *The Changer and the Changed*, produced with Cris Williamson in 1976, sold more copies than any other independent record to that date and was listed as the best independent record for that year by *Billboard Magazine*.

One of the most contested issues affecting women's recording companies was the process of determining which musicians were recorded. Although women entrepreneurs were beginning to actualize ideals of separatism and empowerment, the network's economic base left it vulnerable to racism and classism from within. The companies were put on the defensive regarding charges of racism and elitism and proved not to be immune from the ills of capitalism, in that often those who had the economic resources were the ones who made the decisions and benefited from any economic gains. Other businesses within the women's music network also struggled with these issues. Most of the women who started the businesses and the early-recognized performers were white. Women of color musicians were composing women-identified music at the same time but were hesitant to attempt to enter this budding network because of its built-in racism.

For example, in 1974 Judith Casselberry (musician, scholar, and producer) discovered other musicians in an African American cultural group, Hente, who were composing women's music in San Francisco. She joined with her friend Jaque Dupreé and formed the duo Casselberry and Dupreé. Casselberry describes the difficulty of being booked into the women's music network:

> It was definitely a mixed response because the structure that was being built at that time was being forged primarily by white women. There wasn't readily a lot of room for people coming from a really different cultural place and so us coming into that scene was not always a smooth situation. . . . There were some hard times, but on the other hand, to be fair, I do have to say that there were ways that it was also a very nurturing environment. . . . Even though we would be struggling, we would be talking about things that were real to us, issues of racism or class differences. . . . I think the women's community as a whole and the Women's Music scene as a whole and specifically the festivals, created a space where, even though we weren't always where we wanted to be, it showed us what was possible.[21]

White women were more likely to have the economic means to develop the network and women of color less likely to have equal access to recording contracts with the new women's music labels or to have tours booked by promoters and festivals. This reality slowly changed after many hard-fought battles.

In 1978, Amy Horowitz, who worked closely with Bernice Johnson Reagon (founder of Sweet Honey in the Rock) and Holly Near (founder of Redwood Records, 1973), created Roadwork, a women's production and booking company. It was unique in that it was created with a vision specifically to address racism within the women's music network. Its key mission was to create an environment to combat racism and to produce multicultural productions. According to Horowitz, "Its mission statement was that it would be an organization that would present women's culture within the context of coalition with other movements for social change. That it would be a multiracial cross-cultural coalition."[22] The culmination of this vision was Roadwork's annual festival, Sisterfire, which became renowned for its diversity of performers and workshops geared to address difficult political issues.

Within the framework of the creation and marketing of women's music, women began to fully control the technical and artistic components of the circuit, including audio engineering, lighting design and operation, management, and promotion. Their intention was not only to achieve economic control of their lives but also to create a safe and comfortable women-identified environment for all participants. An entire women's music network developed that provided the economic infrastructure supporting business enterprises of both performers and the wider lesbian/feminist community.

Women's Music Festivals: The Heart of the Network

The heart of this newly emerging cultural network was its music festivals. The first of these unique events was the National Women's Music Festival (NWMF), produced in 1974 in Champaign-Urbana, Illinois, and staged on a university campus. It was originated by Kristen Lems and her sister, politically committed feminists singing as a folk duo, in response to a local folk festival that sought only male singers because, "there just weren't any women good enough."[23] As feminists, they were angry and inspired to create an alternative event to counter it, a woman's folk festival. The NWMF was open to both men and women. The success of this first women's music festival far exceeded the organizers' expectations; however, all was not harmonious as conflicts ensued over whether men should be permitted to attend. The issue was resolved by the university, which threatened to close the festival if it did not admit male audience members.[24]

In the early stages of the development of the women's music circuit, some events were organized for women only, which resulted in protracted and heated debates about the politics of such a concept. The question of whether women's music concerts should be gender exclusive caused significant controversy among musicians, producers, and audience and continues to this day in response to permutations of gender politics. Nevertheless, some concerts held during this phase were only open to women and mirrored the separatist traditions of the Black Panthers, Brown Berets, and other nationalist movements that enabled oppressed minorities within the dominant white culture to forge authentic identities by separating from it.

Although the NWMF was also open to men, the women who worked or performed and the audience were primarily lesbians. Casse Culver, lesbian-feminist singer/songwriter, reflected that becoming aware of the number of lesbian performers at the Festival was the most empowering experience of her life:

> What we discovered there was that we were all lesbians. There were only one or two women who were performing who were straight women. And I tell you, our sense of power just went over the top. I mean, we were so high on the fact that we all existed. And that we're all doing all different types of music. . . . I met all these different lesbians. And just the rush of power, it was almost overwhelming, it was heady. . . . At one point on stage I said, "I want to welcome you all to the First National Lesbian Music Festival." And of course there was this enormous cheer, I mean, just all these women just stood up and just practically took their shirts off to wave them as flags.[25]

The Michigan Womyn's Music Festival[26]

The Michigan Womyn's Music Festival quickly followed in 1976, providing an environment that would safely accommodate an audience composed exclusively of women and one in which women would exercise maximum control of its various elements. It was organized around three defining parameters: to provide 1) an experience of women's music and culture, 2) an environment open to "women only," and 3) a safe space for women and their children. In this space musicians, producers, technicians, political theorists, spiritualists, craftswomen, and audience could enjoy the exhilaration of a communal experience, in which their physical safety and psychological well-being were primary values.

Women who were excited about women's music and wanted to bring women's music artists to rural Michigan founded the Festival in 1976. Its core members were two sisters, Lisa and Kristie Vogel, and their friend Mary Kindig, who created the fledgling organization We Want the Music Collective. According to Lisa Vogel, their political identity as lesbians was coalescing in tandem with not only local lesbian enclaves, but also lesbian communities throughout the United States.[27]

Night Stage, Michigan Womyn's Music Festival. Photo by Boden Sandstrom

Enthusiasm mounted as the women began envisioning the Festival as a re-ality. Starting from the original idea for a two-day concert, collective members immediately began contacting various women within the lesbian-feminist community of Mt. Pleasant, Michigan, most notably Susan Alborell, who ran the local record store (and who still is a Festival coordinator), and women from the food co-op.

Significant controversy emerged, however, over the issue of male inclu-sion at the Festival. Although this issue was initially overlooked by Festival organizers because many had male friends considered sympathetic to feminist politics, eventually it was decided that the Festival would be identified as es-sentially an event for lesbians and thus an inappropriate environment for men if women were camping outdoors. This prompted some of the hetero-sexual women to withdraw from the original group of Festival organizers, leaving the Vogels and Kindig to coproduce the first Michigan Womyn's Mu-sic Festival.

More than 2,000—twice the size of the anticipated audience—attended the first Festival during three days and nights of performances held on one main stage. The second Festival attracted 3,200, and by the third, more than 4,300 women were traveling from throughout the United States and the world to attend the Michigan Festival. Steady growth occurred up to the eighth Festival, which drew approximately 8,500 women. It continues to average between 4,000 and 6,000 participants each year. During major anniversary events, more than 9,000 women attend the Michigan Womyn's Music Festival.

Although the Festival's success was staggering, Vogel referred to the staging of early productions as "primitive." Funds were raised through bake sales and car washes, and all physical structures including stages, kitchens, plumbing, electricity, and wells were built from the ground up. Portable toilets, water tankers, and tent skins were the only facilities that were supplied by companies or individuals extraneous to the Festival organization. Publicity consisted of mimeographed and hand-distributed flyers. At the second National Women's Music Festival in Champaign-Urbana, Illinois, organizers promised a cold beer to anyone who would distribute one hundred flyers in their hometowns to publicize the festival.

This system of connecting in advance with women supporting the Festival at the grassroots level is still one of the most effective means of promoting the Michigan Festival. Each year thousands of brochures are sent to bookstores, women's centers, and other networking centers. Women who manage these enterprises are proactive at ensuring that material is received from Festival organizers; it is to their mutual benefit to stock brochures, thus stimulating business.[28] A website has been designed to further publicize the Festival, but the grassroots efforts have been the key to its success.

The first Festival, held in 1976, ran for three days, during which all music performances were held on the main stage. The Festival expanded over the years to include additional days and stages. Currently three performance venues—the Night Stage, Day Stage, and Acoustic Stage—run for six days, Tuesday through the following Sunday. The Acoustic Stage is currently the locus of choral singing, classical and instrumental music, theater, and dance, while the Day Stage hosts new acts, comedy, and round robins. A round robin is a traditional folk performance with three to six musicians on stage who take turns singing one of their songs. Often the round robins are organized around particular social or political themes.

Part of the unique experience of the Festival is the result of the decision made during its early planning that women would build the entire infrastructure required for the performance. The universe of women who created the physical framework of the Festival consisted of its key organizers, paid workers, work-exchange participants, and volunteers, who are organized through a system that requires all Festival attendees to sign up for work shifts in various areas of the Festival. This has been a tremendously empowering value of the Festival. Each year, at the end of the Festival, all stages and most of the infrastructure are torn down and rebuilt before the next one.

Although planning occurs throughout the year, the women who build the Festival arrive anywhere from three and one-half months to two weeks prior to the opening of the gates, and some remain for several weeks afterward, contributing various skills and crafts including carpentry, truck and forklift driving, lifting and climbing expertise, kitchen management and cooking, sound engineering and lighting design, stage management and production, box office and parking management, child care and health care, graphic design, and professional security and firefighting expertise. Numerous other skilled and talented women who are marginalized in traditionally male-dominated occupations are valued at Michigan on their own terms. For many women, the process of constructing the Festival environment in accordance with their own vision helps erode layers of internalized powerlessness.

By 1980, the Vogels, having taken all of the financial risk, and performing essentially all of the hands-on organizing, assumed full management of the event. Thus Kristie and Lisa Vogel served as coproducers until the amicable dissolution of their partnership in 1983. Lisa Vogel produced the Festival single-handedly from 1983 to 1985, when Barbara (Boo) Price joined her as an equal partner and coproduced until 1994. Vogel then resumed her role as executive producer, assisted by her seasoned team of regular workers.[29]

Throughout the Festival's twenty-eight-year history, the organizers have rigorously engaged in an ongoing process of self-evaluation, including feedback from workers and "festigoers" (an indigenous festival term used for those who attend the festival in contrast to performers or workers) to continually improve its governing process. Confrontations, spontaneous meetings, festival workshops, post-festival conversations in underground press, and currently online chat rooms have all served as the centrifuge in which the Festival's essential qualities could be distilled and refined. Post-festival workers' input meetings and a system for soliciting remarks from festigoers were established over the years. At times ideological conflicts have been heated and tensions have risen, creating discomfort for many participants. It is a tribute to the process, though, that the Festival continues to this day.

As the physical and cultural territory expands, many women experience the Michigan Womyn's Music Festival as a lesbian city in the middle of deep country. Approximately 7,500 festigoers, 800 workers, and several hundred performers attended the twentieth anniversary of the Michigan Womyn's Music Festival (1995). The Festival had grown by then to include over 200 workshops run by women musicians, dancers, healers, trades women, athletes, spiritual leaders, writers, poets, and political theorists and activists, and the craftswomen's area had also been extended to include160 booths.[30] The original single-stage concept of the early Festival years had been expanded to include an open mike and dance lessons at the August Night Café and a six-day Film and Video Festival within the area known as One World.

> We're a very service-intensive event, so besides the typical Festival staffing needs of Production, Parking, Box Office, etc., we have staff working in four Childcare areas, Healthcare, Oasis (emotional support), Sober Support, Over 40's, Women of Color, One World Workshops, DART (Disabled Resource Team), Shuttle, Orientation, Communications, Def Way & Jewish Women's Networking.[31]

Separate but Safe Spaces

Equally important as the organizing parameters of separate, women-only, and safe space for Festival participants was the demarcation of separate, safe space for other than gender-defined identities within the Michigan community. The early festival culture was no less vulnerable to the strains of an endemic racism than the dominant culture from which it chose to separate. Women who had the financial means to organize, attend, or perform at women's music festivals were primarily white. Generally, festival norms—everything from musical aesthetics, to food preferences, to camping acumen, reflected white predilections and experiences that tended to be more accessible to white participants.

Only 42 women of color (20 percent), compared with 180 white performers, performed during its first ten years. Women of color found it difficult to identify with much of the Festival arts programming and only began attending Michigan in greater numbers as greater balance was achieved. However, the Festival did include more women of color performers than most local women's music circuits due primarily to feminist ideological values and to some extent, working-class roots among organizers. Vogel's own commitment to diversity was also a key factor in broadening Michigan's musical and cultural horizons. She became acquainted with women in the New York City music scene as early as the mid-1970s who were performing jazz, funk, and Latin jazz. The initial introduction of these musicians and groups to Michigan audiences met with some resistance among the majority white audience, whose ears were more attuned to pop and folk.[32]

At the twentieth anniversary Festival, twenty women of color groups (the figure does not include mixed groups) performed at the stages, a full 50 percent of all performers, representing South Africa, Costa Rica, Hawaii, Argentina, and the United States, performing gospel, dance, theater, comedy, spiritual, rock, folk, roots music, salsa, and acoustic solo piano music.

According to Vogel, the women of color performers, "came in and they just didn't do a gig. They came in and they laid ownership."[33] Cultural diversity became a core value of the Festival. Some of the groups that have performed over the years are Ulali (Native American), Ubaka Hill and The Drumsong Orchestra (Festival African drumming group), Stefôné & Rites of Passage (Afro-centric/world music), Orquesta D'Soul (hip-hop, salsa), Edwina Lee Tyler (African drumming/singer), Juca (African American fusion), and Toshi Reagon and Big Lovely (rock with R&B).

The venues at Michigan serve many purposes. New artists performing solo or as duos, full rock bands, ensembles, and big bands are showcased, representing a wide range of musical genres including jazz, rock, blues, folk, and classical music. One of Michigan's many contributions has been to expand the concept of women's music to include women's cultural performance. The Festival now features comedy, theater, performance art, and dance. The artistic director of the Dance Brigade, Krissy Keefer, coproduces the opening ceremony, and comedians (Lea DeLaria, Sabrina Matthews, and Marga Gomez), performance artists (Alix Olson, C. C. Carter), circus artists (Lava), and theater troops (Sister Spit's Ramblin' Roadshow, Root Wy'mn, and Urban Bush Women) regularly perform.

In *Eden Built by Eves*, Morris identifies twenty-seven women's music festivals throughout the history of women's music that are staged in every region of the United States from Alaska to Florida. They range in size from the "mother of all festivals" (Michigan) to one of the smallest (50 to 200), Camp Sister Spirit in Mississippi. The festivals have been the vital transformers along the women's music circuit, infusing the artists with creative energy and providing the context for synergy among musicians, songwriters, and performers. They have also facilitated global commerce in women's recorded music and a central marketplace for women-made crafts, clothing, and healing arts and have been among the prime locales for national and international networking among lesbians. The smaller regional festivals provide an environment in which often isolated lesbians can come together and experience their culture. "Many a revolutionary idea, later a national lesbian trend, came to fruition beneath festival trees. And plenty of women come to festivals just to party and girl watch."[34]

Next Generations of Women's Music

Women's music and its network significantly altered women's roll in popular and classical music.[35] Artists such as Melissa Etheridge, who began her career in lesbian bars and at women's music festivals, Ani DiFranco, and the Indigo Girls were able to break through into the basically male world of rock and roll and become mainstream favorites. Many of the women's groups whose music is known as riot grrrls (Sexpods, 7 Year Bitch, Bikini Kill) acknowledge women's music as one of their influences. The combined momentum of the equal rights movements and women's breakthroughs in the music industry changed the face of popular music today. Many women in all popular music genres speak their minds and sing songs that are powerfully expressive of the authentic experiences of women. Women musicians and women working in the industry still have to fight for equal pay, but singers such as Queen Latifah, Tori Amos, Lauryn Hill, Courtney Love, k.d. lang, Alanis Morissette, Me'Shell Ndegéocello, Missy Elliot, Joan Armatrading, and the Dixie Chicks are able to reach greater audiences and become successful while speaking the truth about women's lives.

A defining moment in the performance of women's music in the mainstream was Etheridge's appearance at the 1994 Woodstock Festival, where she sang "I'm the Only One" in front of thousands of screaming fans. Etheridge's vocal power has been compared to Janis Joplin. But she, unlike Joplin, plays a gutsy electric guitar while singing about her passion for women, rather than the hardships of being one:

> But I'm the only one
> Who'll walk across the fire for you
> I'm the only one
> Who'll drown in my desire for you[36]

One of the most far-reaching effects of women's music has been its impact on the personal and professional lives of musicians who perform it, as their musical survival depended on this outlet for true musical creativity. Musicians valued opportunities to play instruments that were considered unconventional for women, front big bands, perform in front of an audience of thousands at the festivals, and compose music that expressed their experience without fear of being artistically dismissed or ignored or unsupported financially. Ellen Seeling, cofounder with Jeanne Feinberg of Deuce, a jazz-fusion duo (or as they describe themselves, a "metal jazz" duo), credits women's music with providing unique professional opportunities for performers:

> I think if it weren't for the Women's Music scene, a lot of the players who are professionals now would not be professionals. They would have given up because of discouragement, would not have cut it because of lack of experience. It gave us stage experience. At the Michigan Festival we played to an audience of 10,000 people—I know very few professional colleagues of mine now who have done that. I know some. It's quite an amazing experience.[37]

Linda Tillery (Grammy-nominated singer, songwriter, producer, and founder of Cultural Heritage Choir) probably best articulates the ongoing legacy of women's music, "The greatest piece of work to come out of Women's Music are the women themselves. We were trying to create whole human beings who had a sense of self-esteem and self-empowerment, to be the best that we could be."[38]

Gender Negotiation

The Michigan Womyn's Music Festival is still the pulse at the heart of women's music because it remains the most dynamic gathering place of women's music artists and their audience. It also continues to be the nexus of an ongoing redefinition of women's music and womanhood itself. The boundaries of women-only space that are negotiated at the Festival not only are defined by the sex or sexuality of those attending the Festival but expand (or contract) according to emerging modes of gender identification.

The Western concept of a binary gender system has been challenged as insight deepens into the role of social forces in shaping gender identification. The idea that gender identity is "performed" has gained currency, as expressed by Judith Butler in Gender Trouble: Feminism and the Subversion of Identity.[39]

As queer theory and gender theory have revealed the complex intersection of one's sexuality and socially constructed gender roles and provided enriched perspectives on lesbian and homosexual identity, the MWMF's stated policy of permitting "women only" to enter the Festival site has required greater analysis and introspection on the part of organizers and participants, alike. A definition of queer theory is, "a body of work which does not represent a specific kind of theory so much as it does a number of interdisciplinary texts which emphasize the constructedness of sexuality."[40] One battleground for a new understanding of the multiplicity of genders has been the annual gay and lesbian pride rallies held nationally and locally every year since the events of Stonewall.[41] Activists have demanded that the rallies include in their titles such gender/sexuality categories as bisexual, transgender, transsexual, etc. As a result, the younger generation has tended to dispense with labels to embrace the term "queer" as a more inclusive reference.

It is not appropriate to refer to all of the music of today's generation, who are active in the women's music circuit, as women's music, because many are claiming new gender identities. Some are rejecting the hegemonic society's gender labels such as "woman" or "lesbian" and are adopting a more inclusive but fluid gender identity under a broader concept of "queer." Thus queer or "trans" (transgender or transsexual) musicians refer to their music as "queer music" or "queer punk." Terry Grant, the founder of Goldenrod, a primary distributor of women's music since 1975, when asked how she would define women's music today replied, "One of the things that I find really tricky about us trying to be inter-generational is that music by definition is not inter-generational. We aren't supposed to like the music of the next generation because that is part of the definition of a generation."[42] Women's music today is being redefined by the challenges posed by these younger women to a binary gender system.

In 1994, Tribe 8 performed at Michigan for the first time. Tribe 8 is an all-lesbian punk-rock band whose music is often referred to as queer punk. Tribe 8 performs loud, often angry music, pushing the limits on many taboo subjects about sexuality and gender. The band has been criticized for their explicit stage shows, during which they sometimes perform mock castrations to raise issues of male and female power. The band performed a mock castration of a rapist on stage and sang about traditionally taboo subjects such as S/M (sado-masochism), incest, and rape, issues that are important to many lesbians. However, their performance was picketed as perpetuating violence against women, and resulted in considerable debate over whether Tribe 8's music is offensive to women and whether they should be permitted to play. In an interview with Andrea Juno, Lynne Breedlove, the leader of the group, explained, "I cut off a rubber dick in the context of talking about gang rape. It's a cathartic ritual; it makes us feel like we are getting some kind of revenge."[43]

A young woman who had attended the Festival for eleven years with her mother said that Tribe 8's music created an opportunity for dialogue among the three generations of lesbians now attending the Festival. The incident involving Tribe 8 was reported in Ms. Magazine after the Festival, marking the first appearance of a major article about Michigan in that publication. The article, "Queer Punk Meets Womyn's Music," reviews the controversy and the following workshop during which the issues were discussed.[44]

Conventions and norms of womanhood are challenged at Michigan in any number of ways. Just as feminists and lesbians challenged the pervasive gender scripts in the hegemonic culture (for example, the model of a heterosexual male-centered family structure), transgender and transsexual communities challenge traditional definitions of gender. For the past several years male-to-female (MTF) transsexuals and their supporters have become activists in their quest for admission onto the Festival grounds.[45] In response, the Festival's policy for admittance has been formally articulated as open to "womon-born womyn only," a biological basis.[46] These self-identified women established "Camp Trans," a separate encampment near the Michigan site. Today, it attracts many younger women who identify as transgender and who claim they feel unwelcome at the MWMF or who are boycotting the Festival because of MTF exclusion. According to the organizers of Michigan, trans-gender women are welcome at the Festival and have been attending Michigan since its inception.

In 1999, in response to an organized entry into the Festival by some trans-sexuals and their supporters, Lisa Vogel reiterated the reason for the Festival's policy in the underground publication, *Lesbian Connection:*

> For the last 24 years, the Festival has been like a petri dish, a laboratory of ideas and expression that have influenced—and been influenced by—the many com-munities and cultures that flow into and out of the Festival. We recognize that the Festival and Son of Camp Trans symbolize and express divergent views on the larger gender discussion that is going on in lesbian and gay communities. We support this discussion and value and respect the Transsexual community as in-tegral members of the broader queer community. We ask that they in turn respect womon-born-womon space. . . . We remain united in our commitment to the MWMF as womyn's space. This is basic to the power and philosophy of what brings womyn from around the world back to Michigan every August. And this is the experience we are committed to celebrating next year at the 25th MWMF. The Transsexual Menace's action in defiance of womyn's space is not an isolated phenomenon. It's part of the misogyny and sexism we've all been organizing against for years. We support deconstruction of gender roles, but we cannot sit by while the definition of woman becomes blurred to the point of denying the real-ity of our existence. . . . As we enter the 21st century, it's up to each of us who value an alternative to patriarchal culture to get clear on our priorities and to rally against this latest challenge to our autonomy and sovereignty.[47]

New festivals such as Ladyfest, which had its start in Seattle, Washington, in 2000, are now open to the trans community, which many of the women who want to keep Michigan for "womon-born womyn-only" support. This festival has had several incarnations in locations in the United States, Canada, and Europe. According to Elizabeth K. Keenan, they are indie-rock festivals for women and have been most closely influenced by the politics of the riot grrl movement of the early 1990s. "The websites of many Ladyfests proclaim that 'Ladyfest is for everyone' (www.ladyfest.org) and profess goals of 'bringing talented, brilliant ladies together in order to nurture a produc-tive and inclusive community.'"[48] (http://www.pazazygeek.com/ladyfest/).[49] It is not within the scope of this chapter to analyze the success or failure of the Ladyfests' political philosophy of inclusiveness.

Networking Today

One of the major defining characteristics of women's music has been the evolution of its infrastructure, which sustained the genre by enabling the music to reach its audience and the audience to support the musicians. This network is much reduced today. Grant pointed out that Goldenrod is the only distributor left out of the sixty to eighty original companies. Ladyslipper, which went into business in 1976, is the major online source for women's music today. Goldenrod bought out Ladyslipper's distributorship, freeing its staff to pursue their dream of digitizing women's music recordings that otherwise would be lost.

Most of the performers starting out today play in clubs, coffeehouses, bars, colleges, in-house concerts, and the remaining festivals. Tam Martin (Beachfront Bookings/Productions), who has been producing and booking women's music artists since 1982, comments, "When I started booking, there was an entire network of women's producers and distributors and festivals. Now there's just a handful left of each. I think we all did our jobs so well that they don't need us anymore!"[50] Significant producers, clubs, and radio shows within the women's music infrastructure that are successful today include Barbara Price's club; Montclair Women's Cultural Arts in Oakland, California; Mountain Moving Coffee House for Women and Children in Chicago—which according to its website is the oldest, longest-running women-only space in the country;[51] Virginia Giordino (producer) in New York City; Olivia Records—which has reorganized itself as a producer of women's cruises featuring women's music concerts; and *Sophie's Parlor*, a radio program devoted to women's music broadcast over Washington, D.C.'s Pacifica Radio since 1972.

However, many of the young women who are producing and performing women's music speak of a budding underground network similar to the early women's music network in that it relies on word-of-mouth and mutual support. Many referrals are exchanged during the festivals. The drive to be financially independent, an essential feature of lesbian separatism, is not as evident. For example, the three women who manage Girl Gang Productions, based in New Orleans, have full-time jobs. The company focuses on producing queer women's bands, most of which are punk bands. They do book some queer men's groups, but only as openers for the women's groups. The shows are usually small-scale productions staged in bars for an audience of around fifty people. The biggest draws so far have been a duo, Bitch and Animal, and spoken-word artist Alix Olson, who often performs with songwriter/singer Pamela Means. They get the word out via their website and an e-mail listserv. According to

Val McKay, one of the producers, "It's all about the service. We're providing a service. We don't have that many lesbian bars or dyke bars in New Orleans so we're making our own dyke spaces in these dives."[52]

Underground Women's Music Today

Michelle Bradshaw (member of an "all girl band," Zonic Aria out of Ottawa, Canada) describes today's women's music as having, "a definite harsher edge." She adds, "I think it's starting to take people over and surprise them a bit who aren't used to Women's Music."[53] McKay defines this harsher edge as being unapologetic:

> Just to see the progression of things in the last 10 or 15 years is just amazing. I think it's being reflected in the music that you are hearing. I'm hearing it with these bands that are coming through. It is unapologetic. It's—"I am who I am and fuck you. I don't care what you think and I am going to be myself and I'm going to sing about what I want to sing about and you know what, if I don't get booked, I don't get booked." What they're finding is that you know there are people like us who will book them and there are women who will come out.[54]

Many of the queer or punk-identified bands do have a harsher edge. The music is not always distinguishable from their riot grrrl or punk predecessors but is often characterized by several different and atypical musical styles or types of instrumentation within one song. Lyrics are also often "in your face" about subjects that may make some audiences uncomfortable.

Bitch and Animal, a duo out of New York City, is probably one of the most popular groups performing at Michigan and for queer audiences. Bitch sings, and plays electric violin, viola, and bass. Animal sings, raps, and plays a variety of percussion instruments and the ukulele. Their style could be considered performance art using a combination of spoken word, song, and music. Bitch refers to it as "radical performance art rock" and Animal as "experiential wild lusty bliss."[55] It has an edgy quality straight from the streets of New York City. They are radical feminists who support gender freedom. Bitch defines her gender identity as woman and Animal defines herself as transgender, butch, dyke, and woman.[56] One of their most requested songs is "Pussy Manifesto," in which Bitch reclaims the word "pussy" from being used as an insult to a source of female power. During a performance she yells out feminist statements that often resignify feminine stereotypes, for example:

> Manifest this Muthafucka #3:
> I'm sick of my genitalia being used as an insult. Are

you? It's time to let my labia rip and rearrange this. Here we go: "That was so Pussy of you to help me move to my new place! Especially since I'm living on the 13th floor. You've really made this a Pussy move!"[57]

Their latest CD is *Sour Juice and Rhyme*, which was coproduced and corecorded by June Millington. Millington is a founding mother of women's music whose first band, Fanny, is known as one of the first all-women rock bands to be signed by a major label. She is also known as the founder of the Institute of Musical Arts, whose purpose is to promote and preserve women's music, as well as for her virtuosity with the electric guitar. Diane Dimassa, who produces the lesbian comic book *Hothead Passion (Homicidal Lesbian Terrorist)*, did the cover design. Bitch and Animal are writing the music for a musical adaptation.

Cover art, Sour Juice and Rhyme, *2003. Graphic design by Diane Dimassa; front cover photo by Mr. Means*

Bitch and Animal's "Secret Candy" is against gender oppression and makes a plea for turning the energy wasted on prejudice into galvanizing a movement for peace in the world:

"Secret Candy" (Chorus and 2 verses)

Chorus:
i ain't got no 'tience this time of year
for phony presidents always pushing fear

Verses:
I still could go to jail for taking off my shirt
and that tranny will still get fucked with for wearing a skirt
and I'll get protested for singing for michigan women and my
pal marshall* is gettin' it just for being him
and my shit—radio won't even play it cuz it's coming from a tit

we need to get together make a spark
take over central park stop this fucking war
be nice to each other that'll even the score
make the world we want to live in so no one's got to give in
past present future you just felt them all
now and then some and then we come
for a moment there's nothin wrong just a song [58]

(*marshall refers to Marshall Mathers, aka Eminem, a popular hip-hop musician.)

Animal raps the lyrics and does "beats" (synthesized rhythm) and Bitch sings backup vocals. Evelyn Harris, a long-time former member of Sweet Honey in the Rock, who currently is singing/songwriting solo, joins in on the chorus.

Their songs can also be very funny and lighthearted, as exemplified by "Drag King Bar," in which the performance alternates between sounding like a square dance and storytelling. Bitch says this song was written, "after a few sloppy nights at Club Cassanova, a party and drag king show that used to happen in the East Village, hosted by mo b. dick."[59]

"Drag King Bar" (2 verses)

Bitch:
Well I was bored with the lesbian scene
I told myself I gotta find another thing
so I strapped on my boots

and I walked down the street
and I rolled right in to the local d.k.b.

Animal:
(drag king bar, that is)
Bitch:
when I waddled in at quarter to eight
well I thought I might be straight
at the drag king bar last night
it's unlike me to look at boys
but when the girls are packing toys
I can dig that scene all right (Bitch and Animal, 1999)[60]

An earlier album features "Boy Girl Wonder," a song about the frustration of being transgender in a two-gender system. Animal's approach is touching, tender, and vulnerable. Bitch accompanies with a very simple bass line in a minor key and harmonizes on the chorus. When the duo performed the song at Michigan a couple of years ago, Animal mimed the lyrics by paddling along the runway in a make-believe canoe while the moon hung overhead. Ani DiFranco produced the song.

"Boy Girl Wonder" (1 verse and chorus)

Verse:
a pink moon is out tonight
and my heart is folding over
because i think she liked me
and i mighta had her
but he's got a real one
and mine's from the store

Chorus:
why is it so lonely
in between boy and a girl
they're so glued down
in this world
and what it means
i'm trans alla that
gender I'm a bender
bi bye girl (Bitch and Animal, 2001)[61]

Many younger artists who travel the women's music circuit are not necessarily queer-identified but are nonetheless equally outspoken in their music, such as

Kinnie Starr (spoken word/hip-hop), Melissa Ferrick (singer/songwriter/guitar), Magdalen Hsu-Li (singer/keys/alternative punk), and Toshi Reagon. Another artist known for her straightforward approach is Nedra Johnson, whose sound could be described as rhythm and blues combined with funk and folk. She has a beautiful, soulful voice, and her music embraces lesbian love and spirituality and often features overtly political content. She is an accomplished bass, guitar, and keyboard player. One of her best known songs, "Testify," is an upbeat R&B tune featuring a favorite women's music drummer, Lisette "Peaches" Smith.

> "Testify!"
> My baby got sanctified booty
> I swear I'm saved
> by what she do to me!
> G-d smiled down and said,
> "Blessed are ye that knows a good thing.
> when a good thing is what you see."
>
> Testify!
> I want to be a witness for the Lord.
> Praise to the one above
> for the faith it takes to love!
>
> Testify!
> Folks say G-d made Eve and Adam,
> not no Adam and Steve.
> When we make love there is no doubting
> that my G-d made that girl and me!
>
> And I wanna sing and shout!
> Hallelujah!
> I wanna be a witness for the Lord
> and praise the one above
> for the strength it takes to love
> I wanna testify![62]

Two other current performers representative of an unapologetic sentiment are Alix Olson and Pamela Means. Alix Olson is a spoken-word artist who describes her art as "poetry attack with music." She won the 1999 OutWrite National Slam. Her work combines poetry, rap, and vocalization. She is a socialist and feminist who is totally unafraid of speaking political truths. Olson also performs and records with Pamela Means, a Boston singer/songwriter and musician who accompanies her dynamic political messages on guitar. Olson and

Nedra Johnson. Photo by Toni Armstrong Jr.

Alix Olson and Pamela Means. Photo by Kristin Dodge

Means share their resources and often tour together. Olson has her own label, Subtle Sister Productions.

"Built Like That" is a popular example of their dynamic synergy, with Means playing guitar and singing backup vocals along with synthesized drum accents. A sample verse and chorus:

"Built Like That" (verse and chorus)

Verse:
some art's real nice to look at.
some art's all neat and clean
my art forgot her tampon
and she's bleeding through her jeans
yeah my art don't need no tampon
she'll just bleed through her jeans

Chorus:
my art's not just made like that,
no no my art's just meant for that,
my art's just built like that,
my heart's just built like that[63]

Unwilling to temper their unabashedly political message, often Means and Olson are advised, "Why don't you shift your politics just a little and you could be really successful?"[64] However, their unflinchingly direct approach remains untempered, as evidenced in songs such as "O.D.," accompanied by the beat of a military marching drum, played by Kim Zick, the mood given an eerie cast by the minor chords of Lydell Montgomery's electric violin.

"O.D."*(three verses)

iraq iran north korea try to stand
bush bin laden and saddam
each of them with dirty hands
meet dick cheney oil merchant
former head of halliburton
had an oil transport plan
a pipeline through Afghanistan

then chairman cheney left the post
to join the george who lost the vote
now next in line he often quotes
whisperings of ancient rome[65] (Means 2003)

(*O.D. (oleaginous diplomacy) is government initiatives on behalf of oil companies.)

Passing the Torch

Even though the quest for a music expressive of an authentic experience of gender and sexual identity has been characterized by intergenerational struggle, a genuine appreciation of the legacy of women's music endures. McKay makes the link: "The things that they were singing about then were completely revolutionary and paved the way for all of us. Even these bands who don't necessarily understand Michigan need to understand historically the context and the fact that it took very large ovaries to start this festival and to have an all-women production."[66]

In many of the interviews for *Radical Harmonies*, the younger women frequently acknowledge the founders of women's music as mentors and sources of inspiration. Toshi Reagon, daughter of Bernice Johnson Reagon and protégée of June Millington, paid tribute to both. Ani Difranco, Bitch and Animal, Slade Bellum (drummer of Sexpods), Jackie Strano (Hail Marys), and Amy Ray (Indigo Girls) all were inspired by the roots of women's music. When Animal first met Alix Dobkin (singer/songwriter who wrote some of the first overtly lesbian songs) she said, "when I first met her, I really felt the sense of her seeing me. . . . I remember even she might have said something about passing the torch."[67] These younger women were inspired by the music that was authentic to women and to lesbian experience and by the sense of autonomy gained through participation in the women's music network.

The theme of the 2003 Michigan Womyn's Music Festival seemed to be one of heartfelt appreciation between the generations. Many of the founders of women's music continue to keep the world attuned to the music and its affirming messages for women just as they have always done, but perhaps with greater confidence and recognition. There are new albums from Rhiannon (formerly with Alive), Cheryl Wheeler, Tret Fure, Gretchen Phillips (formerly with Girls in the Nose), Adrienne Torf, Sweet Honey in the Rock (thirtieth-anniversary album), Ruth Barrett (Goddess chants and songs), Cris Williamson, and Holly Near. Carol McDonald, founder of Ginger and the Gingerbreads and Isis, two of the groundbreaking all-female rock bands, has a new record company, the Second Coming. The trio Betty currently has a show on Off-Broadway, *Betty Rules,* and Sweet Honey in the Rock is currently touring with Toshi Reagon and Big Lovely to celebrate their anniversary milestone.

Two performances at Michigan in 2003 were notable in paying tribute between older and younger generations of musicians. At the Night Stage on

Saturday night, the torch was symbolically passed back and forth between Sweet Honey in the Rock and Toshi Reagon and her band Big Lovely as they alternated selections between the a cappella singing of the former and the rocking sounds of the latter. It was a deeply moving and memorable evening, enhanced by a full moon and starlit sky shining on a female audience, a combination that makes the Michigan Womyn's Music Festival a unique and unforgettable experience.

Holly Near and Cris Williamson also performed a medley of their old tunes as well as soloing new ones on the Acoustic Stage, a performance inspired by their recent collaboration on the album *Cris and Holly*. Near was accompanied by the extraordinary pianist Adrienne Torf. Prior to their performance, Torf performed her own set, which included pieces from her new album *Collaboration*, a moving collaboration between Torf and her recently deceased partner, the acclaimed poet June Jordan.

Near invited two young women to join her, Rocio Mendoza, whom Holly has been mentoring, and Allison Hunt, her stepdaughter. Considerable warmth flowed from the audience, as befit Cris and Holly's status as respected "elders," which the performers amply returned. Near told the crowd that, "The next generation brings new energy and ideas to the table and that along with the experience elders bring, we form a vibrant social change community that continues on century after century."[68]

One of the songs Near sang was "I Am Willing." According to Near, "The song has a hymn-like quality, a prayer without religious affiliation, a spiritual commitment to being alert and active and fascinated by being alive and on this unique planet."[69] Grammy Award winner Leslie Ann Jones, one of the best recording engineers in the country and a great supporter of women artists, recorded it. She is currently the director of Music Recording and Scoring at Skywalker Sound in California, the sound studio for all of George Lucas's (movie director) projects, and has been nominated for a Grammy for Best Engineering Recording.

"I Am Willing"

I am open and I am willing
To be hopeless would seem so strange
It dishonors those who go before us
So lift me up to the light of change

There is hurting in my family
There is sorrow in my town

There is panic in the nation
There is wailing the whole world round

May the children see more clearly
May the elders be more wise
May the winds of change caress us
Even though it burns our eyes

Give me a mighty oak to hold my confusion
Give me a desert to hold my fears
Give me a sunset to hold my wonder
Give me an ocean to hold my tears[71]

Cris Williamson and Holly Near, album cover art, Cris and Holly. *Photo copyright 2003 Susan Wilson*

Conclusion

It is often through performance that socially constructed identities are either reinforced or changed. Performance as formal event is defined by its occurrence within a space that is energized and elevated from the mundane and has served as an arena to examine and experiment with modes of gender representation. Music has been and continues to be a powerful catalyst within the political arena because it has the ability to act as both a physical and spiritual force. Music can convey feelings and memory via symbolic representation, and because it is not easily quantified, can convey emotion and meaning that is not readily expressed in words. But when artful lyrics are added, music can stir emotions and channel them to unite groups of people toward effective political action.

When women's music emerged during the second wave of feminism, it expressed the voice of an oppressed gender, in the process encouraging and empowering women to fight for women's rights. Early feminist women rock bands such as Fanny, Ibis, and the Deadly Nightshade, among others, began reflecting the aesthetics and ideological values of this movement, which were manifested through not only the lyrics, but the very reality of rock and roll performances by all-women's bands. What followed was the empirical necessity and spontaneity of the women's music infrastructure that lesbian feminists collaborated in creating, having come out of their isolation to find each other at the early music festivals. It was a healing force and helped lesbians come out of the closet to find each other and inspired women to be powerful.

Within this underground cultural network women-identified women and lesbians were finally able to take full artistic and managerial control of the unique cultural expressions emerging from it as well as the industry that supported it. It is not possible within this chapter to credit all of the women performers who have contributed to this body of work and who continue in their respective fields today. Suffice it to direct anyone interested to Goldenrod and Ladyslipper's websites for catalogs of this work (see note 49). It is equally difficult to name all of the women who gained skills in navigating the shoals of the music industry and who succeeded in building careers within it or to convey the effects of women's music on its audience.

The skills and knowledge gained by starting independent recording companies and maintaining one's own image in a male-dominated industry have been invaluable to the younger artists both within and outside the scope of the genre of women's music. The synergy of this underground network as a cultural force with those of feminism and the gay and lesbian rights movement created a contemporary cultural environment in which women musicians can unhesitatingly give voice to issues vital to themselves and other women and to control their finances within the industry.

Part of the dynamic within this network was the need for women-only spaces in which to experience women's music and negotiate issues vital to this community. Within the confines of the hegemonic culture, lesbians and women-identified women felt the need to establish a separate physical and psychological environment to experience and continue creating a lesbian culture. Over the years, women worked through important issues concerning discrimination and oppression stemming from ethnicity, race, gender, religious orientation, national or regional heritage, language, disabilities, and political affiliations. The third wave of underground performers is tackling these difficult issues less tentatively, if not at times with a blatantly aggressive edge. Many of the younger women in hip-hop and punk have a similar approach.

In essence, women's music is dynamic, and as such is defined by its sociopolitical context. As the context changes so does the genre. A subgenre of queer music or queer punk emerged whose artists delivered a challenge to the center of the women's music network, its major Festivals. The network, as Martin pointed out, does not exist in its past incarnation; however, in some ways women's music is more accessible due to the longevity of Golden Rod and Ladyslipper. Within these companies the mainstream and underground musicians have found common ground and have become more aware of each other. The network evolved because of the successes of feminism and women's music artists.

During the 1990s women and lesbians gained the full attention of the popular music industry. In 1997 *Rolling Stone* dedicated its thirtieth-anniversary issue to "Women of Rock."[72] In the current decade, in all popular music genres there are women who are able to sing about their true experiences without having to objectify themselves as women in order to succeed. The pressure is still there to become a sex object, as demonstrated on innumerable covers of *The Rolling Stone*, in which artists such as Christina Aguilera and Britney Spears undress for the cameras. However, many new artists come on the scene writing about women-identified experiences: Alicia Keys's "A Woman's World," the Dixie Chicks' "Wide Open Spaces," Martina McBride's "Country Angel," Lauryn Hill's "That Thing That You Do," Avril Lavigne's "Complicated," Sleater-Kinney's "Dykes Rule," Shelby Lynne's "If I Were Smart," Eve's "My Enemies," Melissa Ferrick's "Shatter Me," and Aaliyah's "We Need a Revolution." Women have also broken into the male-dominated world of DJ-ing in hip-hop. *Pink Noises* (www.pinknoises.com), a

Web magazine launched in 2000 to promote women in electronic music, was nominated for the Best Music Site for the 2003 Webby Awards.

Perhaps some of the most interesting new research to be done in the field might be an extension of Kay Gardner's analysis of the musical aesthetics of women's music. Given the rich and growing body of work, a comparative analysis of women's music and mainstream music might reveal whether what the journalists now refer to as women's music has not in fact adopted some of the aesthetic features of what had been mainly an underground phenomenon.

Women's music today is more above ground than underground and harder to distinguish from women-in-music today. As June Millington would say, "This is the good news!"[72] Sweet Honey in the Rock celebrated its thirtieth-anniversary concert Eveningsong in large, sold-out major venues, sharing the stage with Bernice Johnson Reagon's daughter, Toshi Reagon, and her band Big Lovely. Big Lovely includes Judith Casselberry (vocals and guitar), who is finishing her Ph.D. in anthropology at Yale University; Jen Leigh, a young electric guitar player who definitely has her "chops" down; and two male members of the band, drummer Fred Cash and Chicken Burke on bass. Although exciting as a cross-generational performance, the Washington, D.C., concert was particularly inspiring in evoking a history through songs of D.C.'s struggle for the right to vote in a medley including civil rights freedom songs.

Women's music was and continues to be a political force celebrating the rights of all people. This last decade of women's music has been one of collaboration, whether between generations, women of the queer underground circuit, or women and men making music together on the basis of common political aspirations. Whether uniting to lend their voices to the cause of social justice and harmony, to preserve and extend the rights of women, or to redefine the boundaries of gender, women of the women's music circuit will continue to work together and learn from each other.

Biography

Boden Sandstrom, Ph.D., is a lecturer at the University of Maryland, specializing in gender studies and concentrating on world popular music and women's music in the United States. As a political activist, she was a founding member of Female Liberation in Boston, Massachusetts, helping to create The Second Wave, a feminist journal, and was active in the anti–Vietnam War movement. She is coproducer of the documentary Radical Harmonies, about an underground women's music network that emerged during the second wave of feminism. She recently won the Philip Brett Award sponsored by the Gay and Lesbian Study Group of the American Musicological Association for exceptional musicological work in the field of transgender/transsexual, bisexual, lesbian, and gay studies. She is also an experienced sound engineer, having been the owner of

Woman Sound, one of the first all-women sound companies. She has done research and has published on gender issues within technological fields and the effect of technology on fieldwork.

1. *Radical Harmonies*, directed by Dee Mosbacher, produced by Dee Mosbacher and Boden Sandstrom (Woman Vision, 2002). Order from www.woman-vision.org.

2. Barbara O'Dair, *Trouble Girls: The Rolling Stone Book of Women in Rock* (New York: Random House, 1997), xxii.

3. Buffy Childerhouse, *From Lilith to Lilith Fair* (New York: St. Martin's Griffin, 1998), xii.

4. Ruth Scovill, "Women's Music," in *Women's Culture: The Renaissance of the Seventies*, ed. Gayle Kimball (Metuchen, N.J.: Scarecrow Press, 1981), 148.

5. Scovill, "Women's Music," 148.

6. Scovill, "Women's Music," 154–55.

7. Scovill, "Women's Music," 157–60.

8. Laura Post, *Backstage Pass: Interviews with Women in Music* (Norwich, Vt.: New Victoria Publishers, 1997), 5.

9. For example, such traditions as laments, wedding songs, spiritual repertoire, lullabies, and European ladies orchestras can be compared. See *Music, Gender, and Culture*, ed. Marcia Herndon and Susanne Ziegler (Wilhelmshaven: Florian Noetzel Verlag, 1990); *Women and Music in Cross-Cultural Perspectives*, ed. Ellen Koskoff (Chicago: University of Chicago Press, 1989); and *Music and Gender*, ed. Pirkko Moisala and Beverly Diamond (Chicago: University of Illinois Press, 2000).

10. Cynthia Marion Lont. "Between a Rock and a Hard Place: A Model of Sub-culture Persistence and Women's Music" (Ph.D. dissertation, Iowa City: University of Iowa, 1984), 242.

11. Bonnie J. Morris, *Eden Built by Eves* (New York: Alyson Books, 1999), 14.

12. Much of the following information is from Boden Sandstrom, "Performance, Ritual and Negotiation of Identity in the Michigan Womyn's Music Festival" (Ph.D. dissertation, College Park: University of Maryland, 2002). See this source for more information on women's music and its cultural network and the Michigan Womyn's Music Festival.

13. "A term coined by Marsha Lear to refer to the formation of women's groups in America, Britain and Europe in the late 1960s." Maggie Humm, *The Dictionary of Feminist Theory* (Columbus: Ohio State University Press, 1995), 251.

14. "Feminist theory which is dedicated to creating a separate and radical women's culture. . . . Cultural feminists describe how a powerful female culture of music, art, poetry, science and medicine would be anti-authoritarian and anti-structure." Humm, *Dictionary of Feminist Theory*, 53.2.

15. Gayle Kimball, ed., *Women's Culture: The Renaissance of the Seventies* (Metuchen, N.J.: Scarecrow Press, 1981), 2.

16. Toni Armstrong Jr, "An Endangered Species: Women's Music By, For, and About Women," *HotWire: The Journal of Women's Music Culture* 5, no. 3 (1989): 18.

17. Gillian Garr, *She's a Rebel: The History of Women in Rock & Roll* (Seattle, Wash.: Seal Press, 1992).

18. Lont, "Between a Rock and a Hard Place," 242.

19. Charlotte Bunch, "Perseverance Furthers: Separatism and Our Future," *The Furies* 1, no. 7 (1972): 3.

20. Jane E. Pipik, "Woman-Identified Music: Moving On," *Heresies* 3, no. 2 (1980): 88–89.

21. Judith Casselberry, interview by Boden Sandstrom, October 2000.

22. Amy Horowitz, interview by Boden Sandstrom, January 20, 2001.

23. *Radical Harmonies.*

24. *Radical Harmonies.*

25. Casse Culver, interview by Boden Sandstrom, June 12, 2001.

26. The Michigan Womyn's Music Festival (MWMF) is referred to as either "Michigan" or the "Festival" throughout the chapter. People who are familiar with the MWMF generally refer to it with these shorthand expressions. The organizers chose to spell women as womyn, which was one of several alternative spellings used by some feminists during the 1970s to eliminate any reference to man or men in words that denote female.

27. Boden Sandstrom, "Performance, Ritual and Negotiation of Identity in the Michigan Womyn's Music Festival" (Ph.D. dissertation, College Park: University of Maryland, 2002), 100.

28. Sandstrom, "Performance, Ritual and Negotiation of Identity," 106.

29. Sandstrom, "Performance, Ritual and Negotiation of Identity," 103.

30. We Want the Music Collective, *The Michigan Womyn's Music Festival*, (Berkeley, Calif.: WWTMC, 1997), 1.

31. We Want the Music Collective, *Michigan Womyn's Music Festival*, 4.

32. Sandstrom, "Performance, Ritual and Negotiation of Identity," 173–74.

33. Sandstrom, "Performance, Ritual and Negotiation of Identity," 173–74.

34. Morris, *Eden Built by Eves*, 9.

35. This chapter does not address the role of women in classical women's music.

36. Melissa Etheridge. "I'm the Only One," on *Yes I Am Melissa* (Island Records, 1993). © Melissa Etheridge.

37. Sandstrom, "Performance, Ritual and Negotiation of Identity," 85.

38. *Radical Harmonies.*

39. Judith Butler, *Gender Trouble: Feminism and the Subversion of Identity* (New York: Routledge, 1999).

40. Brett Beemyn and Mickey Eliason, eds. *Queer Studies: A Lesbian, Gay, Bisexual, and Transgender Anthology.* (New York: New York University Press, 1996), 1.

41. Stonewall is the name of an historic event for the gay community. It is thought to be the first time gays fought back against police who raided the homosexual bar, Stonewall, in New York City in 1969.

42. Terry Grant, interview by Boden Sandstrom, August 15, 2003.

43. Andrea Juno, *Angry Women in Rock*, Vol. 1 (New York: Juno Books, 1996), 46.

44, Evelyn McDonnell, "Queer Punk Meets Womyn's Music," MS *Magazine* 5, no. 3 (1994).

45. Transsexuals are men who have been hormonally and surgically altered to change their sex from male to female or who are in various stages of preparation. They are sometimes referred to as M-to-F or MTF transsexuals or transsexual women. FTM is women to men in the same context.

46. These are alternative spellings that some radical or lesbian feminists used during the women's rights movement of the 1970s and 1980s to eliminate any language with the words "man" or "men" when referring to the female sex. Womyn and wimmin are plural and womon is singular for woman.

47. Lisa Vogel, "Festival Forum: Michigan Womyn's Music Festival," *Lesbian Connection* (November/December 1999): 5–7.

48. Elizabeth K. Keenan, "'I Went to School in Olympia . . . Where Everyone's the Same': Space and Place in a Feminist Rock Music Festival" (paper presented at the annual meeting of the International Association for the Study of Popular Music, Charlottesville, Virginia, October 2004), 1–6.

49. For a comprehensive catalog of women's music see their websites at Ladyslipper, Inc. (www.ladyslipper.org) and Goldenrod Music (www.goldenrod.com).

50. Tam Martin, e-mail to Boden Sandstrom, September 15, 2003.

51. www.glhalloffame.org

52. Val McKay, interview by Boden Sandstrom, August 18, 2003.

53. Michelle Bradshaw, interview by Boden Sandstrom, August, 18, 2003.

54. McKay, interview.

55. Animal and Bitch Loud, e-mail to Boden Sandstrom, February 8, 2004.

56. Animal and Bitch Loud, e-mail.

57. www.bitchandanimal.com

58. Bitch and Animal. "Secret Candy," on *Sour Juice and Rhyme* (Righteous Babes Records, Inc., 2003). © Righteous Babes Records, Inc.

59. Bitch Loud, e-mail to Boden Sandstrom, January 26, 2004.

60. Bitch and Animal. "Drag King Ba," on *What's That Smell?* (Dive Deep Productions, 1999). © Dive Deep Productions.

61. Bitch and Animal. "Boy Girl Wonder," on *Eternally Hard* (Righteous Babes Records, Inc., 2001). © Righteous Babes records, Inc.

62. Nedra Johnson, "Testify," on *Testify* (BigMouth Girl and Goldenrod Records, 1998). © Nerdra Johnson/BigMouth Girl.

63. Alix Olson, "Built Like That," on *Built Like That* (Feed the Fire Productions, 2001). © Feed the Fire/Poosamoos.

64. Alix Olson, interview by Boden Sandstrom, August 15, 2003.

65. Pamela Means, "O.D.," on *Single Bullet Theory* (Wirl Records, 2003). © Wirl Records.

66. McKay, interview.

67. *Radical Harmonies.*

68. Holly Near, e-mail to Boden Sandstrom, September 28, 2003.

69. Near, e-mail.
70. Holly Near, "I Am Willing." on Holly Near and Cris Williamson, *Cris and Holly* (H&C Records, LLC, 2003). © Hereford Music.
71. "Women of Rock," *Rolling Stone* 773 (November 13, 1997).
72. *Radical Harmonies.*

Bibliography

Animal and Bitch Loud. E-mail to Boden Sandstrom, February 8, 2004.

Armstrong, Toni, Jr. "An Endangered Species: Women's Music by, for, and about Women." *Hotwire: The Journal of Women's Music Culture* 5, no. 3 (1989): 17–19, 57.

Bitch and Animal. "Boy Girl Wonder." On *Eternally Hard.* Righteous Babes Records, Inc., 2001.

———. "Secret Candy." On *Sour Juice and Rhyme.* Righteous Babes Records, Inc., 2003.

Bradshaw, Michelle. Interview by Boden Sandstrom, August 18, 2003.

Bunch, Charlotte. "Perseverance Furthers: Separatism and Our Future." *The Furies* 1, no. 7 (1972): 3–5.

Butler, Judith. *Gender Trouble: Feminism and the Subversion of Identity.* New York: Routledge, 1999.

Casselberry, Judith. Interview by Boden Sandstrom October 2000.

Childerhouse, Buffy. *From Lilith to Lilith Fair.* New York: St. Martin's Griffin, 1998.

Culver, Casse. Interview by Boden Sandstrom, June 12, 2001.

Etheridge, Melissa. "I'm the Only One." On *Yes I Am Melissa.* New York: Island Records. 1993.

Garr, Gillian. *She's a Rebel: The History of Women in Rock & Roll.* Seattle, Wash.: Seal Press, 1992.

Grant, Terry. Interview by Boden Sandstrom, August 15, 2003.

Herndon, Marcia, and Susanne Ziegler, eds. *Music, Gender, and Culture.* Wilhelmshaven: Florian Noetzel Verlag, 1990.

Horowitz, Amy. Personal Interview by Boden Sandstrom, January 20, 2001.

Humm, Maggie. *The Dictionary of Feminist Theory.* Columbus: Ohio State University Press, 1995.

Johnson, Nedra. "Testify." On *Testify.* BigMouth Girl and Goldenrod Records, 1998. © Nerdra Johnson/BigMouth Girl.

Juno, Andrea. *Angry Women in Rock.* Volume 1. New York: Juno Books, 1996.

Keenan, Elizabeth K. "'I Went to School in Olympia . . . Where Everyone's the Same': Space and Place in a Feminist Rock Music Festival." Paper presented at the annual meeting of the International Association for the Study of Popular Music, Charlottesville, Virginia, October 2004.

Kimball, Gayle. *Women's Culture: The Renaissance of the Seventies.* London: Scarecrow Press, 1981.

Koskoff, Ellen, ed. *Women and Music in Cross-Cultural Perspectives.* Chicago: University of Chicago Press, 1989.

Lems, Kristin. *Radical Harmonies.* Directed by Dee Mosbacher. Produced by Dee Mosbacher and Boden Sandstrom. Woman Vision, 2002.

Lont, Cynthia Marion. "Between a Rock and a Hard Place: A Model of Subculture Persistence and Women's Music." Ph.D. dissertation, University of Iowa, 1984.

Loud, Bitch. E-mail to Boden Sandstrom, January 26, 2004.

McDonnell, Evelyn. "Queer Punk Meets Womyn's Music." MS *Magazine* 5, no. 3 (1994).

McKay, Val. Interview by Boden Sandstrom, August 18, 2003.

Martin, Tam. E-mail to Boden Sandstrom, September 15, 2003.

Means, Pamela. "O.D." On *Single Bullet Theory.* Wirl Records, 2003. © Wirl Records.

Moisala, Pirkko, and Beverly Diamond, eds. *Music and Gender.* Chicago: University of Illinois Press, 2000.

Morris, Bonnie J. *Eden Built by Eves.* New York: Alyson Books, 1999.

Radical Harmonies. Directed by Dee Mosbacher. Produced by Dee Mosbacher and Boden Sandstrom. Woman Vision, 2002.

Near, Holly. e-mail to Boden Sandstrom, September 28. 2003.

Near, Holly. "I Am Willing." On *Cris and Holly.* H&C Records, LLC, 2003.

O'Dair, Barbara. *Trouble Girls: The Rolling Stone Book of Women in Rock.* New York: Random House, 1997.

Olson, Alix. "Built Like That." On *Built Like That.* Feed the Fire Productions, 2001. © Feed the Fire/Poosamoos.

———. Interview by Boden Sandstrom, August 15, 2003

Pipik, Jane E. "Woman-Identified Music: Moving On." *Heresies* 3, no. 2 (1980): 88–89.

Post, Laura. *Backstage Pass: Interviews with Women in Music.* Norwich, Vt.: New Victoria Publishers, 1997.

Sandstrom, Boden. "Performance, Ritual and Negotiation of Identity in the Michigan Womyn's Music Festival." Ph.D. dissertation, College Park: University of Maryland, 2002.

Scovill, Ruth. "Women's Music." In *Women's Culture: The Renaissance of the Seventies,* 148–62. London: Scarecrow Press, 1981.

Vogel, Lisa. "Festival Forum: Michigan Womyn's Music Festival, *Lesbian Connection* (Nov./Dec. 1999): 5–7.

———. Interview by Boden Sandstrom, January 24, 1995.

———. Interview by Boden Sandstrom, August 17, 1996.

———. E-mail to Boden Sandstrom, October 25, 1999.

We Want the Music Collective. *The Michigan Womyn's Music Festival.* Berkeley, Calif.: WWTMC, 1997.

"Women of Rock." *Rolling Stone* 773 (November 13, 1997).

~

CHAPTER SEVEN

Women's Musical Composition:
An Interview with Kay Gardner

Gayle Kimball

GK: Do you still think women compose in a circular form, different from male composers?

KG: Yes. I didn't know at the time of the first edition about the principle of sacred geometry, the golden mean or the divine proportion. This is called phi; phi = .618. Phi relates to circular form in that the climax is toward the middle. The golden mean is usually thought of as being in art, architecture, and certain forms of nature. The proportion is found in pine cones and sunflowers; it is found in our DNA and the formation of the human brain. Unlike art and architecture, which operate in space, music operates in time. To compose using the divine proportion, I multiply the length of my piece by .618 and that tells me where to put to the climax. I was doing this organically before I learned about it from Pozzi Escot, a music professor at Wheaton College, Massachusetts, and the New England Conservatory of Music. She did several presentations at women's classical gatherings and told us that Hildegard of Bingan used the golden mean in her compositions. The same form was used to design medieval cathedrals. In other words, the music was written in the same form as the buildings. The twentieth-century composer Anton Webern wrote his doctoral dissertation on the use of the golden mean in medieval music.

GK: Do women compose in circles rather than linearly with the climax at the end, more often than men?

KG: There's a cyclical organic form that women who are not academically trained create in, and some who are highly academically trained use, because they know it's the golden mean. Women are more in touch with natural cycles, because we menstruate. The earth, nature, is female. She contains both male and female, but nature is innately female because she gives birth. I'm very connected to the biological connection with earth in musical composition.

The Sapphic or Lesbian mode (known today as the mixolydian mode) and the Lydian mode are also elements of female composition. Modes are musical scales, or sequences of tones that fall between octaves. The Greek modes were named after ancient tribes, and the invention of the Lesbian and Lydian modes has been attributed to women. There was no such tribe as "mixolydian," but because the invention of what is called the "mixolydian mode" is credited to Sappho of Lesbos (by Plutarch, 46 BC), it makes sense to call it the Lesbian mode.

Another musical mode said to be invented by women is the Lydian mode. The Lydians were originally from Asia Minor; however, according to Monique Wittig, they were a tribe of Amazons who settled on Crete. The Lydian mode was banned by Plato in his book *The Republic* because he said it was "too female" for Platonic society, a notably misogynist society. The Lydian mode is used to communicate with sea life, with dolphins and whales. Years ago, when Paul Winter recorded "Common Ground," he used the Lydian mode to communicate with dolphins and whales.

GK. Do sea creatures "sing" in the Lydian mode?

KG. I'm not sure. We can't hear the whales' deepest tones because whales are so huge their sounds are below our hearing range. What we're actually hearing are the overtones, the high scales that occur over the fundamental deep roaring sounds. Once we get to the fourth octave of overtones, perhaps the whales' scale or mode is created. This is called the Saraswati raga (a raga, like a mode, is, among other things, a sequence of tones between octaves). After I decided to compose in the mixolydian and Lydian modes because women invented them, I made a combination of the two, which I thought was my invention. But I found out three years later that it's actually the East Indian scale, named after Sarasvati, the Hindu goddess of music and the sciences, whose consort is Brahma. The 5,000 scales in South India are named half after gods and half after goddesses, so Saraswati is a female scale.

GK: What happened with the New England Women's Symphony after its birth in 1978?

KG: NEWS folded after six performances because of lack of money. Boston wasn't really the place to have it because so many other orchestras are there. A few years after NEWS died, California women decided to start a women's symphony in San Francisco. It was originally called the Bay Area Philharmonic. Nan Washburn, who was assistant director of NEWS, moved to San Francisco and became artistic director and researcher for the Bay Area Philharmonic, called the Women's Philharmonic. (Washburn is now conductor of the West Hollywood, California, Symphony and another orchestra in Michigan.)

GK: Have more female classical composers come to light in the last two decades?

KG: Publishers (Alfred and Mel Bay) now are selling collections of women composers' music. Many more recordings of women's compositions are being made on many record labels. Women's works, including mine, are being programmed by more and more orchestras. Within the past five years, it's become cool to include a woman composer. Last year the Bangor Symphony Orchestra (where I live in Maine) for the first time in its entire one-hundred-year history played a program of all women's compositions. I was guest conductor for that concert. Before that, they'd played about two women's works total. In one hundred years! Now they play women's compositions once in a while.

In the nineteenth century, women weren't published at all or were published under their father's or brother's name. When Felix Mendelssohn went to play for Queen Victoria, she requested one of his "Songs without Words," not knowing it was composed by his sister, Fanny. The only way she could have her work published was as part of her brother's collection. Publishing women's works just wasn't done.

The NEWS concertmaestra, Jean Lamon (now conductor of Taffelmusik in Toronto), went to the microfilm library at Harvard University to do research and found a listing for M. Grimani, a nun who lived in Vivaldi's time. We later found that her first name was Maria. Many piano students who learned pieces from the collection 59 *Favorite Piano Pieces* studied "Scarf Dance" by C. Chaminade. It wasn't until I got to college that I learned that the C. stood for Cecile. Sometimes when there's just a first initial, it's a good clue that the composer was a woman.

GK: Are there other centers of interest in women composers? Other women's orchestras, conductors, and organizations that encourage women musicians?

KG: Columbus, Ohio, has a women's symphony, though I don't think it specializes in women's works. The Women's Philharmonic in San Francisco started in the early 1980s. Miriam Abram was the original business manager. She interviewed us about why the New England Women's Symphony wasn't able to continue, so they wouldn't make the same mistakes. The original conductor of that orchestra was Elizabeth Min. The conductor, Marin Alsop, has been moving along quickly. I first heard of her in New York City when she directed a group of women called String Fever. Recently she was with the St. Louis symphony and has since moved on, conducting internationally.

The International Alliance for Women and Music (IAWM) has its administrative office at the University of Nebraska Press, which publishes the quarterly IAWM journal. It includes articles, interviews, job opportunities, and concert reviews. *Women in Music: A Journal of Gender and Culture* is an annual journal published by the Music Department at Indiana University of Pennsylvania.

GK: How has your composing evolved?

KG: I still consider myself a classical composer, even though I never formally studied composition. For the most part, my music has been put into the New Age category, even though I was composing spiritual and meditation music before there was such a thing as New Age. My largest composition is *Rainbow Path*. It took me until 1984 to get it finished and recorded. It was based on the chakras, after I found the Saraswati connection. A *Rainbow Path* was orchestral and has a movement for each of the seven energy centers associated with the human organism. In concert, I play it on piano with projections of mandalas painted by Gina Halpern. I've also used silk scarves soaked in pure essences associated with the chakras. The recording of *Rainbow Path* is still selling after twenty years, and it's the piece I get the most response from. It takes the listener through all the chakras and helps her feel clear and whole. That piece took me eight years. I'd hoped it would have a healing effect; I certainly wrote it with that intent. Over the years I spent creating it, I had to live with the relationship of tone and color before I knew enough to write. I started with the piece for the third chakra, the center of will. Then I wrote the piece for the Third Eye, the sixth chakra. I needed both those attributes in order to finish the entire work.

The largest piece I've written is *Ouroboros* (the ancient symbol of a circled snake with its tail in its mouth)—*Cycles of Life: Women's Passages*, which came as a commission to write a piece that celebrated the ages of women's lives. With text by Ila Suzanne and Charlie Hutchins, the oratorio grew to an hour-long work with solo voices of women ages eight to eighty, a women's chorus and orchestra. It was first performed at the National Women's Music Festival in 1993. It's been recorded and has since been performed by M.U.S.E., the Cincinnati Women's Chorus, and the Denver Women's Chorus.

Since conducting was my main training, I didn't expect to move from orchestral and chamber music to the music and healing field. I wouldn't have imagined that I'd be so involved in choral music now, as my training was instrumental, but now I have a choir at the local Unitarian-Universalist church, and I direct Women with Wings, a singing spiritual circle. We've just finished a CD of the chants that the women in the group have created.

Having a mixed choir at the church has gotten me more interested in the choral literature. Recently I composed three choral hymns to Innana, an ancient Sumerian goddess, based on translations from the cuneiform text. These are big pieces with large instrumental ensembles as accompaniment. I've also set [to music] the words of Kahlil Gibran and the Sufi poet Hafiz (who was after Rumi), who writes beautiful poetry that doesn't feel male to me. (The Sufis address the deity as they would address a lover.) Other poets whose work I've set to music recently are May Sarton and Starhawk.

GK: What makes music conducive to meditation?

KG: Intent is the key. When I'm creating a piece of music, I really feel that whatever my intent is goes to the listener or, if it's a musician, to the participant. If I have clarity in my intent, it will come across in the music. The way I center myself is to build an altar near where I compose. For example: I wrote music inspired by Susan Griffin's poem "Dancing." I put symbols of earth, air, fire, and water on the altar, and a picture of Judith Jameson (director of the Alvin Ailey Dance Company) dancing. The poem spoke to me about women dancing through whatever difficulties we have as women in this culture, the beauty and strength of women dancing. The altar was my focus, constantly reminding me of my intent.

With the Innana pieces, my altar included an image of the goddess Innana. It's almost as if my concentration on the altar dictates how the compositions are to proceed. These Sumerian hymns are celebratory, in honor and praise of their most important deity. In Innana's aspect as goddess of thunder, I used percussion as accompaniment. In a section about her blessing the land, I used winds and strings. For her aspect as the powerful mother goddess, I used a double brass quartet.

GK: How do you define women's spirituality?

KG: To me, it's a relationship to the divine as female. After almost twenty years of devotion to the Goddess, I was ordained as a priestess of Isis in Ireland by Lady Olivia Robertson, who founded the international Fellowship of Isis, along with her late brother, Lawrence Durdin-Robertson and his wife, Pamela. The Fellowship has around 20,000 members worldwide. Isis is one of the 10,000 names for the great mother. She was worshipped in Egypt, traveled to Rome, and was brought by Romans as far north as Germany and England. Because my grandfather grew up in Egypt, I've always related to Egyptian arts and artifacts. Through them I was introduced to the myths and images of Isis. Mary is an outgrowth of Isis; she is seen in paintings and sculptures holding her baby on her lap, just as Horus sat on Isis's lap. The hieroglyph for Isis is a throne, and she was the throne on which the Egyptian pharaohs sat. I especially like Isis because she's a winged goddess; I feel nurtured and uplifted by those wings. In Women with Wings, the singing and chanting group in Bangor, which I helped found, we celebrate ourselves as goddesses with wings.

In my ordination I had to pick three goddesses whose aspects I most resonated to: I selected Isis as Great Mother, Kwan Yin for compassion, and Saraswati for music. Isis is the organizer; she has her fingers in everything. That's how I relate to her. I feel the energy of Isis as an embodiment of female divinity. She and the other goddesses are in my heart, my ancient remembering.

GK: How do you produce and distribute your music?

KG: I have fourteen albums on CDs. My last vinyl LP was in 1986. I prefer the warmer analog sound, but these days it's almost impossible to find recording engineers or studios using anything but digital technology. I suspended Even Keel, my own independent recording label, after my third recording, *Moods & Rituals*. This recording fell between *Emerging* and *A Rainbow Path*. It's an album of solo flute improvisations. I needed more time to collect funds to do the orchestral album, *A Rainbow Path*. Also *Moods & Rituals* was a way to introduce my music to the New Age listeners to whom I hoped to market my future recordings. When I reached a fundraising impasse, Ladyslipper Records agreed to produce *A Rainbow Path*. It was their first album. I was convinced that this composition was important and would sell for a long time. Fortunately I was able to convince Ladyslipper's guiding light, Laurie Fuchs, also a visionary. The album is still in their catalog, still sells on a regular basis, and for a number of years produced a quarter of my royalty income.

Ladyslipper has produced most of my recordings. I get personal attention and royalties when I'm supposed to get them. Ladyslipper is a nonprofit organization devoted to disseminating music and art by women. Based in Durham, North Carolina, you can see their catalog online at www.Laddyslipper.org. Ladyslipper began as a distributor of Olivia albums and tapes of women musicians like Meg Christian, Holly Near, Margie Adam, and Chris Williamson. (Olivia is no longer in the women's music business; they organize cruises for women and their roster of women performers entertain on the cruises.) Now Ladyslipper has a catalog of literally thousands of annotated recordings by women and an active website where one can browse and listen. The main distributors of women's recordings are Ladyslipper and Golden Rod in East Lansing, Michigan.

I've worked with two other record companies. The Relaxation Company out of Roslyn, New York, sponsored my CD, *Drone Zone* as part of their healing music series. My other recorded work is a nine-hour teaching set called *Music as Medicine: The Art & Science of Healing with Sound*. It includes me talking about my work in sound healing, using lots of recorded examples of curative music from classical, folk, and world music genres. (The material expands on my book *Sounding the Inner Landscape: Music as Medicine*.) It's on the Sounds True label, an outfit in Colorado, near Boulder. Sounds True was founded by Tami Simon, whom I met years and years ago when she was a radio interviewer and recording engineer for women's music concerts and local New Age–type conferences. Tami now heads Sounds True, a multi-million-dollar company with a catalog of audio recordings featuring many, many spiritual and new-consciousness teachers. I'm honored to be included in their roster of authors.

Back to women's music in the 1970s, we got into producing and distributing women's music because of our politics; we were into it to make change. Most of us are lesbians, and because most lesbians weren't tied to family as much as straight women, we had more flexibility and were able to get out to promote our work. Historically, lesbians and single women—leaders like Jane Addams and Emma Goldman, Susan B. Anthony—have been the instigators of most social change movements—gay rights, civil rights, child labor, and labor movements. The gay rights movement, begun with the Stonewall incident, was sparked by a lesbian couple.

GK: What's happening with young musicians?

KG: One of my favorite younger composers is Augusta Reid Thomas, the Chicago Symphony's composer-in-residence. She uses the whole orchestra as a palette, painting with sound. Her music is almost muscular. When I programmed pieces for my appearance with the Bangor Symphony Orchestra, I selected a piece by Chen Yi. She's brilliant. She just received a Charles Ives grant for $100,000 to compose. Her compositions are very dramatic and very theatrical, very emotional. The piece I conducted was based on folk music she learned while sentenced to a communal farm during the Cultural Revolution. Current classical women's music tends to be visceral. That isn't so true of the music of such historical composers as Fanny Mendelssohn and Clara Schumann. Right now I could think of a number of women composers, each having her own approach. Today's women's music is completely diverse, there's no right way, no one school of composition. Young composers are not being dictated to by their teachers. We are becoming the teachers. Many younger women in the field have no idea what we did to bring women composers to recognition. It will take probably another twenty years before this work is acknowledged. Sometimes herstory has to skip a generation until we're proud of what our grandmothers did.

Younger women in the pop music field have started independent labels. Anni Difranco is the best known. They are independent and strong women, learning how to be businesswomen as well as musicians, although they may not know those of us who opened the doors in the 1970s, doors that are now wide open. They take for granted composing, recording, having control over their own careers, not having a recording company executive tell them how they have to present themselves to the market. That's the whole reason we founded the women's music industry. We wanted to be ourselves.

There are a lot of wonderful younger songwriters: Dar Williams is one, Nedra Johnson is another. I see many of the best every summer at the Michigan Womyn's Music Festival, now in its twenty-seventh year. As far as my style of music, I don't hear many instrumentalists at that festival, and it would be hard to tell whom I might have influenced. I knew when we began that women's music would eventually be assimilated into the mainstream. That was one of our goals. When I think of Lilith Fair, though, the backup musicians and techs are mostly men. As long as music is commercial, controlled by male-owned interests, it will stay, in the main, patriarchal. But we were role models, giving young performers the opportunity to be strong, independent women with minds of their own, with fewer restraints.

Comedy is the other healing art besides music that is very evident at the festivals and on Olivia cruises. Kate Clinton performs very intelligent comedy. She's probably the best known in women's music circles. Vickie Shaw, Susanne West-enhoffer, and Ellen DeGeneris are brazen. Probably the first comic in the age of TV was Phyllis Dyler, joking about her husband "Fang," then the strongly femi-nist Rosanne Barr. The standup comedians talk about menstruation and other womanly subjects, and they skewer the human condition but from a woman's viewpoint. In these days when we have so much tragedy we need humor.

GK: What will you be doing twenty years from now?

KG: I'll be eighty-one. I'll still be composing, of course. And I'll be enjoying my garden, which by then should be large and prolific. [Sadly, Kay unexpect-edly passed on soon after this interview.]

Biography

Kay said, "Music is my religion," beginning in 1960, when she first began performing in coffeehouses in California. She studied piano and flute throughout her childhood. She received a master's degree in music performance from SUNY Stonybrook. In the early 1970s, Kay decided to combine all of her talents toward the goal of making and promoting women's music. She became a founding member of the feminist and openly lesbian women's band, Lavender Jane. Later in the 1970s, Kay founded the New England Women's Symphony in Cambridge, Massachusetts and, as conductor, made a special effort to program works by women composers.

By the 1980s, Kay had shifted her focus to studying the healing effects of music on the human body. As a result, she created A Rainbow Path. She also wrote Sounding the Inner Landscape, showing how music is medicine. Her original compositions consisted of orchestral and choral works, recordings, publications, and videotapes.

Kay's devotion to the revival of consciousness of the goddess began in the 1970s and grew stronger throughout her lifetime. In 1993, she worked with the Bangor Uni-tarian Universalist women's community to create a sacred singing circle, Women with Wings. She was ordained a priestess by the Fellowship of Isis in Clonegal, Ire-land, in 1998. She founded the Temple of the Feminine Divine and a three-year or-dination program called the Iseum Musicum. Kay was a performer, composer, partner, mother, grandmother, priestess, and activist. Challenged to describe her politics, she said she was a musician first, a woman second, and a lesbian third.

PART THREE

LITERATURE

CHAPTER EIGHT

∽

Our (M)others, Ourselves

Irena Praitis

Poetry written by women today is so diverse, so dynamic, and so rich that it is impossible to typify. The prior norms and structures, the inherited myths and archetypes that were once so often the focus of poems by women—that needed to be the focus to be shown inadequate and rejected—have lost much of their grip. A vast sea of voices rises in affirmation, chorusing the complexities and splendor of reality in as many ways as there are voices to sing. And oddly, despite all of the diverging viewpoints, sometimes antagonistic starting points, and downright contradictory positions held among poets writing today, all of these voices together don't result in dissonance but in a strange harmony that exists despite and perhaps because of its divergences.

As I read contemporary poetry, I am increasingly impressed by the sources of inspiration, the foundations of story, and the lyric intensity. And if I were to conjure a contemporary muse, I do not imagine some remote, mystical figure an artist evokes. No, when I read contemporary poetry by women, I feel that the muse emerges in process: the process of awareness, the process of recovery, the process of connecting, and the process of creating in and of itself. The muse is movement. The muse is discovery, creation, and forging connections. The muse refuses to be contained within one image, one story, one moment, one figure to be returned to, and, instead, emerges in the relations between the poet and the world, the poet and the poem, the poet and herself, the poet and the beloveds around her.

We can read the linguistic experimentation and deconstructive awareness of language poets who challenge definitiveness by breaking words and sentences into foundational sounds and rhythms; of postmodernists who rely on fragmentation, intellectual inquiry, and wry humor; of lyricists who find new pathos in traditional rhymes and meters; of historicizing poets who recover and represent events from the past; of consciousness-raising poets who foreground the political in their work; and of poets who write about family, friends, and their own bodies; and many, many others. There is such an outpouring and uplifting that I can imagine the walls that had to be breached to enable such a flow of creativity. And while this achievement of diversification and proliferation has become so commonplace as to be paid the highest compliment of increasingly being viewed as the norm, there is still much to recover about struggles over voice, artistic expression, and publication, and still much to achieve. This essay offers a small glimpse at an amazing creative foment that will continue to change the way we think about and live within the world around us.

Ashworth

In the first edition, Debora Ashworth focused on female archetypes in women's poetry.[1] Ashworth discovered poets struggling against archetypes and developing new strategies for dealing with the limitations of patriarchal myths and their psychically damaging effects. In exploring the virgin/whore archetypal myth, Ashworth noted that many women rejected the either/or categorization at the foundation of the myth and often present female speakers who fit both categories. The poets of the 1960s and 1970s addressed the myths, challenged them, and lost their fear of them. They recognized that many myths bear an "oppressive impact on . . . life" (1981, 184) and that they are an "inauthentic source of power" (184). Rather than rely on patriarchal myths and social norms, the poems show how each story, each poem, each relationship has its own reason for being. A mythic precedent, determined by society and perpetuated by imbalances of power, is not necessary for cultural validation because new ideas of validation are being developed.

As did the artists and thinkers of the European Renaissance of the fifteenth and sixteenth centuries, when classical knowledge was increasingly questioned by individual discovery, the poems by women in the 1960s and 1970s affirmed that being itself, and knowing on the individual level, provide truth enough for art. New stories emerge as poets acknowledge the authority of their own experiences and the wide applicability of personal experiences. So poets create new, more fluid myths that refuse stasis and universalism. Once archetypal figures (mothers, fathers, heroines) refuse singularity between presentations and within presentations. Poets offer new multivalent symbols that shift from poem to poem and context to context the way light affects iridescence; a color, an image, a word names and renames, sifting through implications.

Women writers have a long tradition of looking to female literary forebears, and writers of the 1980s and 1990s also looked to predecessors and sought out foundations and stories that had been buried or suppressed. What has changed over the past two decades are the starting points for these forays into the past, with more perspectives, more traditions, and more voices looking to the past. Women from a wide range of ethnicities, social classes, and philosophies are acknowledging, searching for, and discovering predecessors. Through the continuing recovery of the past, writers redefine the present and open possibilities for the future. To trace the current incarnation of this poetic ethos and symbolic framework and to show the ways that women uncover and reclaim a past that has been discredited, I focus on one particular symbolic figure, that of mother.

The Mother

The mother figure is a symbol with a long history and multiple valences. Archetypal renderings of motherhood offer impossible models by which women have been measured; in contradiction to these models, our lived experience teaches us the limitations of archetypal renderings and so we know that there are many mothers to be written about honestly and fully. As Adrienne Rich notes in *Of Woman Born*, "this cathexis between mother and daughter—essential, distorted, misused—is the great unwritten story."[2] Women have been writing of mothers for generations, and yet there is still much to be discovered outside of traditional and institutional conceptions. And in the exploration is "the germ of our desire to create a world in which strong mothers and strong daughters will be a matter of course" (1986, 225). For writers, exploring the mother/daughter relationship is vital for self and artistic understanding. Not only do mother figures offer representations of personal and familial relationships, they also symbolize the relationships between poets and their predecessors.

Literary inheritance has sometimes been construed in terms of a family romance,[3] but as with most conceptions of "family," and most depictions of "romance," these terms are all too often associated with cultural constructions scarcely applicable to the lived experiences of actual people. As associations and love interrelationships between people challenge the idea of the "traditional family," and as the idea of "romance" is undergoing revision in many artistic venues, so too women writing poetry challenge standard conceptions of romance, family, and literary inheritance. For just as individual experiences within individual families and within individual selves are fluid, dynamic, and constantly evolving, so too are literary lineages. And in both senses, in personal and literary histories, as Rich states "until a strong line of love, confirmation, and example stretches from mother to daughter, from woman to woman across the generations, women will still be wandering in the wilderness" (Rich 1986, 246). What emerged over the course of the twentieth century, but especially in the 1980s and 1990s, were more and more perspectives from which to consider women, mothers, and forebears. The many peoples that make up U.S. culture and world culture offer numerous starting points and paths of exploration regarding women, their mothers, their predecessors, and their own mothering. More and more in recent decades, these many different voices have been heard.

An exploration of mothers in poetry offers one way to trace the various dynamisms of poetic lineage, of forebears, of those who bore and came before. The intricacies of these relationships with mothers, as presented by poets, provide a slant of light within which to view the dynamic complexities of our most complicated relationships: those we have with those who came before. Within this poetic space of illumination, we begin to witness the changing interactions between poets and their predecessors, between the present and the ideas of the past.

Walker and Ostriker

Numerous critical studies about women's poetry (by Margaret Homans, Patricia Yeager, Paula Bennett, and Annette Kolodny, to name a few) emerged in the mid-1980s.[4] Two texts that particularly exemplify how women artists and thinkers establish solid foundations for forays into the past are Alice Walker's In Search of Our Mothers' Gardens and Alicia Ostriker's Stealing the Language.[5] These books offer strong exemplifications of the connections between women artists and the traditions they inherit. They look toward the past and offer an awareness of the social systems and structures that often lead to the suppression of female writers and that contribute to the erosion of female literary history. Walker and Ostriker offer truths that exist under the façades-presented-as-truth, and their work marks the strengthening of a framework for the recovery and affirmation of what had not been fully sung before.

In her search for literary predecessors, Alice Walker, an African American writer born in 1944, found not only forebears, but also a strong sense of possibility, creativity, and endurance from the literary world and also nearer to home. After recovering the work of Zora Neale Hurston, a Harlem Renaissance writer of the 1930s, Walker affirms how Hurston's work enables and supports her own. In relation to one of her stories that drew from Hurston's work, Walker states, "I would not have written the story . . . had I not known that Zora had already done a thorough job of preparing the ground over which I was then moving" (1983, 13). This recovery of Hurston's work serves as an affirmation of both Hurston and Walker. Walker sees Hurston's work as making her own possible. For Walker, literary predecessors are allies, friends, supporters, encouragers, and survivors. It is no surprise, then, that in *In Search of Our Mothers' Gardens* (first published in 1974), Walker discusses how her female creative forebears were not always recognized as such, and were, in actuality, dwelling quite close to home. The "crazy, loony, pitiful, women" Walker discovered in novels by such writers as Jean Toomer, were, as Walker asserts, "without a doubt, our mothers and grandmothers . . . driven to a numb and bleeding madness by the springs of creativity in them for which there was no release" (1983, 232–33). Using the stories of literary predecessors and unacknowledged familial artists, Walker affirms that women writers "must fearlessly pull out of ourselves and look at and identify with our lives the living creativity some of our great-grandmothers were not allowed to know" (237). Walker sees her mother in herself. She recovers her mother's creativity in her own: "No song or poem will bear my mother's name. Yet so many of the stories that I write, that we all write, are my mother's stories" (240). Strengthening a framework for a literary history based on respect, admiration, hope, and a sense of familial connection—not in terms of a family romance but in terms of family love—Walker relays a strong sense of possibilities in female literary lineages: "Guided by my heritage of a love of beauty and a respect for strength—in search of my mother's garden, I found my own" (243).

Alicia Suskin Ostriker, a European American poet and critic, offers a feminist history that traces female literary lineages in *Stealing the Language*. Finding a complex dynamic in these lineages, Ostriker notes that, "like every literary movement, contemporary women's poetry in part perpetuates and in part denounces its past" (1986, 10). Also exploring literary predecessors through a familial metaphor, Ostriker notes, "When we think back through our mothers we find weakness; we also find power. As writers from Virginia Woolf to Alice Walker make clear, women poets need strong mothers" (16). And strong mothers are exactly what Ostriker finds over and over again in her text. Allowing for a complex and shifting dynamic, Ostriker, like Walker, explores the ways that literary foremothers are essential to the creativity and artistic expression of contemporary women writers. The strength of the women who came before fuels the strength of women writing now, and the limitations that women who came before struggled against are addressed, struggled against, and increasingly overcome now. Both Walker and Ostriker are keen to reveal the gritty experiences of women artists. Rather than rely on mythic archetypes about mothers, these writers seek actual experiences. The observations of Walker and Ostriker encourage women artists to delve into their personal and literary pasts to uncover and tell the story of what they find there. Individual story and personal experience emerge in contemporary poetry in defiance of traditional archetypes.

Poets and Their Poems

In exploring the relationship with their mothers, contemporary women writers allow for increasing complexity. The poetry develops from their own sense of history, their own sense of family, their own sense of a mother. Poets legitimize personal experience and challenge the imposed restrictions of archetypes not developed from the experiences of women. These poems about mothers are affirmations because they embrace the complexity of female individuality and personal experience. Contemporary women poets are not stepping into expected roles, and they are also not just challenging expected roles. Rather, these poets are telling their own stories about their own experiences, and in the process realizing that it is often in the particular—in the actual experience of the individual and the community—that points of connection are made between people.

As a culture, we are developing a strong sense of multiplicity. But there is the danger of touting multiplicity without fully hearing singular and contradictory voices. If we all simply repeat the idea of multiplicity, without actually opening up the possibilities for voices—some strident, some contradictory, some amenable to our own beliefs, some not—then we are developing a univocity of perspective on a token multiplicity. And so, lest we become a group of people agreeing with one voice that multiplicity is what we want without really getting beyond that agreement to actual voices, may we remember the importance of listening closely to each voice. It may be a group's story as told by an individual, a story that strives to be universalist, a voice that stresses the particular, or a voice we barely hear and move closer to to catch its nuances. May we remember that we are not only listening to different people speaking different words, but to different poems, different stories, and different structures that may challenge our own truths and understandings and that may require the development of different modes of listening. In the readings that follow, I offer four poets and highlight their unique styles.

Lorna Goodison

In her collection of poems, *I Am Becoming My Mother*, Jamaican poet Lorna Goodison (b. 1947) traces her lineage.[6] She looks into the past and discovers and recovers what has fed her life and what feeds her becoming. In the poem that shares the volume's title, there is an addended parenthetical comment: "May I inherit half her strength." She traces inheritance and strength, celebrating what we receive and learning from those who came before. In this poem we learn that this mother:

> Could work miracles, she would make a garment from a
> square of cloth
> in a span that defied time. Or feed twenty people on a
> stew made from
> fallen-from-the-head cabbage leaves and a carrot and a
> cho-cho and a palmful
> of meat.   (1986, 46)

Food, shelter, covering from cold: this mother brings the essential forward and is intricately connected with another mother figure that Goodison writes of called Nanny.

In "Nanny," Goodison presents and celebrates the history of a warrior and Jamaican national hero. Nanny, one of a band of fugitive slaves who were known as Maroon warriors and who led assaults against the British, speaks her history in Goodison's poem. At the poem's opening, this warrior woman writes of her womb being sealed "with molten wax" (44), and thus she appears, initially, to relinquish the possibility of motherhood. Yet, as the poem continues, we discover that her adoption of "the condition of the warrior" (44) enables another form of motherhood. Nanny feels the birth of a people. Her body would "quicken/at the birth of every one" (44) of her people's children. She becomes a mother in a symbolic sense, and her generosity, her concern for her people, her love of them, fuels her capacities as a healer and as a warrior. The capacities she develops to "sense and sift" (44) between different impressions, and the warrior skills she masters to "smell danger," feed her capacities for rebellion, and also feed her solitude as she becomes "most knowing/and forever alone" (44). Her song, though sometimes a moan, persists.

When Nanny's "training was over," an apparent betrayal occurs. Nanny is sold "to the traders" (44). And yet she presents this event as necessary for her subsequent heroism. She travels with all her "weapons within her" and a marked defiance: "I was sent, tell that to history" (44). Nanny's was a planned resistance, a trained-for rebellion, a salvation capacity that she understood from the beginning. No matter what the writers of history might say regarding her status, in her own words, as rendered by Goodison, Nanny knew her capacities and how she would use them. As Goodison shows throughout the poem, Nanny offers a new blending of characteristics as she embodies nurturing, healing, and the skills of a warrior. The last two lines of the poem could serve as a mantra to anyone in times of trouble. Nanny, the mother of her people, the healer of her people, the resister of oppression, ensures her legacy:

> When your sorrow obscures the skies
> Other women like me will rise. (44)

Because of her example and her presence in a recovered history, Nanny endows her lineage with endurance and possibility. Goodison celebrates that strength by sharing Nanny's story, and offering it as the rallying cry of a strong mother indeed.

Sandra Cisneros

In Latina poet Sandra Cisneros's (b. 1954) prose poem "Smart Cookie" from *House on Mango Street,* we are reminded of the mothers Alice Walker's essay alludes to, who were artists in whatever realms were open to them, and who encouraged their children to reach beyond limitations.[7] In Cisneros's poem, we overhear a mother talking about her youth to her daughter in the hopes that her daughter will not stumble. Through the daughter's description, we can see the artistic potential and intelligence of this mother who "can speak two languages," "sing an opera," and "fix a T.V." (1991, 90). Finding expression through domestic tasks, this mother "draws with her needle" but also yearns for more: the ballet, the opera, plays (90). While she "stirs the oatmeal" (91), she instructs her daughter verbally, offering admonitions against succumbing to societal pressures. The mother herself had succumbed, but she instructs her daughter to follow a different path. She passes on her own story. She gives examples of those who followed expected paths, "Izaura whose husband left and Yolanda whose husband is dead" (91), and ended without achieving their goals. She values education and rails against the stereotypes that cause suffering. The daughter listens, surprised at her mother's vehemence:

Then out of nowhere:
Shame is a bad thing, you know. It keeps you down. You want to know why I quit school? Because I didn't have nice clothes. No clothes, but I had brains. (91)

The "out of nowhere" moment at the end of the poem reveals the daughter's sudden realization of the importance of storytelling. The mother uses her own life as an example. The mother and daughter both look to the mother's life and see its potential and the limits on that potential. There are elements to be followed—the artistic expression, the concern for others—and there are elements to be broken through—the shame, the limitation. This mother, who offers nourishment to her child in the form of food and wisdom-filled story, who offers beauty in the form of song and embroidery, knows something her daughter doesn't yet know, and she strives to strengthen her daughter to endure what she herself could not endure. This mother, this forebear, begins to build the bridge that will enable her daughter to eventually leave Mango Street and then to return for the others "left behind," the ones "who cannot out" (110).

Brenda Hillman

The poem "Mother's Language" from European American Brenda Hillman's (b. 1951) volume of poems *Loose Sugar* is introduced by the line "the lyric you worked really hard to retrieve" (1997, 108), indicating that the poem's creation involved struggle and that struggle is felt in the body of the poem.[8] As the parenthetical pre-title to the poem suggests, the speaker's attempt to describe "mother's language," and "mother's language" itself, exemplify struggle:

> (the lyric you worked really hard to retrieve)
>
> *Mother's Language*
> Maybe you dwelt for a brief time in a language given up for you
> or found reasons to combine brightnesses like a picture of a
>   Brazilian village made of butterfly wings—;
> why are children still thought of as incomplete?
> Your fingers were so smooth
>   because your fingerprints had been stolen!
> To this very day,
> before or after a photo, thinking sentences will heal you,
> you stand so straight your speech is slow.
> You speak to her so well now!
> And if what she thinks she gave up is not what she
>   gave up, there is a desperate sweetness—(108)

Throughout the poem, the language that belongs to the mother (and the relationship to that language identified by the speaker) repeatedly evokes both possibility and difficulty. The language internally affects the body and the mind, "thinking sentences will heal you" (108), and externally references spaces one can occupy and lose, where "you dwelt for a brief time in a language given up for you" (108).

As if to further manifest the struggle with language in the poem, the words themselves become sites of multiplicity that make specific reference difficult to determine. The "you" repeated throughout the poem could constitute a self-reference since the introductory line can be read as the writer speaking to herself about language, the lyric, and her relationship to it. But the "you" could also reference the mother described throughout the poem who stands "straight" and whose speech is "slow" (108). Each "you" then, can reference the mother/subject or the daughter/writer. The multivalence in which writer/daughter and subject/mother are one offers an indication of the complexities of familial relationships. What the poet/daughter says of the mother/subject is equally applicable to the writer. Hillman's poem touches on Rich's idea that "we are, none of us, 'either' mothers or daughters; to our amazement, confusion, and greater complexity, we are both" (253). But the poem's possibilities continue to unfold beyond this duality. The "you" of the poem could also be a second person reference, and so the reader is also implicated in the poem's descriptions. Through this mingling and twining of the writer, the mother, and the reader, Hillman's sense of authorship, readership, and experience of a mother/daughter bond becomes a site of intense dynamism. We are all connected. We are all implicated. The poet writing the poem is the mother creating a daughter. The mother in the poem is the mother who created the poet who is creating the poem and the mother written about. The poet writing the poem is the daughter understanding and relating to the mother's struggle with creation. The reader reading the poem is involved in the act of seeking meaning and is brought into the cycle of creation and its awareness since the poem is born and reborn for each reader. Mother, daughter, writer, and reader can all identify with the "children still thought of as incomplete" (108). Mother, daughter, writer, and reader search for ways to "combine brightnesses." Mother, daughter, writer, and reader, cling to the "desperate sweetness" (108) at the end of the poem, a sweetness evoked by the generativity of the mother/daughter, writer/reader relationships.

Kimiko Hahn

Drawing on a combination of literary and familial ancestors, Japanese and German American poet Kimiko Hahn (b. 1955) offers a poetry that embraces the women of the past for their capacity to survive and endure. In "Resistance: A Poem on Ikat Cloth," from her volume of poems *Air Pocket*, Hahn weaves

the past with the present and the future in a poem that pays homage to mothers and literary lineages.[9] Citing a wide array of sources, from Lady Murasaki,
to Virginia Woolf, to Japanese folklore, to Ono no Komachi, Hahn tells a
mother's story, relays a daughter's experiences, and creates a fabric that both
adorns and offers a map of resistance to oppression. Early on in the poem
Hahn cites the folk tale *Shitakirisuzume*, or "The Tongue-Cut Sparrow," and
we learn of a "sparrow" that "wept for her tongue" (1989, 59). The clipped
tongue of the sparrow from the folktale becomes symbolic of the speaker's
mother and of women throughout literature, history, and folklore who have
been silenced by oppression or violence. Drawing on a folktale, one of the
common sources for cultural archetypes, Hahn minimizes the generalizing effects of such archetypes by pulling the strands of individual story and experience through the web of the archetype so the archetypal story gains its reso-
nance through the individual stories that expand on it. Rather than gaining
preeminence as an archetypal story, the folktale is seen as material for elabo-
ration as opposed to a limiting or structuring element. The tongue-cut sparrow story becomes one story among many, not the story that explains or makes
other stories possible. The archetype becomes as personal as the personal story
and is viewed in terms of its own individual merits. As the poem proceeds, we
see direct or symbolic recurrences of this tongue-clipped sparrow in Murasaki's
works, those of Virginia Woolf, and in the speaker's mother as well as the
speaker's own life. Oppression and the physical violence it perpetrates on bodies repeatedly emerge in this poem. And yet, through the strength of the
women presented, both as tellers of tales and protagonists in stories, and survivors of lives lived, the poem offers resistance to oppression. Sometimes the
resistance seems to do as much damage as the oppression,

> So she flapped her wings
> and cried out
> but choked
> on blood   (60)

and yet the resistance continues across epochs, across lineages (both poetic
and familial), across national and social lines. As the poem draws to a close,
carefully limning the edges of the fabric it represents, we discover that the resistance will continue because it has been passed down through generations
of writers and women:

> and in the rhythmic chore
> I imagine a daughter in my lap
> who I will never give away

but see off
with a bundle of cloths
dyed with resistance. (68)

Whether working through the rhythm of weaving, or writing poems, or
the creation of generations, or surviving oppression, the speaker of the poem
endows her daughter with the capacity for endurance, resistance, and survival. Because the stories and poems are told, because the stories are repeated, because the stories are lived and expanded, resistance to oppression
emerges and continues.

Each of the poets I've examined has uniquely discovered that the best way
to challenge limiting archetypes is with the power of individual stories that
explore the possibilities of individual experience and give credence to the capacities of individual awareness. Because the poets of recent decades have
drawn from so many different heritages and provided such a wide range of
stories and foundations, they have shown that archetypes, in actuality, are individual stories. Archetypes are not universal or evidence of a deep structure,
and so women poets need not revere them as models or fear them as limitations. In addressing archetypes, poets of the last four decades have worked
with each other. Women of the 1960s and 1970s brought a human dimension to archetypes and reinvigorated archetypal voices with everyday experience. Poets of the 1980s and 1990s took the next step and diversified the
qualities and insights of that human dimension. They broke through the universalizing paralysis that so often accompanies archetypes by bringing even
more stories and possibilities to readers. As the poems above show (and as
many more poems of the past two decades reveal), paradoxically, individual
experience forges more connections between people than overarching
rubrics and archetypes. The distinctions and detailed complexities of the poems and stories of women writing in the past two decades offer numerous
points of connection and association even as they each sing their own notes
in a building chorus of poetic possibilities.

Conclusions and Beginnings

The development of individual voice and story does not constitute a complete erasure of archetypes. But archetypes become more multifold, emerge
from numerous foundations and sources, and are seen more as starting points
than as full maps. And so we are reminded by many contemporary poets that,
when there are patterns (mother-daughter bonds, one literary generation

looking to another), there aren't inherently set structures. And even when there are structures (familial, poetic, literary), there aren't inherently limits.

This is an essay, and its space is finite, but each of us has the capacity to reach toward the infinite in our writing and in our reading. So let us read the work of each other, so we may mother each other, give birth to each other, be daughters to each other. Read, read, read, those whose names you recognize—Joy Harjo, Gloria Anzaldúa, Sandra McPherson, Louise Erdrich—and those whose names you don't recognize but that you will learn—Aimee Nezhukumatathil, Kate Light, Jeanne Clark, Pamela Stewart. Read and share the names you know with others—Lucille Clifton, Mary Oliver, Julia Alvarez, Marilyn Chin. Read their names— Cathy Song, Theresa Hak Kyung Cha, Lorna Dee Cervantes, Jeannine Savard. Write to me and remind me. Write to others and inform them about Aurora Levins Morales, Leslie Marmon Silko, Louise Glück, and many, many more; Audre Lorde, Wendy Rose, Beckian Fritz Goldberg, Kim Addonizio, and many, many, many more rising.

My list of poets is not the least bit comprehensive. And it could never be, for it would have to be as broad, intricate, and beautiful as we ourselves are. All of us. For we include, we enfold, we give life to. There has been a renaissance as women have increasingly found their voices from more places than ever before. This is a new world because we are increasingly seeing this world—the people in it, the perspectives developed, the different cultures— and in this world we are hearing each other's poems and stories. We are hearing that these stories do not need to be the same to be understood and shared. We are learning and relearning empathy in this world that grows closer and closer by the day in so many ways—geographic, economic, and political being the least of those ways. We are in close contact. We know we are ourselves. And we know we are also others. We know difference not as disjunction but as possibility, as powerful, as generative. Our difference makes us strong. Our difference helps us survive difficulty. Our difference is what holds us together. For as we increasingly affirm our differences, we increasingly cherish and respect the spaces between us. Even as spaces divide our differences, there arises inevitably the awareness of a multitude of connections, a world of synecdoche: where each part—different as each of us is—is representative of the whole, of something larger, of something wonderfully diverse. And in that awareness there is connection and reconnection, with no final, definitive connection possible. There are lines to be traced, poems to be written—in the spaces, in the connections, in all the ways we come together and don't. That is our glory. That is our triumph. That is poetry.

Biography

Irena Praitis is an assistant professor of literature and creative writing at California State University, Fullerton. She earned her M.F.A. and Ph.D. degrees from Arizona State University. Her poems, essays, and reviews have appeared or are forthcoming in *Cold Mountain Review*, *The Iconoclast*, *Cultura, Lenguaje, y Representación*, *The Mid-America Poetry Review*, *Rattle*, *Connecticut River Review*, and other journals.

1. In *Women's Culture: The Women's Renaissance of the Seventies*, ed. Gayle Kimball, XXX–XXX (Metuchen, N.J.: Scarecrow Press, 1981).
2. Adrienne Rich, *Of Woman Born: Motherhood as Experience and Institution*. Tenth Anniversary Edition (New York: W. W. Norton, 1986), 225.
3. Harold Bloom, *The Anxiety of Influence* (New York: Oxford University Press, 1979); and Alicia Suskin Ostriker, *Stealing the Language: The Emergence of Women's Poetry in America* (Boston: Beacon Press, 1986).
4. Paula Bennett, *My Life a Loaded Gun: Female Creativity and Feminist Poetics* (Boston: Beacon Press, 1986); Margaret Homans, *Bearing the Word: Language and Female Experience in Nineteenth-Century Women's Writing* (Chicago: University of Chicago Press, 1986); Annette Kolodny, "A Map for Rereading Gender and the Interpretation of Literary Texts," in *The New Feminist Criticism: Essays on Women, Literature, and Theory*, ed. Elaine Showalter (New York: Pantheon Books, 1985); Patricia Yaeger, *Honey-Mad Women: Emancipatory Strategies in Women's Writing* (New York: Columbia University Press, 1988).
5. Alice Walker, *In Search of Our Mothers' Gardens* (New York: Harcourt, Brace, Jovanovich, 1983); Ostriker, *Stealing the Language*.
6. Lorna Goodison, *I Am Becoming My Mother* (London: New Beacon Books, 1986).
7. Sandra Cisneros, *The House on Mango Street* (New York: Vintage Contemporaries, 1991).
8. Brenda Hillman, *Loose Sugar* (Hanover, N.H.: University Press of New England, Wesleyan University Press, 1997). "Mother's Language," copyright 1997 by Brenda Hillman and reprinted by permission of Wesleyan University Press. All rights reserved.
9. Kimiko Hahn, *Air Pocket* (New York: Hanging Loose Press, 1989).

References

Ashworth, Debora. 1981."Madonna or Witch: Women's Muse in Contemporary American Poetry," 178–186. In *Women's Culture: The Women's Renaissance of the Seventies*, ed. Gayle Kimball, Metuchen, N.J.: Scarecrow Press.
Cisneros, Sandra. 1991. *The House on Mango Street*. New York: Vintage Contemporaries.
Goodison, Lorna. 1986. *I Am Becoming My Mother*. London: New Beacon Books.
Hahn, Kimiko. 1989. *Air Pocket*. New York: Hanging Loose Press.

Hillman, Brenda. 1997. *Loose Sugar*. Hanover, N.H.: University Press of New England, Wesleyan University Press.

Ostriker, Alicia Suskin. 1986. *Stealing the Language: The Emergence of Women's Poetry in America*. Boston: Beacon Press.

Rich, Adrienne. 1986. *Of Woman Born: Motherhood as Experience and Institution. Tenth Anniversary Edition*. New York: W. W. Norton.

Walker, Alice. 1983. *In Search of Our Mothers' Gardens*. New York: Harcourt, Brace, Jovanovich.

~

CHAPTER NINE

Flora Liked Fauna:
The Woman–Nature Connection
in Contemporary Women's Fiction

Carol Burr and Elizabeth Renfro

Revision—the act of looking back, of seeing with fresh eyes, of entering an old text from a new critical direction—is for women more than a chapter of cultural history: it is an act of survival. Until we can understand the assumptions in which we are drenched we cannot know ourselves. And this drive to self-knowledge is more than a search for self-identity: it is part of our refusal of the self-destructiveness of male-dominated society. . . . A lot is being said today about the influence that the myths and images of women have on all of us who are products of culture . . . . [A woman] goes to poetry or fiction looking for her way of being in the world, since she too has been putting words and images together; she is looking eagerly for guides, maps, possibilities; and over and over . . . she comes up against something that negates everything she is about.

—Adrienne Rich[1]

As American women increasingly entered the cultural dialogue called story-making through an explosion of literary expression in the decade of the 1970s, they had to decide whether to reject the patriarchal stories that constitute the American social and literary tradition or to harness these stories for their archetypal power. Radical demythologizing to escape the gender definitions created and perpetuated by these stories is marked by angry recognition of the detrimental effects of the dominant myths—Greek, Roman, and European folklore—that have shaped Western civilization. The effect on women of Venus, Cleopatra, Cinderella, Snow White, and Sleeping Beauty as models of femininity and objects of male desire is deconstructed in many novels of the 1970s. Female authors often gave narrative voice to the modern equivalents of these silent, static figures and resistance to their powerlessness. Marge Piercy is perhaps the best example of such antitraditional work in such novels as *Small Changes*. Harnessing patriarchal stories, the other approach women took to entering the cultural dialogue, involves looking to non-Western social/literary traditions and shifting the traditional meanings of these stories by exposing their ambiguities. Authors like Maxine Hong Kingston are in this category.

Both approaches are dangerous, the former because deconstructing tradition without an alternative tradition leaves the anger unresolved, and the latter because such male-defined, male-dominated, and male-centered material can easily pull the female back into a gendered (and therefore silent) situation through social assumptions she cannot fully understand. How, in the first case, can one reject such powerful stories when they are built into the social institutions—family, religion, education—that shape the self? How, on the other hand, does one raise to consciousness the very air she breathes? What all these women artists found is that it is difficult, as Margaret Atwood notes in *Survival*, to escape victimhood even after one has done all the work of recognizing this state of powerlessness.[2] As is true of all aspects of the women's movement, women writers since the 1970s have continued to build upon their foremothers' efforts to reject victimhood, sometimes taking the arguments further and sometimes moving in new directions.

Women writers of the 1970s often expressed their sense of entrapment in traditional stories and their desire for voice through analysis of the ways in which most of the traditional tales see women as having a direct connection to nature. In European traditions, this connection is seen as dangerous, a shared wildness that needs taming and controlling by patriarchy, and—simultaneously—as a nurturing and procreative mandate defining women's place (and purpose in life) as mothers and self-less caregivers. Non-Western cultures (particularly indigenous cultures like those of American Indians) give higher value to nature and therefore offer, if unintentionally, a source of power to women. Even in highly patriarchal societies like China, the worship of nature provides at least a potential avenue for achieving agency. The connection with nonhuman features of landscape, particularly those one associates with home and being "at home," can be seen as either a rejection of the patriarchy's devaluing of both women and nature or as a reinterpreting of women's place in nature-worshipping cultures, but in any case one's ability to see, to respond directly from one's sensory response, shapes the self and opens the way to a radically different story of that self. As Simone de Beauvoir states in *The Second Sex*,

> Nature is one of the realms women writers have most lovingly explored. For the young girl, for the woman who has not fully abdicated, nature represents what woman herself represents for man, herself and her negation, a kingdom and a place of exile; the whole in the guise of the other.[3]

Here de Beauvoir is looking to nature as men look at women, as "Other," but an other that does not require abdication, the victimhood Atwood describes. This relationship is between equals, based on knowledge lovingly gathered and shared. Because it builds on patriarchy's identification of women and nature, it creates an ironic source of power that counters women's powerlessness in relation to man. These devalued "Others" can together create the fluid and generative self that Judith Butler theorizes as deconstructing all notions of gender essentialism.

Sherry Ortner builds on de Beauvoir's analysis in "Is Female to Male as Nature Is to Culture?", a chapter in her book *Making Gender: The Politics and Erotics of Culture* (1996):

> [M]y thesis is that woman is being identified with—or, if you will, seems to be a symbol of—something that every culture devalues, something that every culture defines as being of a lower order of existence than itself. Now it seems that there is only one thing that would fit that description, and that is "nature" in the most generalized sense.[4]

Like de Beauvoir, Ortner understands that culture is set against nature and by extension against woman, but she also notes that "women . . . tend to enter into relationships with the world that culture might see as being more 'like nature'—immanent and embedded in things as given—than 'like culture'—transcending and transforming things through the super-imposition of abstract categories."[5] This unmediated relationship with the natural, while held lower by patriarchal aspects of culture, gives women a powerful ally in the formation of self and in relational ways of living in the world.

Going back at least to Sappho in ancient Greece, there have been women writers whose sense of self came from their sense of place (which might or might not be seen in natural terms), but contemporary writers have consciously used this primary relationship with nature to demythologize the connection or to harness patriarchal stories of male domination of woman and nature. Ecofeminist writers such as Susan Griffin argue that women have always been mythically connected to nature, so why should women not own this connection and make it a source of strength? In *Made from This Earth* (1982) Griffin states,

> He says that women speak with nature. That she hears voices from under the earth. That wind blows in her ears and trees whisper to her. . . . But for him the dialogue is over. He says he is not part of this world, that he was set upon this earth as a stranger. He sets himself apart from woman and nature.[6]

Like Carolyn Merchant, author of *The Death of Nature: Women, Ecology, and the Scientific Revolution* (1980) and *Reinventing Eden: The Fate of Nature in Western Culture* (2003), Griffin recognizes that such myths are intended to silence and control women by claiming that wildness in nature is the same wildness in women, and men must "civilize" both. But what potential power there is in this linkage between women and nonhuman aspects of nature! Ecofeminism, a term coined in the 1970s and only now becoming a visible movement, asserts that women should embrace the archetypal connection with nature that men through their myth-making power have assigned to them, and contemporary fiction writers are consciously claiming and using it to re-vision women's own senses of self and place within the cosmos.

The resulting literature posits the body/earth as a power base by shifting the literary focus from social relationships to relationships between the self and nature. Thus, in their fiction, whether they take the approach of radical demythologizing or of reworking traditional stories, women writers tend to address certain issues and experiences pivotal—and interrelated—in women's lives and self-conceptions—for example, motherhood, home, and family; sexuality; religion and spirituality; community—through an exploration of the woman–nature connection that is one of the foundations of patriarchal ideology.

One of the more direct—some have even said propagandistic—forms of deconstructing and harnessing cultural myths taken by women writers has been through creation of feminist fairy tales for both child and adult audiences. *Ms. Magazine* began running as a regular feature some of these reworked tales in the 1970s as a tear-out section designed for progressive parents. In these stories, girls were taught not to fear the dark forest, nor were they trained to aim all their aspirations toward capturing the attention of a prince who would make them the keeper of his castle and mother of his children. The stories included both reversals of traditional stories, with girls and young women taking on the heroic roles, plus stories illustrating more androgynous female and male characters. Marlo Thomas's *Free to Be You and Me*

(1974) is in this latter vein, and the approach has continued to be popular. Other women, like Charlene Spretnak (*Lost Goddesses of Early Greece* (1978), Paula Gunn Allen (*Spider Woman's Granddaughters*, 1989), Carolyn McVicker Edwards (*The Storyteller Goddess*, 1991), and Barbara Walker (*Feminist Fairy Tales*, 1996), have produced collections of traditional myths and tales from a variety of cultures. These stories, too often subsumed in the traditional androcentric stories, create female characters who are strong and powerful, in large part through embracing the positive aspects of the woman–nature connection.

Well-known scholars and fiction writers have also taken up Adrienne Rich's call to action. Anita Diamant's *The Red Tent* (1998) takes the Old Testament story of Jewish Patriarch Jacob and retells it from the perspectives of his two wives, Rachel and Leah (and of his two concubines). The novel not only reclaims these mythic women's voices and experiences but also imagines a woman-centered form of early Judaism blended with the goddess religions of the Middle East. Diamant's novel illustrates how antiwoman traditions and practices in Judeo-Christianity may have developed as a reaction against women's power and strength, as patriarchy itself overtook earlier, woman/mother-nature centered spiritual practices and lifeways. Ursula K. LeGuin's short story "She Unnames Them" (1985) is a reworking of the Genesis story, in which Eve realizes that the naming of all creatures that Adam (man) has done has resulted in a hierarchical fracturing of the natural interrelationship among all beings. Because Eve, unlike Adam, recognizes her (and all humans') connection with nature, she takes on the task of "unnaming" all the creatures—and herself. After attempting to explain what she has done and why to the unresponsive Adam, she and the creatures leave, implicitly to create their own "brave new world."

In her short story "Buffalo Gals Won't You Come Out Tonight" (1987), LeGuin draws upon Native American myths of creation and relationship, as a little girl from the dysfunctional world of mainstream culture is unexpectedly dropped into the mythic—more real—world and taught a new way of being to take back with her to "her" world.

Linguistics scholar Donna Jo Napoli has written a series of what are labeled "young adult" novels (*The Magic Circle*, 1993; *Song of the Magdalen*, 1996; and *Zel*, 1996), deeply introspective psychological "revisioning" of the traditional, male-centered stories of Hansel and Gretel, Mary Magdalen, and Rapunzel. In each of these, the central female character is given the voice, complexity, and strength missing in the traditional renderings. In *The Magic Circle*, for example, which is told from the "witch's" perspective, we find the protagonist is actually an herbal healer and midwife whose life-affirming power is the result of her spirituality and closeness to nature. Her transformation to an evil witch is presented in a complex exploration of the sin of pride damaging human relationships to God and nature.

Another of the fairly direct fictional approaches to challenging the androcentric power of patriarchal stories that became popular in the 1970s is utopian/dystopian novels and science fiction/fantasy. The rediscovery of Charlotte Perkins Gilman's *Herland* (1915) is credited by Ann J. Lane with sparking a "rebirth" of the utopian novel "as a uniquely feminist expression." The era saw the publication of such utopian/dystopian and science fiction/fantasy books as Ursula LeGuin's *The Left Hand of Darkness* (1969) and *The Dispossessed* (1974), and Joanna Russ's *The Female Man* (1979). These novels critiqued the rigidity of gender roles and behaviors that Western culture presented as natural results of nature and/or divine mandate, and instead, in the tradition of the liberal feminism of the time, proposed alternative visions of androgyny. Monique Wittig's *Les Guérillères* (1969; English translation 1971) and Marge Piercy's *Woman on the Edge of Time* (1976) took a slightly different approach in their reconstructive visions, presenting (as had Gilman in *Herland*) the beauty of woman-centered culture, reflecting the growing impact of cultural feminism's valorization of women's innately nurturing and creative strength. Gerd Brantenberg, in her 1977 (English translation 1985) novel *Egalia's Daughters*, took yet another slant, using satire to critique both patriarchal culture and what she saw as simplistic cultural feminist visions of matriarchal cultures and myths and implicitly arguing for more realistic and complex understandings of the multiple sources of oppression women face—including socioeconomic class, race, and sexuality.

The interest in utopian/dystopian and science fiction/fantasy fiction as a way to critique and reconstruct patriarchal myths has continued among these and other women writers (e.g., Doris Lessing's *The Marriages Between Zones Three, Four, and Five*, 1980; Atwood's *The Handmaid's Tale*, 1986; Jean Auel's *Clan of the Cave Bear* series, 1981– ; and Octavia Butler's *Dawn*, 1987). Ecofeminist utopian writers like Starhawk have developed their own myths in utopian novels like *The Fifth Sacred Thing* (1993) and *Walking to Mercury* (1997). Starhawk uses earth-based goddess worship to attack environmental depredation and argue for sustainability and earth-friendly politics.

This form of revisionary fiction has been also enriched and influenced by Latin American magical realism and surrealism, as seen in Brazilian writer Clarice Lispector's *The Smallest Woman in the World* (1944; first English edition 1972), Laura Esquivel's *Like Water for Chocolate* (1990), and American novelist and poet Ana Castillo's *So Far from God* (1993). Each of these authors has her own approach, ranging from Lispector's understated but biting satire on the "othering" of woman (and her complicity in it) to Esquival's sensuous and haunting evocation of women's powerful nurturing. In *So Far from God*, Castillo's hilarious yet wrenching telenovela portrayal of two generations of Chicana women, we see the women's participation in their own subjection as they accept the patriarchal stories, but we also see the great strength of their revisionary powers and nurturance for both humans and the earth, grounded in their demythologizing of patriarchal stories and in their reclaiming of ancient indigenous stories of women's powers.

Most recently, Margaret Atwood, author of the dystopian novel *The Handmaid's Tale* (1986), takes on the effects of human arrogance on nature in her *Oryx and Crake* (2003). The first novel focuses on the terrifying effects of patriarchal control of the female body. The latter is an ironic look at the ways good and evil become tangled when humans use their species superiority to control every living thing. The novel's title itself suggests the problem, giving the name of an extinct antelope to the selfless female character and the name of a flightless bird to the male scientist, who single-handedly wipes out the human race. The narrator is an unloved and sophomoric young man who becomes the god of the lab-produced "Crakes," life forms that ironically parallel Adam and Eve. Atwood seems to say that humans are intelligent enough to destroy the planet or to save it by destroying themselves.

While woman-centered demythologizing by means of fantasy has been flourishing, women also have been harnessing traditional materials to empower the woman–nature connection. Barbara Kingsolver is such a writer. With degrees in biology and ecology and a commitment to ecofeminism, her novels consistently demonstrate the power of nature and indigenous ways against the human and ecological effects of patriarchy. In *The Bean Trees* (1988), she creates the character, Turtle, a three-year-old Native American who helps the narrator, Taylor Greer, find her center in nature and traditional native ways. They end up in Arizona, where Taylor becomes involved in helping Guatemalan refugees. Taylor clearly is sensitive to her physical environment, but until late in the novel, her relationship with nature and its corresponding descriptions are elliptical. Only as Taylor begins to claim her Cherokee ancestry as a means to adopt Turtle do her thoughts become rich with images of nature:

> I thought of my Cherokee great-grandfather, his people who believed God lived in trees, and that empty Oklahoma plain they were driven to like livestock. But then, even the Cherokee Nation was someplace.[7]

When they reach Lake o' the Cherokees, Taylor finds peace for the first time:

The sun was setting behind us but it lit up the clouds in the east, making one of those wraparound sunsets. Reflections of pink clouds floated across the surface of the lake. If I didn't let my mind run too far ahead, I felt completely happy.[8]

Through Turtle—child and symbol of the native connection with nature—Taylor achieves agency and finds a place to stand.

Kingsolver's more recent novel *The Poisonwood Bible* (1998) continues to explore the importance of nature to a woman's power. Here, she clearly sets masculine control over nature against female relationship with nature to show the ecological and spiritual damage patriarchy causes. The novel begins with Orleanna Price, one of five female narrators, seeing an okapi (once thought to be the unicorn) in Georgia. This rare creature comes to symbolize Africa, where Orleanna and her four daughters are taken by her missionary husband. Kingsolver makes a clear connection between economic and religious colonization and her female narrators: "But still I'll insist I was only a captive witness. What is the conqueror's wife, if not a conquest herself?"[9] Because Orleanna, and to varying degrees her daughters, recognize Africa as nature writ large enough to overwhelm any hubris, they survive while Reverend Price does not:

But Africa shifts under my hands, refusing to be party to failed relations. Refusing to be any place at all, or any thing but itself: the animal kingdom making hay in the kingdom of glory. So there it is, take your place.
. . . We aimed for no more than to have dominion every creature that moved upon the earth. And so it came to pass that we stepped down there on a place we believed unformed, where only darkness moved on the face of the waters.[10]

By using biblical stories and language, Kingsolver unpacks the Judeo-Christian notion of nature as the handmaiden of man, there to be formed and utilized, with no will of its own. The powerful and unforgiving forces of nature bring down the conqueror and his captive witnesses, but the story ends with a dead daughter watching her mother and three living daughters reconnecting with Africa and its power to humble and forgive the conqueror.

Two other major writers who harness the woman–nature connection in patriarchal myths are Toni Morrison and Leslie Silko. In Morrison's most recent novel *Paradise* (1997), the first of her novels with a place as its title and central focus, she examines the different relationships a group of blacks have with the community they founded to escape racism. In attempting to get away from white racism, the black leaders called Eight Rock have failed to see its connection with patriarchy, a system of gender inequality that ultimately unravels the community. This sexism expresses itself in the treatment of the wives of the community and more violently in the treatment of a group of women living in what had been a convent. In the climactic scene that both launches and concludes the novel, a group of men come to kill the women, "[t]o make sure it never happens again. That nothing inside or out rots the one all-black town worth the pain."[11] The women of the convent are earthy, literally and metaphorically. They work in the soil, make wonderful bread, enjoy their bodies, heal with herbal remedies—all manifestations of the dangerous woman–nature connection. The men are attracted and appalled by their attraction. They need to destroy such sensuousness to maintain their black purity: "They think they have outfoxed the whiteman when in fact they imitate him. They think they are protecting their wives and children, when in fact they are maiming them."[12] But as Morrison clearly shows, patriarchy is inseparable from racism; to internalize one is to adopt the other. The women of the convent expose that connection by their shameless relationship with the natural world.

Less successfully but equally clear in its exploration of the woman–nature connection is Leslie Marmon Silko's most recent novel *Gardens in the Dunes* (1999). This incoherent mix of well-realized sections on Indian ways and unconvincing sections on upper-class Anglo lives uses botany to put her almost allegorical characters on a moral grid. Those who live by nature are contrasted with those who use it for economic gain and, in keeping with the woman–nature connection, it is the women who live in symbiotic relationship with the land while the men, wittingly or unwittingly, abuse the natural world and are punished for their abuse. Indigo, the main Indian character, grows up near the old gardens of the Sand Lizard people, one of the last of a tribe driven from their sand dune home but hanging onto their tribal ways.

The main white character, Hattie Abbott, is an educated young woman from a prominent East Coast family, ostracized for arguing in her dissertation that Jesus had female disciples and Mary Magdalene wrote a gospel suppressed by the church. Indigo and Hattie meet at Hattie's husband Edward's home near the boarding school where Indigo has been taken after losing contact with her family. Indigo has escaped and hidden on their property and been discovered by a pet monkey Linnaeus (not so subtly invoking Carl Linnaeus, father of plant taxonomy). From this point Hattie appears to educate Indigo, while the narrator shows Hattie moving closer and closer to Indigo's way of envisioning the world, a movement that culminates in Hattie's efforts to share Indian ways, particularly their belief in a messiah whose harbinger is crows.

Women writers continue to explore venues to power through their writing. To the extent that nature is made to function as metaphor, it participates in patriarchal stories that women must reject or subvert to find their voice. In this way, connecting with natural places can be seen as part of the ongoing war with the mythic meanings that nature, like women, has been made to carry. It is not clear whether third wave feminists will, like Starhawk and other goddess worshippers, continue to be interested in ways to harness and empower the woman–nature connection, but their interest in identity formation and multiculturalism suggests many fruitful ways this connection could be used. Similarly, some of the more serious of the late twentieth- to early twenty-first-century "chick lit" writers (e.g., Julia Alvarez, *How the Garcia Girls Lost Their Accents*, 1992, or Joanne Harris, *Chocolat*, 2000), while often labeled "fluff," are also exploring the meanings of individual identity and empowerment for women, though it remains to be seen whether this genre will move more deeply into the roles of nature and cultural mythos in the (mis)naming of woman.

Regardless of the degree to which woman's desire and aptitude for human-natural world relationships is hardwired or culturally taught, many contemporary indigenous women writers can help women who have lost contact with that aspect of the self because of industrialization and urbanization rediscover their environmental affiliations But when a woman is blessed with an early and intense exposure to landscape, she has a chance to develop a relationship so woven into her sense of self that nature is given full "humanity," and her voice comes from an engendered rather than antipatriarchal position. Elizabeth Meese puts it this way:

> I am beginning to believe that women's ascribed roles cause them to confer a special significance on the topography of this outer, physical place. Man may use place symbolically—as a sign of power, heritage, or history, but rarely in modern literature do they see in the land itself a definition of life and character.[13]

This place-centered pattern in women's writing is not intended to point to essential differences between women and men but, as Meese states, the result of ascribed roles, cultural constructs that have placed women in metaphorical relationship to nature and thus opened an unintended avenue to personal power. This power is not controlling but affiliative, a way to perform the self through a collapse of the subject–object split and a joyous merger of embodied voices.

Biography

Carol Burr holds a B.A. from Middlebury College, a master's from Columbia University, and a Ph.D. from Case Western Reserve University, all in English literature.

She has taught in the English Department at California State University, Chico, since 1970 and is director of the Center for Multicultural and Gender Studies. Her research areas are nineteenth-century British and women's literature. She has edited two collections of essays on northern California women (cburr@csuchico.edu).

Elizabeth Renfro has been teaching at California State University, Chico, for almost thirty years, first in the Department of English and since 1995 in the Center for Multicultural and Gender Studies. Her research and publications have focused on feminist theory, multicultural and women's literature, California Indian history, and LGBTQ studies (erenfro@csuchico.edu).

1. Adrienne Rich, *On Lies, Secrets, and Silences* (New York: W. W. Norton, 1979), 35, 39.

2. Margaret Atwood, *Survival: A Thematic Guide to Canadian Literature* (Toronto: House of Anansi Press, 1972), 38.

3. Simone De Beauvoir, *The Second Sex* (New York: Alfred A. Knopf, 1952), 362.

4. Sherry Ortner, *Making Gender: The Politics and Erotics of Culture* (Boston: Beacon Press, 1996), 25.

5. Ortner, *Making Gender*, 37.

6. Susan Griffin, *Made from This Earth* (New York: Harper & Row, 1982), 83.

7. Barbara Kingsolver, *The Bean Trees* (New York: Harper & Row, 1988), 195.

8. Kingsolver, *Bean Trees*, 209.

9. Barbara Kingsolver, *The Poisonwood Bible* (New York: HarperCollins, 1998), 9.

10. Kingsolver, *Poisonwood Bible*, 10.

11. Toni Morrison, *Paradise* (New York: Alfred A. Knopf, 1998), 5.

12. Morrison, *Paradise*, 435.

13. Elizabeth Meese, "Telling It All: Literary Standards and Oral Narratives by Southern Women," *Frontiers* 2 (Summer 1977): 63–67.

CHAPTER TEN

Feminist Eyes Wide Open

Marge Piercy

To be a political and feminist writer means to be conscious of the implications of what you write. All fiction and most poetry is political, whether or not it is so perceived by critics and readers, because the work contains and expresses attitudes toward what is masculine and what is feminine, who deserves to win and who should lose, and what does winning or losing mean. It embodies attitudes about who is worth paying attention to and who it is permissible to make light of or use for humor. It embodies attitudes about class: Are people with more money more emotionally complex and more intelligent than people with less money or fewer possessions? Who is it all right to love and/or have sex with, and what is all right to do with your partners? Is violence sexy? Are children real people? Do animals, or does the environment, matter? All narrative contains such attitudes whether we recognize them or not.

Attitudes and opinions are most noticeable to critics and to readers when they are different from those the person is used to hearing expressed, perhaps contradictory to ideas that the individual has come to take for granted. Reviewers do not perceive books as having a political dimension when the ideas expressed in the novels—the attitudes toward wealth and poverty, social class, sex roles, what masculine and feminine are, what's normal—are congruent with their own attitudes or those they are used to hearing discussed over supper. When reviewers read novels whose attitudes offend them or clash with their own ideas, they perceive those novels as political and polemical, and they attack them. But all fiction and poetry contains attitudes that are political, even when they are merely assumed as the way things are.

From the time I began to hear stories and to read them, I began telling myself stories, generally by fitting myself into those tales I encountered. But they always needed changing. I did not wish to be a princess rescued. When I played pretend with my girlfriends, I wanted to be the one who saved, not the one who was saved. I had to rewrite those stories to play the parts that I found attractive, so I began my career in fiction by subverting received tales.

In some sense, I am still doing so, taking the recognized stories of history, such as World War II or the French Revolution, and finding the female heroes. I am not inventing history in those cases but excavating it, turning it about, changing the perspective. In *Gone to Soldiers* and *City of Darkness City of Light*, I did not make up the roles of women who were fighters, thinkers, political activists, resisters—I simply dug them out of the rubbish heap of what is regarded as unimportant and set them in the center of my narrative.

Often, in poetry, I do something similar, as in my interpretations of the months in the lunar cycle or my treatment of various tales and myths, from the frog prince to Frankenstein to Gertrude, Hamlet's mother. I find it interesting how the story changes when you alter viewpoint, especially when you take the viewpoint of someone who had previously been the villain or a minor character.

Simply to survive as a feminist writer is something of an accomplishment in and of itself, but I hope I have done more than that in my work. Certainly I have produced a reasonably sized body of work so far that I stand behind, that reflects my values and I hope some of yours, in a wide variety of forms. I do writing of several kinds, and each feels quite distinct to me. I have published sixteen books of poetry, sixteen novels, a play, a book of essays and interviews, short memoirs, and a book-length memoir, *Sleeping with Cats*. I even edited an anthology of women's poetry and wrote a how-to guide with Ira Wood, *So You Want to Write: How to Master the Craft of Fiction and Personal Narrative*. Writing remains fascinating to me. I hope to do a lot more of it.

Often writing with a feminist perspective means taking apart a received narrative and examining its assumptions and sometimes turning it on its head. We go into a genre such as the utopian novel, for instance in *Woman on the Edge of Time*, or the myth of the golem as it has been interpreted through non-Jewish sources, such as Mary Shelley's *Frankenstein*, as in *He She and It*, and use it to examine personhood and autonomy. We take World War II or the French Revolution and find the historic roles that women played and create a female-centric narrative.

Being a feminist novelist also involves sometimes going into characters that the generally middle-class reader would find alien and off-putting in real life, such as the homeless woman, Mary, in *The Longings of Women*. Once you as the reader have spent some time inside the mind of someone like Mary, you may not dismiss homeless women quite so easily again.

A lot of my memoir, *Sleeping with Cats*, is centered on particularly female activities: early lesbian experiences, first experience of sex with a male, pregnancy, self-abortion, decision not to bear children, struggling for recognition as a writer (particularly difficult in my time for a woman writing seriously about women), and trying to find a domestic situation that supported my aspirations instead of undermining them. A man from the working class would have experienced some of the same problems and experiences I did, but many of mine would be quite dissimilar. His life too might not have had a spine of cats.

I had imagined that writing a memoir would be easy; after all, I didn't need the research that typifies my preparation for a novel. Didn't I know all about me? It is far more a matter of taking out than of putting in, but the putting in can be quite painful, I learned. Reliving parts of my life I prefer not to remember or to think about, events and periods that were painful, humiliating, embarrassing, or guilt-provoking, was not a pleasant stroll down memory lane. When I examined my life closely, I discovered I wasn't as good a person as I had previously believed, for instance.

Poetry

My poetry appears to me at once more personal and more universal than my fiction. My poetry is of continuity with itself and with the work of other women. No one who reads a lot in women's anthologies can avoid being struck by how we are all opening new ground for each other, how we create new kinds of poems, call attention to old daily experiences never named and thus never recognized, how we help each other along the way.

I speak mostly in my own persona or in a voice that is a public form of it. Some poems come out of my own experiences and some from the energy of others' experiences coming through me, but they are all fused in the layers of my mind to my voice. I stand up in public and say them to audiences. That makes me directly and immediately accountable for the poems. I can see what is working and what is not; I can hear where I have failed to hew my rhythms, to set just the right word in. I can hear my failures of nerve. I can hear where I relied upon rhetoric that came to me used rather than making it clear out of our daily language. I can hear muddiness that is laziness, not working through until the simplicity emerges from the noise.

I want my readings to be an emotional as well as an intellectual and literary experience, an affirming experience—one in which we together touch what we hope for and what we fear, what makes us weaker and what makes us stronger, where we have been and where we are wanting to go. I try to have some notion of who is in the audience, to create a program and an order that can work.

The first level is that of the psyche. Poetry is a saying that uses verbal signs and images, sound and rhythm, memory and dream images. Poetry blends all kinds of knowing, the analytical and the synthetic, the rational and the pre-rational and the gestalt grasping of the new or ancient configuration, the separate and fused hungers and satisfaction and complaints and input of the senses, the knotted fibrous mass of pleasure and pain, the ability to learn and to forget, the mammalian knowing (the communication you share with your dog or cat), the old reptilian wisdom about place and intent. Poetry has a healing power because it can fuse for the moment all the kinds of knowing in its saying.

Poetry can also heal as a communal activity. It can make us share briefly the community of feeling and hoping and grieving. It can create a rite in which we experience each other with respect and draw energy.

Fiction is as old a habit of our species as poetry. It goes back to tale, the first perceptions of pattern, and fiction is still about pattern in human life. At core, it answers the question, what then? And then and then and then. A strong difference between fiction and poetry is that poetry is almost independent of reviews for getting out to people. Poetry readings are important, as is inclusion in anthologies. There are many alternate sources of information about poetry, and many shades of opinion are represented in writing about it. There is no single source or single few sources of rating, as there is with novels. In venues like *The Women's Review of Books*, you find a feminist perspective (1983–2004). Elsewhere, no way. Academics and sponsors of readings like poets who win prizes, but those are seldom the poets who mean the most to an audience.

Novels

I would divide the novels I have written into two categories. One type (*Going Down Fast, Small Changes, Summer People, Fly Away Home, The Longings of Women, Three Women*, and *The Third Child*) is more like the usual take on the contemporary novel, a novel of relationships among a small group of people, focused on personal issues, although large issues often enter.

The second category (*Dance the Eagle to Sleep, Woman on the Edge of Time, Braided Lives, Gone to Soldiers, He, She and It*, and *City of Darkness, City of Light*) comprises books more about time, maybe Time with a capital T, and

about history both past and future. They are more speculative novels and often do not meet the expectations of reviewers, although these are often the
novels that people find most important to them. Two of them would be classified as historical novels, as is the novel I began writing in 2003. Three of
them would be classified as science fiction or speculative fiction. One would
be classified as autobiographical fiction, although it is a fairly free fantasy
based on elements of my life. It is a far cry from my memoir.

Ira Wood and I have collaborated on a novel, *Storm Tide*, and on *So You
Want to Write*. We have taught more than thirty workshops together. We
would probably do more collaborating if there wasn't such a prejudice against
coauthored fiction. It is usual to collaborate in the theater or in film, but it
is looked down upon in fiction and in poetry. We also work together on our
press, Leapfrog. It is more his project than mine, but I am an editor. We like
collaborating because, first of all, it's less work, about two-thirds of the work
of doing it all yourself. Second, writing is a lonely profession, so companion-
ship is strongly appreciated. Third, you give each other immediate feedback
and correction. But your publisher won't be happy.

My novels feel very different to me, each a small world. A novel is something
I inhabit for two or three years, like a marriage or a house. It owns me. I live inside it. Then it is done, and I pick up and go to find a new home, often with a
feeling of terrible desolation and loss and depression. What will become of me?
What will I do now? How will I live? What will I think about? While I am writing a novel, it occupies me and stains my life. The first draft is scary to me. I
can't risk interrupting it for long, as the flow may be broken. The momentum is
important, pushing off into space, building a bridge in midair, from one side of
a river to the other. I am afraid the whole thing is unsound. Sometimes my identification becomes dangerous. In the past, I lost a sense of myself in my characters until I had trouble functioning. I learned mental disciplines mostly in studying Kabala, which prevents that from happening now. I still immerse myself in
the viewpoint of the character while I am writing to the point that when I stop,
I sometimes feel disoriented. But I have learned to let go when I stop work. My
subconscious may be solving problems. I keep a little notebook beside my bed
for just such occasions. However, my attention, once I have finished work for
the day, is focused on the here and now, on those around me.

I like revisions. It's work that has more play in it, less spinning from the
gut. I know I can get through it: The problems are large, perhaps, but smaller
than the horizon. Between third and fourth drafts, I circulate my manuscript
to friends. I show it to seven to ten people, some writers and some not. That
is the time I care most what people say about my work. I can put criticism to
work then.

As a political writer I frequently have a fair amount of research to do on a novel. For *Woman on the Edge of Time,* I studied the brain and psychosurgery, to see how it feels to be in a mental institution. I had much research to do preliminary to thinking about a good future society. For *Gone to Soldiers,* the database was seven times longer than that, my longest novel. *He, She and It* required research into globalization, global warming, and 1600 Prague, as well as the golem legend. *City of Darkness, City of Light* required a large database on the French Revolution. I am accumulating a large database for my nineteenth-century novel.

When I started using personal computers, just about as soon as there were any, collecting and organizing my research data became easier. Otherwise I would drown in notes. I clip periodicals heavily and keep files on things I think possibly useful. Novelists are always hungry for information. I am always way behind clipping things, let alone reading them. My house is full of glaciers of yellowing newsprint creeping through the rooms. I do a lot of research online. I've been on the Internet since well before there was a World Wide Web, and I use it every day, but it can never replace library research. I do interlibrary loans just about every week, so that even living in a village, I can access the books I need.

I wrote six novels before the first one that was published, *Going Down Fast.* That has the least women's consciousness of any of my novels, but then it was written from 1965 to 1967, when I had the least of any time in my life. One of the earlier books that could not be printed was close to a feminist novel, *Maud Awake,* and that was one of the things about it besides its great length that made it impossible to publish in the mid-1960s. *Going Down Fast* marked the first time I had written with a male protagonist, in part. It was my love-hate musing on Chicago, where I lived for four years, the hardest of my life so far.

Nothing else like *Dance the Eagle to Sleep* came out of the 1960. I doubt that it would find a publisher today: The politics are too harsh and direct. It had enough trouble finding a publisher in 1969. Twenty houses turned it down before Doubleday took a tiny chance on it with a minuscule advance and a two-book contract that tied me up till 1975. It has more in it to me of what the heart of the New Left felt like than anything else I've read, and I think that a lot of people who were passionately involved felt or feel that way about the novel.

Small Changes was an attempt to produce in fiction the equivalent of a full experience in a consciousness-raising group for many women who would never go through that experience. It was conceived from the beginning as a very full novel that would be almost Victorian in its scope and detail. I needed that level of detail in the lives of my two women protagonists. The novel is as much about who is doing the housework as it is about who is sleeping with whom.

In *Woman on the Edge of Time*, my intent was to create an image of a good society, one that was not sexist, racist, or imperialist: one that was cooperative, respectful of all living beings, gentle, responsible, loving, and playful. The result of a full feminist revolution. To try to imagine people of such a society was my hardest task. I think that Consuelo Ramos is one of the best characters I ever created, the fullest and deepest.

The High Cost of Living concerns the price of moving from the working class to the college-educated working class, and about loneliness and the rigidity that prevent us from loving each other. It's about labeling and about lying.

Vida has as protagonist a political fugitive, a woman who has been living underground since 1970. Set in the 1960s and the 1970s, it deals with two sisters, both politically committed, and some of the inner and outer forces that make one woman a feminist and another more oriented toward the male Left. On another level, it is a love story about two people trying to build love and truth on the margin of danger and desperation.

Braided Lives is about what the world was like for ordinary women growing up in the 1950s, when abortion was illegal and a matter of do it yourself or makeshift operations performed without anesthetics, when rigid sex roles and Freudian ideas governed many relationships, when any choice other than heterosexual marriage and early childbearing was considered a sign of deep sickness. It is also a novel of the formation of a woman writer, her annealing in the forge of her time. It is the closest to an autobiographical novel I have written, but as a reader can tell, comparing it with my memoirs, it is by no means autobiography.

Fly Away Home is a divorce thriller. I started with an interest in arson, acquired when I lived in Bedford Stuyvesant in Brooklyn, and began to notice how uncommonly many fires we endured in our neighborhood. I clipped articles about arson for years; the problem was how to render the material interesting to middle-class readers. I finally had the notion of making the detective a woman whose husband is leaving her and who is forced to understand his financial dealings because of the divorce.

For seven years, I worked on a novel about World War II, *Gone to Soldiers*, and I have been constantly asked why a woman would write a novel about World War II; I have to respond, why not? War is not a male preserve. Modern war is visited upon populations as well as upon armies. More civilians died in Vietnam than combatants. Wars are always fought in someone's country, and everyone in that country is therefore a participant. Bombs do not fall only upon men aged eighteen to thirty-five; they kill and maim women, old people, children, babies, cats, dogs, tigers and water buffalo, birds, reptiles, and the landscape and future of a place. Women experience wars even when they do not fight in them, and frequently, women end up fighting, if not in official armies, in the unofficial armies that have been part of most wars in my lifetime.

For instance, the image of the Resistance hero in World War II is a man with a gun. In reality, the resistance consisted of many different activities, publishing and distributing clandestine papers and newssheets, creating false identity papers, passing people across borders, warning people of actions aimed at them, hiding refugees, hiding prisoners, hiding downed airmen, hiding Jews, both adults and children, and passing people over borders into safety. Sabotage was an important function. Women made up a large part of most resistance activities and were usually the couriers. Often, they were also the spies, the observers, extremely active and overrepresented in all the so-called rat lines used to pass escaped prisoners, downed airmen, and refugees along to safety. They also were active in sabotage and in guerrilla warfare. War is too important in our time to leave only to men to write about it, especially in the limited ways that men have often thought about and felt about war.

Summer People is focused on relationships, with the viewpoints shifting among the characters in that personal net. I used four viewpoints, three women and a man. It is a morality tale set in the area where I live. I wanted to write something light, bright, tight. I called it an operetta to myself as I was writing it.

The late Isaac Asimov once wrote that all science fiction falls into the categories of what if, if only, and if this continues. Certainly *Woman on the Edge of Time* was mostly a novel of, if only! However, *He, She and It* falls more in the category of, if this continues. It is set partly in the future, seventy years from now, and partly in 1600. I wanted to look at extrapolations from where we are now. I wanted to create a world in which the consequences of a great many choices and actions of the present have arrived. A world in which there is no ozone layer, and therefore to go outside unprotected is dangerous. A world in which global warming has melted the icecaps, raised the oceans, created deserts or estuaries where many of the great bread- and rice-growing regions of the world are now located, on which billions are dependent for food. I wanted to look at consequences of our choices in the same concrete way that I looked at wishes made flesh in *Woman on the Edge of Time*.

I had been fascinated by the myth of the golem since I heard it as a child and wanted to explore through it the meaning of being human. As someone not a member of "man-kind" this was a particularly subversive narrative to me. But the larger intention of this novel, as of much of my writing, is a desire to take control of the stuff of our dreaming mind, the stuff of our fantasies, the stuff of the stories we tell ourselves about our lives, and to remake them from my own perspective. To re-imagine, to subvert, to make over the myths of our culture, whether I am working in poetry with Eve or Ruth, with Jacob or the princess and the frog, with Golem/Frankenstein/robocop/Data, with the French Revolution or World War II—the symbols of the Tarot, in Laying Down the Tower, the wealth of moon associations in The Lunar Cycle.

The Longings of Women centers on three women whose lives are peripherally connected, who face crises involving identity, security, and a sense of place, a desire for home. One is a university professor in a failing marriage. Another is a mall rat, a working-class Becky Sharp. The third is a homeless woman of sixty-one, Mary Burke, who was a mother and homemaker married to a Washington bureaucrat. After divorce, she slowly spiraled downward economically, until she was homeless. When I was researching the novel, I became accomplished at recognizing homeless women in malls and managing to engage them. These are not women who talk to themselves, who wear obvious old clothes in grungy unwashed layers and push around shopping carts. They can pass for middle-class women, and their survival depends on their ability to do that. Many work at part-time or minimum wage jobs and cannot manage high rents and huge deposits for rent and utilities.

Storm Tide, a collaboration with Ira Wood, is about small town politics and unconventional relationships. It is set on the Cape and our fragile local environment. It is also about the way that people define success and failure.

Three Women concerns three generations of a family: Beverly, a feisty, independent woman of seventy-two who was a union organizer; and her only daughter Suzanne, who is a lawyer who teaches in a law school at a university and also takes on cases that interest her, mostly appeals. Suzanne has two daughters, half sisters. The youngest, Rachel, is close to her mother. The oldest, Elena, has been at war with her mother since puberty. In high school, she got into serious trouble. Elena, twenty-seven and still smoldering, is the third of the women through whose eyes we watch the story unfold.

Often I like to give the reader several viewpoints. None of the characters is a spokesperson for me or my ideas or my politics. I think of the meaning of all of my novels as coming together in the mind of the reader. I think with multiple viewpoints; often each character has something to add to the total picture, and the reader will create her own truth and synthesis from the characters and the story, from the milieu of the book and its themes. Each of you who reads my novel will read your own version of it. I'm not a control freak, and I understand you create your own interpretation. The novel is about generation conflict and generational rapprochement—if it's possible between people used to finding fault with each other, women thoroughly comfortable with the roles they have assumed in their family and with the roles into which they have been cast—or shoved. Can we break out of these roles and actually learn to listen to each other, to be together?

A recent novel, *The Third Child,* revolves around the love affair of two college students from politically and racially different backgrounds. It deals with contemporary national politics and the aftereffects of the death sentence. My new novel, *Sex Wars,* published by Morrow/HarperCollins, deals with the turbulent post–Civil War era, in so many ways like our own in its controversies about the rights of women and minorities, election fraud, sexual expression, censorship, the role of religion in public life. The viewpoint characters are Elizabeth Cady Stanton, Victoria Woodhull, Anthony Comstock, and an immigrant woman, Freydeh, who manufactures condoms in her kitchen.

I continue to find the lives of women and girls in the past, the present, and the imagined future fascinating to write about. So much of our lives and our thoughts remain unexplored.

I have published sixteen novels. Whether writing science or historical or contemporary fiction, I have explored the lives of women, choices open to them, their problems and passions, victories and defeats. My memoir *Sleeping with Cats* examines my first sixty-five years. My sixteen books of poetry include *The Moon Is Always Female, My Mother's Body, Circles on the Water, What Are Big Girls Made Of, Early Grrrl, The Art of Blessing the Day: Poems with a Jewish Theme,* and recently, *Colors Passing Through Us.* My poems have been set to music many times; quoted on T-shirts; used at weddings and memorials, in religious services, in unions, at rallies, and in women's health clinics; and sewn on quilts.

I have been active on women's issues since 1967, when we started a women's caucus in Students for a Democratic Society in New York City. I was part of the first women's center in New York, starting consciousness-raising groups. I had helped women get abortions for years, but I became active on that issue in the late 1960s and continue to be today. It is one of my hot button issues. I've organized or been involved with many groups: Cape Cod Women's Liberation, Bread and Roses, NOW, Roots for Choice, Massachusetts NARAL. I've done hundreds of benefits. What means the most to me, however, is my writing.

CHAPTER ELEVEN

Writing in a Political Context: Interview with Robin Morgan

Gayle Kimball

GK: What are highlights for you as a writer since the original chapter?

RM: *Sisterhood Is Global* came out in 1984, a thirteen-year project. For the rest of the 1980s I was on the road doing speaking. *The Demon Lover*, a study of male psychology of violence, came out in 1989. It was re-released in 2002 after 9/11. It started as a study of violence in the United States, but I discovered a major shift had occurred since I compiled *Sisterhood Is Global*: I could no longer think "locally," even with my book for children called *The Mer Child*. All my writing reflects that consciousness, whether in metaphors or issues. Then *Saturday's Child*, my memoir, came out in 2000.

Now I'm finishing up editing *Sisterhood Is Forever*. With sixty contributors, it's labor intensive, but in the wake of the election of George W. Bush, I'm glad I did this. It provides analysis of where we're going, trends, and tactics to prevent the rollback of women into the twelfth century. We could easily lose gains like *Roe v. Wade*. Many of the chapter authors are young women, and others highlight the establishment of our feminist anti-establishment "establishment," including Anita Hill, Gloria Steinem, Carol Gilligan, Andrea Dworkin, Faye Wattelton, Eve Ensler, and Grace Paley. This is my eighteenth book, not including *The Burning Time*, a novel I just finished, which will be out in 2006. It takes place in Ireland in 1324; I did a lot of research years ago about who the witches really were and how certain women fought back.

In my personal life, the marriage ended in 1983. I look back in bemusement at my tone about Kenneth in the first interview. I fell in love with a woman, later conducted a rather passionate commute to New Zealand for over ten years. The "whole story," as they say, is in *Saturday's Child*, the memoir.

My writing was greatly affected by taking over as the editor-in-chief of Ms. in late 1989. I said I would do it for a year, if it were autonomous from the corporation that then owned it and ad-free. But I got talked into staying almost to 1994. We did the relaunch, and it won more awards and sold better than it ever had, with an emphasis on fiction, poetry, and investigative journalism, including global news coverage. The success means magazines don't need to dumb down. For the first time since the early days of Ms., we wooed major writers by telling them they wouldn't be cut or censored. Ursula K. Le Guin, Margaret Atwood, Toni Morrison, and Sandra Cisneros were only a few of the writers I was pleased to publish.

But I soon discovered my own existence as a creative human being was drowning. It stretched to almost four years before I managed to extract myself from the job, and took off for New Zealand for six months. During this time with Ms., except for writing editorials, I hadn't done any "real" writing, although I did publish books already in the pipeline. Editing one hundred pages every eight weeks, with a staff of only thirteen people—that took obsession. I had nothing left over for my writing. When I left Ms., I naively assumed I'd have this explosion of repressed creativity, but nothing happened. So much intensive journalism had hurt my ear and cramped my style; the length and tone of my prose got truncated.

The New Zealand relationship ended, plus I slipped and ruptured a spinal disk. Not a happy camper, I came back to New York City with writer's block and severe depression. But (like a woman) I functioned; there were only two days in the next four years when I couldn't get out of bed. I hacked journalism for money, and I wrote introductions to other people's work. But the real work I couldn't do in the face of grief and physical pain. Normally, my way of surviving bad times is to write my way through it, especially poetry. And the memoir was way over due at my publisher's. Then FedEx lost the files for the memoir while I was visiting professor at the University of Denver for three months. In all, a hard time. And I couldn't seem to write.

The voice came back, first as poems—a considerably different voice, older, a mature voice with far better craft. I'd think, "Shit, that's very *good*. Did *I* write that?" A happy ending after a hellish time. I'd made myself a pledge that if the voice came back, the joy of writing, the joy of art, would never be put second to *anything* although the women's movement is a jealous goddess. But writing can be a form of activism. A book like Sisterhood Is Forever is a political act. But now I say "No" more if somebody else can do it, since I certainly am not indispensable. I try to restrict my time away from my desk to where I uniquely can be of activist use.

My memoir Saturday's Child was a process of discovery for me. I had to use all my skills as a poet, political writer, novelist, etc., to make it work for the reader. Certainly as I age, I see the increasing value of humor. My writing shows greater simplicity, greater transparency. It's more intimate. It was new to be as honest in prose as I had been in poems (especially those in *A Hot January*). There's a way in which I feel freer; as in many indigenous cultures, older women achieve status for their store of knowledge and experience. I don't know if the memoir is a form of this, but at sixty-one, I've never felt more womanly and more audacious—and I've always loved audacity. I wouldn't flinch from writing a male character now, while I would have before, feeling women need more attention. Now I have the freedom to create *what the work needs*, after a desperate, debilitating silence.

GK: What's happened to the renaissance of women's culture in these last two decades?

RM: Women's culture had a huge explosion and then it "normalized." The United States is a particularly ahistoric country. Some things get absorbed so quickly. We've seen movies like *Thelma and Louise* and *The Turning Point*, a lot of women's movies, not chick flics, and musicians like Cindy Lauper and many others who came out as feminists. Nicole Kidman said in a recent interview, "Of course I'm a feminist, anyone with half a brain is," indicative of the mainstreaming of what was at first a marginal phenomenon.

We see the mainstream in popular culture; on TV, if you tune in to *Friends* or *Everybody Loves Raymond*, or *The West Wing*, you'll see women characters are saying and doing what was considered radical feminism twenty years ago. We're seeing more institutional establishment—as in the Museum of Women in the Arts in Washington, D.C., and not only on the coasts.

The women's movement is an international phenomenon now, moving into regional areas with the help of the Internet. Since *Sisterhood Is Global* came out, at least three or four contributors from countries like Chile and Morocco have been published in the United States and found audiences. This indicates a change of consciousness for U.S. women and hopefully for men. We're acknowledging our differences *and* our similarities.

I've spent quite a few months in Palestinian refugee camps. Around a hut housing fourteen people, always the women would manage to grow vegetables and flowers. With so little space and water in the Gaza Strip (the Israeli settlers use 96 percent of the water), I'd ask women why they "wasted" water for flowers. Laughing, they'd say, "You know why, because the soul has to be fed." Women use their art as a political code for freedom. The colors that the women used during the Infantada were the forbidden colors of the Palestinian flag. Embroidery is their great art form.

In Chile under dictatorship, women made cloth paintings sewn with soft cloth dolls, and on these *arpilleras*, they painted symbols for justice and liberty. I have a number of them, they're real art forms. In the Philippines, I traveled to the mountains in the north to talk with the indigenous Igorot tribe that has been royally screwed by all Philippine administrations. These women work the rice paddies. You see the words for peace, freedom, and love, spelled out in the rice fields—in English! At first I thought I was hallucinating, while swaying on a rope bridge high over a gully looking down on the fields. But this is yet another art form. And it's political.

These are four examples of women using art as political code and creating beauty in the teeth of despair. When I think of women's culture, I think of those examples. A book called *African Canvas* (by Margaret Courtney Clark) includes stunning photographs of clay huts painted by African women in geometric designs of such stunning sophistication; they're almost three dimensional, with colors to die for.

Themes in women's culture are connectivity, in contrast to the compartmentalization and separation of patriarchy. It pigeonholes race, age, sex, ability; separating love from sex, law from justice, and creating national borders—which acid rain doesn't care about at all. Feminist energy lies in *making the connections*. Take a crucial international issue like population control. Patriarchal "experts" used to consider it not "a woman's issue." For years, the global women's movement has been saying you can't just inflict population control on the women of the global South; it has to be offered, combined with literacy and job training—and especially *choice*. Women don't want to have so many children when they have a choice and can control the programs. Of course there's a response in lower birth rates when all the elements are in place. It's all about making connections.

Now we're seeing concerns over draconian Bush administration policies. But some people will only wake up and act when disaster is at the door to give a wake up call. People now are afraid of the word liberal; they see it as radical. People use the language of the reactionaries, "pro-life," when it's *anti*-life, and "partial birth abortion," instead of late-term or emergency abortion. Damm right, we're radical, out to change institutions, criticize marriage, speak up against war, and say what we passionately believe. That kind of honest, real ethics can filter up to left-of-center politicians. *We* make *them* look *moderate*, which allows them to move into a more progressive stand. I see a heightening of intensity on both sides. It's exciting—but it makes me cranky. I had planned to spend more time at my desk for the next twenty years of my life. Then 9/11 hit; then after the elections it was even harder to say no. But I realize in my gut the best political activism I can offer is on the page.

GK: How has feminist publishing evolved?

RM: U.S. feminist publishers have been hard hit by the economy. Thank the goddess The Feminist Press is alive and well after thirty years. But the publisher KNOW doesn't exist, nor does Shameless Hussy and many others. But new publishers are emerging around the world, such as Kali for Women in India, and Spinniflex in Australia. Ms. has merged with the Fund for Feminist Majority, founded by Eleanor Smeal. It's a wonderful match; I was the glad midwife behind it. In the 1990s, Ms. had become more superficial, dropping international coverage—and the readership fell tremendously. It's in transition with a new editor. With fresh blood, I think it will again become more feminist, more intelligent, livelier.

GK: What about the organization you founded, the Sisterhood Is Global Institute (SIGI)?

RM: SIGI was recently based in Montreal. It moves every five or six years to another country so it won't be under the hegemony of one country—but that's a logistical nightmare. In the 1990s, we focused almost exclusively on Muslim women. In one sense it fell away from being a think tank, due to the crying need for activism. Now it's in a transition period again, going to expand to include other areas of study. I chair the advisory board (www.sigi.org).

In the last twenty years a vast global women's movement has emerged, which gives us different context. SIGI is one of hundreds of nongovernmental organizations. Simone de Beauvoir and I set it up as a global think tank. Now it's in a transition period again, going to expand to include other areas of study. SIGI is one of hundreds of nongovernmental organizations. Internet influence is huge. Two-thirds of all illiterates are women, yet at the U.N. conference on women in Beijing, lines of women used the computer centers. The Internet means you can't contain feminism. International protest sprung up for the women sentenced to be stoned for adultery in Nigeria, for the women in Afghanistan. We see cross-cultural communication, boycott, letters, e-mails. It's amazing: How did we function in the 1960s without the Internet?

GK: In the first interview, you said that the women's movement was a "profoundly religious revolution."

RM: I would disagree now with the word "religious." But I do think that feminism is the next step in human evolution. Spiritual, metaphysical. . . . I don't know that either word is necessary. Religious and spiritual are words being used by genuinely psychotic people in charge of our government, people who want to deregulate guns but regulate sexuality and reproduction. Each of us can be an agent of evolution. We can be conscious of that in our behavior, in the way we raise our children, and carry ourselves with responsibility, though not with guilt (which is paralyzing and counterproductive).

Feminism is the politics of the twenty-first century because of its inclusiveness and its capacity to connect. It's the most diverse movement this country has known in terms of its constituencies and issues: welfare, disabled women, corporate whistle-blowers, racism, environment, homophobia, ageism, electoral politics. All these issues (and more) are women's issues because we're the majority of the population. The potential is to connect these issues.

We've been multitasking for ages; the average woman does six things at a time. That's reflected in the women's movement, that's part of its power. Something in the species is hardwired for altruism, as explained by Carol Gilligan in her essay and Natalie Angier in hers in my new *Sisterhood* anthology. So, while our reproductive freedom is threatened, and we lack a just economic system and ERA, more women *are* writing, composing, and painting. I think again of art as code, of the secret women's language in China, as described in *The Word of a Woman* (second edition).

GK: What about the role of young women in feminism?

RM: Starting in the mid-1960s, the media said only young women were interested; now they say only older women are feminists. I lecture quite a lot around the world, and it's mostly younger women who come. There are often 800 people there, wonderfully outraged, for all the right reasons.

Gen X and Y voices are loud and clear in the anthology. There's a girls' movement of young teens, as expressed in the magazine for girls called *New Moon*. They critique the media images of girls and women. Young women have a lot of the same themes as we did, body images and eating disorders, violence against women, nervousness about the erosions of *Roe v. Wade*. I hope *Sisterhood Is Forever* will make them aware of the erosion of all of our rights. In Eleanor Holmes Norton's piece she talked about her generation as catalytic feminists, while young women are functional feminists, who want to move on, and up the ante. They understand that issues are entwined: racism, classism, ableism, homophobia, and disability.

GK: In the original chapter you advocated "a life-urgency need for us to refuse simplification." Has that happened?

RM: The complexity *has* begun; but I could use a lot more of it. Feminism in those twenty years has infused and pervades a lot of pop culture and also serious writers. We're beginning to get a complexity that comes out of cross-hatching. For me the two greatest living U.S. writers happen to be feminists, Toni Morrison and Ursula K. Le Guin. Le Guin has been pigeonholed as a sci-fi writer. Her sci fi is bloody brilliant, and she also writes other fiction, poetry, and essays. Her short story, "Findings" in *Unlocking the Air and Other Stories*, gives us the essential definition of women's culture; it's about a woman and a man writing a story and gives a new meaning to the word "pithy." The differences are so absolutely clear. I heartily recommend reading it.

What makes Morrison and Le Guin great is the compassionate sweep of their vision and the depth of their understanding of human nature. As craftswomen they give a particular attention to detail that only a woman would notice. They notice human relationships, details about housework. It's seeing the magic in the practical, like the Filipina rice paddies. Women provide an existential, spiritual, esthetic dimension to politics.

GK: How has your thinking about women's innate images evolved?

RM: I was worried that everything had to be circular and vaginal. That phase is not over. But Eve Ensler's *Vagina Monologues* has focused enormous attention on violence against women. We're not done if the word "vagina" is unutterable. But I do long for a time when "the first woman to . . ." doesn't make the news because it's so common; I long for a time when women address anything they want to.

GK: Are women still obsessed with love, more so than men?

RM: Obsession with love is catching, but it takes longer than twenty years. *Father Courage: When Men Put Family First* is an important book by Susanne Braun Levine about what happens when men put family first. To a man, every guy she interviewed said, "I don't want to be like my father." That's an interesting phenomenon. There is something afoot, a grassroots phenomenon, but I don't see it reflected in the halls of power. Bill Clinton made it safe for a president to cry. Even Bush cried over the Afghan people (then abandoned them). Such changes are tiny but incremental.

After 9/11, Camille Pagilia claimed moronically that the adoration of firefighters and police officers was the return of the he-man, wistfully announcing (again) that feminism is dead. But as I hit the road promoting *The Demon Lover* (which explains the eroticization of violence) this time the men *got* it. In Tennessee and Oklahoma, Georgia and Montana, men stood up and testified about violence. Paglia really got it wrong about firefighters. The shock of the catastrophe was so huge, it moved them past inhibition; they cried and sobbed in each other's arms. Saving, nurturing, human emotion were permitted for men, a paradigm shift over a century. But the reaction to it was the drumbeat for war in the Middle East, branding dissent as unpatriotic, and jingoism.

GK: Why is President Bush popular?

RM: The population of this country has always been about one-third to the right, one-third to the progressive-left, and one-third undecided. Republicans have learned grassroots precinct organizing, which Democrats used to do (and *should* be doing). Clinton moved the Democratic Party to the center, and his legacy is that less competent pols than he are trying to be imitation Republicans. Gore trying to be an imitation Republican didn't work; he lacked Clintonian charm and populist wit. If you don't offer the middle third of the electorate a choice, they go with the lowest common denominator—patriotism. I was so depressed after Bush stole the election in 2000 and got away with it.

Both parties accept such huge amounts of money, it means Democrats are in an awkward position to critique Republicans with their hands in the same pocket. Republicans have control of both houses of Congress, so they have no place to go but down—but their legacy with judiciary appointments will be disaster. Progressive movements didn't educate people enough about how critical the judiciary appointments are. It's very sad to have to refight *Roe v. Wade* yet again.

GK: Where are we headed?

RM: We're seeing eruptions of feminism, not the third but the 10,000th wave, all over the world. In Ellie Smeal's chapter on building feminist institutions to last, she advocates changing the system systemically. All the academics in the new *Sisterhood* anthology wrote about that, so we can't be buried again like the suffrage movement. The next step is to *change the institutions* so we don't have just token female leaders, rather a total transformation of the imbedded estrangement from women. We need to examine and change all the pipelines to power; for instance, gubernatorial slots are the pipeline to presidency. In business, the fastest growing demographic is women's small entrepreneurism—yet Sandy Learner invented Cisco systems, and then found herself fired because she was a woman. Still ownership is one way to go. All this boils down to "it's time to change the system, not just get a slice of the pie."

It's time for multidimensional feminism, where issues of race, sexual preference, age, class, and ability are not ancillary to, but part and parcel of, feminism. If you read the nineteenth-century suffragists, they took on religion, sexuality, financial independence, abolition of slavery, and class differences—but all that got narrowed into the struggle for the vote. So we had to do it all over again. That's the key, to transform institutions. We've got to demand not just what we can get, but what we *want.*

Biography

An award-winning writer, feminist leader, political theorist, journalist, and editor, Robin Morgan has published eighteen books, including six of poetry, two of fiction, and the now-classic anthologies *Sisterhood Is Powerful* (1970) and *Sisterhood Is Global* (1984; 1996); *Sisterhood Is Forever: The Women's Anthology for a New Millennium,* came out in 2003. A founder of contemporary U.S. feminism, Morgan has also been a leader in the international women's movement for twenty-five years. Her latest books include *A Hot January: Poems 1996–1999; Saturday's Child: A Memoir,* and the updated *The Demon Lover: The Roots of Terrorism.* A recipient of the National Endowment for the Arts Prize (Poetry), the Front Page Award for Distinguished Journalism, the Feminist Majority Foundation Award, and numerous other honors, she lives in New York City. Her novel *The Burning Time* will be published in Spring 2006 by Melville House, which will also publish her new nonfiction book, *Fighting Words for a Secular America,* in September 2006.

CHAPTER TWELVE

~

Third Wave Girlie Culture

Jennifer Baumgardner and Amy Richards

Excerpt from chapter 4 of *Manifesta: Young Women, Feminism, and the Future*. New York: Farrar, Straus and Giroux, 2000.

The backbone of feminism isn't so different from one generation to the next. We want to distinguish ourselves from doormats, as early twentieth-century feminist Rebecca West and her cohorts did, as Betty Friedan's generation did. And our values are similar, although our tactics and style often differ. (Suffragist Alice Paul was surely horrified when some early Second Wave feminists, including Shulamith Firestone, wanted to stage an action in D.C. to give *back* the vote as part of a 1969 Vietnam protest.) The difference between the first, second, and Third Waves is our cultural DNA. Each generation has a drive to create something new, to find that distinctive spark.

The word "generation" is an apt pun here, because what distinguishes one era from the next is what we generate—whether it's music, institutions, or magazines—and how we use what has already been produced. Marlo Thomas grew up on Toni dolls and Nancy Drew stories. In her mid-thirties, she created one of the Third Wave's first glimpses of feminist culture, the 1973 book and record *Free to Be . . . You and Me*. When Thomas and Friends created this early manifesto to freedom, in which a football player sang about crying and girls wanted to be firemen, they couldn't have imagined the guys with earrings and girls with tattoos and shaved heads who would emerge a decade or two later—their former readers.

Thomas didn't choose to be influenced by Toni dolls any more than we chose to be influenced by *Free to Be*—or by MTV. Our generation watched powerful, fashionable private detectives solve crimes and bond together in prime-time sisterhood on *Charlie's Angels* but couldn't help noticing that they did all the work while a male voice, always out of reach, told them what to do. We were a generation in which many girls grew up thinking that *Playboy* was for them, too, to sneak peeks at while Mom and Dad were occupied, or to lead tours of neighborhood kids out to the garage for the unveiling of an old copy featuring Miss November 1972. As girls, we saw the culture reflect a bit of our particular vernacular: Valley Girls who shop and register pronouncements about the relative grodiness or radness of all things. We were a generation that was forced to experience equality when it came to the newly coed gym classes, and reveled in Title IX's influence on sports for girls. These products of culture are mundane to us, simply the atmosphere in our temporal tank.

The fact that feminism is no longer limited to arenas where we expect to see it—NOW, *Ms.*, women's studies, and red-suited congresswomen—perhaps means that young women today have really reaped what feminism has sown. Raised after Title IX and "William Wants a Doll," young women emerged from college or high school or two years of marriage or their first job and began challenging some of the received wisdom of the past ten or twenty years of feminism. We're not doing feminism the same way that the 1970s feminists did it; being liberated doesn't mean copying what came before but finding one's own way—a way that is genuine to one's own generation.

For the generation that reared the Third Wave, not only was feminism apparent in the politics of the time but politics was truly the culture of the time—Kennedy, the Vietnam War, civil rights, and women's rights. For the Third Wave, politics was superseded by culture—punk rock, hip-hop, zines, product, consumerism, and the Internet. Young women in the early 1990s who were breaking out of the "established" movement weren't just rebelling; they were growing up and beginning to take responsibility for their lives and their feminism.

The following is a sampling of what the Third Wave grew up with:

- In 1984, Madonna came out with the album *Like a Virgin*. Lying on her back on the album's cover photo, elbows propped, looking sexy, bored, and tough as hell, she wore fluffy crinolines, black eyeliner, and a belt that said "Boy Toy." She was bad, and looked at you like she wanted it bad. *She* wanted it. Then there were the dozens of incarnations that followed for the material girl. The video identities: stripper, pregnant girl from the neighborhood, dominatrix, men's-suit-wearing activist for female sexuality (*C'mon girls, Do you believe in love?*), and a kick-ass version of the vulnerable, victimized Marilyn Monroe. (Which is why, no doubt, Madonna's fans were mostly young women, while Marilyn's were mostly men.) And Madonna's off-camera identities: strongest thighs in all pop music, bitch, best friend to all the fabulous lesbians, "serious" actress with affected English accent, beatific single mother, and most powerful performer in the pop firmament. Throughout all this she was sending a message, teaching by example: Be what you want to be, then be something else that you want to be. (And earn a billion bucks while you're at it.)

- In 1988, when *Seventeen* had just been liberated from being run by an ex-nun, and *YM* still stood for *Young Miss* (rather than the current *Young & Modern*), a revolutionary new teen magazine debuted for girls. It was called *Sassy*, and it managed to put on makeup and fashion without prescribing it and created a camp aesthetic for girls. It took the pressure off beauty and fashion by turning away from *Go from So-So to Sexy!* toward wardrobes donned simply because they were pleasurable: *Dye your hair with Jell-O! Dress like a mod from the sixties! Wear a little Catholic schoolgirl outfit with a down vest! Wear a furry hat with mouse ears! Wheeeee!* Writer Christina Kelly's two-page pastiche, called "What Now" (essentially an archive of Kelly's taste), vaulted this teen fashion magazine into the counterculture. "What Now" profiled a zine of the month, legitimizing the DIY (do-it-yourself) publications at a time when zines were the only place where people who were too young, punk, or weird, such as Riot Grrrls, could publish. Bands like Jon Spencer Blues Explosion and Guided by Voices got their first teen or women's press in *Sassy's* "Cute Band Alert." For once, a teen magazine was actually in touch with youth culture. But the salient point here is not so much that the *Sassy* creators were hip, although they were, as that they were hip to feminism. They told girls to get their own guitars, that it's okay to be a lesbian, and that it's even okay *not* to go to the prom. (*Ms.* may have believed this, too, but *Ms.* wasn't written with teenage girls in mind.) The *Sassy* editors were drawing from wells that were below the radar of *Ms.* and over the heads of nonfeminist competitors *Seventeen, Teen,* and *YM.*

- In 1991, twenty-eight-year-old Naomi Wolf published *The Beauty Myth.* This book analyzed body image and the consumer trappings of femininity —magazines and makeup and, by extension, porn—from the perspective of a new generation. Wolf was writing for us, about us, and she was one of us: a woman reared in the wake of the Second Wave. Gorgeous and articulate, she drew the reader in the way a fashion magazine did—with pretty pictures (at least, in the Scavullo portraits that accompanied interviews)—and then got you mad with her feminist research. Her critique was one that young women conversant in the coded language of eating disorders could recognize (six glasses of water and hard-boiled egg whites from the salad bar for every dinner equals anorexic masquerading as fitness fanatic; pointer fingers with scratches equal bulimic), as could the girls who felt hostile and ugly when they looked at magazines and porn. As one of the first itinerant feminists of the Third Wave, Wolf traveled to college campuses across the United States, talking to young women. This touring led her to conclude that "girls are still understood more clearly as victims of culture and sexuality than as cultural and sexual creators," so she set out to change that assumption. Her next book, *Fire with Fire: How Power Feminism Will Change the 21st Century*, told women to embrace power, and *Promiscuities* recast the slut as a rebel.

- In 1991, a loose-knit group of punk-rock girls in Olympia, Washington, and Washington, D.C., rescued feminism from two hazards: one, the male-dominated punk-rock scene, and two, their own cohorts, women who didn't use the term *feminist*. Seizing radicalism and activism from the dump in which they thought it had slumped since the mid-1970s, Riot Grrrls weren't pushing a rational feminism. They scrawled *slut* on their stomachs, screamed from stages and pages of fanzines about incest, rape, being queer, and being in love. They mixed a childish aesthetic with all that is most threatening in a female adult: rage, bitterness, and political acuity. In bands such as Bikini Kill, Bratmobile, Huggy Bear, and Heavens to Betsy, these Grrrls shot up like flames, influencing countless girls and showing them feminism before dissipating, seemingly, around the mid-1990s.

- In 1993, a xerox-and-staple zine of fewer than twenty pages called *Bust* presented an embraceable, nourishing reflection of young women and their lives—and called it girl culture. "The Booty Myth" was a *Bust* story about black women's sexuality, "Elektra Woman and Dyna-Girl" was fiction about two young white girls who staged play-date rapes, "I Was a Teenage Mommy" was self-explanatory, as was "Blow Job Tips for Straight Women from a Gay Man." These articles were juxtaposed with buxom images from vintage soft-core porn, images now in the control of women. In *Bust*, porn was demystified, claimed for women, debated. Vibrators tried and tried again. Childhood heroines revisited (Judy Blume! Farrah! Cynthia Plaster Caster!). Seventies artists and writers with varying degrees of credentials were recast as Second Wave she-roes (such as sex revolutionaries and authors Erica Jong and Nancy Friday). "We're not apologizing for the culture we've been raised with and not overvaluing masculine culture," said Debbie Stoller, the coeditor of *Bust*.

"Barbies, for example, are seen by the main culture as kind of dumb, and playing with trucks is more important—but, in fact, when we played with Barbies it was complicated and interesting, and it's something we should tell the truth about." Rock critic Ann Powers codified Stoller's definition in the fall 1997 Girl issue of Spin: "Girl Culture girls have transformed what it means to be female in the nineties. Unlike conventional feminism, which focused on women's socially imposed weaknesses, Girl Culture assumes that women are free agents in the world, that they start out strong and that the odds are in their favor."

All of this Girlie culture, from Madonna to Bust, is different from the cultural feminism of the 1970s. It promoted a gynefocal aesthetic (as a form of politics), too, but sometimes in the service of a "separate but equal" alternative world. (In keeping with the previously proposed Femitopia.) Cultural feminism put the y in womyn and brought us women-owned Diana publishing, the aforementioned Olivia Records, and all-ladies collectives such as the Michigan Womyn's Music Festival, which has been going strong annually since 1976 and allows males only under the age of six to grace "the Land" (as the nature preserve upon which everyone camps is always called, with reverence). But for this generation, having or loving our own culture isn't the same as cultural feminism—a separate ghetto (or utopia) for women—it's just feminism for a culture-driven generation. And if feminism aims to create a world where our standard of measurement doesn't start with a white-male heterosexual nucleus, then believing that feminine things are weak means that we're believing our own bad press. Girlies say, through actions and attitudes, that you don't have to make the feminine powerful by making it masculine or "natural"; it is a feminist statement to proudly claim things that are feminine, and the alternative can mean to deny what we are. You were raised on Barbie and soccer? That's cool. In a way, establishing a girl culture addresses what Gloria Steinem was trying to identify when she wrote Revolution from Within—the huge hole that grows in a woman who is trying to be equal but has internalized society's low estimation of women. "It was as if the female spirit were a garden that had grown beneath the shadows of barriers for so long," she wrote, "that it kept growing in the same pattern, even after some of the barriers were gone."

What does the Third Wave garden look like? Planted near Madonna, Sassy, Wolf, Riot Grrrls, and Bust are influential xerox-and-staple zines such as I (heart) Amy Carter, Sister Nobody, I'm So Fucking Beautiful, and Bamboo Girl; the glossy-but-still-independent zines such as HUES, Roller Derby, Bitch, Fresh and Tasty, and WIG; chickclick and estronet websites like

Disgruntled Housewife, Girls On, and gURL; webzines such as *Minx* and *Maxi*; feature films like *Clueless, Go Fish, All Over Me, The Incredibly True Adventure of Two Girls in Love, Welcome to the Dollhouse,* and *High Art*; art films by Elisabeth Subrin, Sadie Benning, Pratibha Parmar, and Jocelyn Taylor; musicians such as Ani DiFranco, Brandy, Luscious Jackson, Courtney Love as the slatternly, snarly singer, Courtney Love as the creamy Versace model, and Erykah Badu, Me'shell Ndege'ocello, Bikini Kill, Missy Elliott, the Spice Girls, Salt-N-Papa, TLC, Gwen Stefani, Team Dresch, Foxy Brown, Queen Latifah, Indigo Girls, and all those ladies featured at Lilith Fair; products galore, Urban Decay, Hard Candy, MAC, and Manic Panic; on the small screen, *Wonder Woman* (in comic-book form, too), *Buffy the Vampire Slayer, My So-Called Life, Xena, Felicity,* and Alicia Silverstone in Aerosmith videos; Chelsea Clinton; the New York club Meow Mix and other joints with female go-go dancers getting down for women; funny girls loving Janeane Garafalo and Margaret Cho; angry women loving Hothead Paisan and *Dirty Plotte* comics; Jenny McCarthy, who somehow satirized being a pinup even as she was one; controversial books like *Backlash* and *The Morning After*; uncontroversial ones like *The Bust Guide to the New Girl Order* and *Listen Up*; the West Coast mutual-admiration society of sex writers Lisa Palac and Susie Bright; Monica Lewinsky; the Women's World Cup; the WNBA; and hundreds more films, bands, women, books, events, and zines.

We, and others, call this intersection of culture and feminism "Girlie." Girlie says we're not broken, and our desires aren't simply booby traps set up by the patriarchy. Girlie encompasses the tabooed symbols of women's feminine enculturation—Barbie dolls, makeup, fashion magazines, high heels—and says using them isn't shorthand for "we've been duped." Using makeup isn't a sign of our sway to the marketplace and the male gaze; it can be sexy, campy, ironic, or simply decorating ourselves without the loaded issues (à la *dye your hair with Jell-O!*). Also, what we loved as girls was good and, because of feminism, we know how to make girl stuff work for us. Our Barbies had jobs and sex lives and friends. We weren't staring at their plastic figures and Dynel tresses hoping to someday attain their pneumatic measurements. Sticker collections were no more trivial than stamp collections; both pursuits cultivated the connoisseur in a young person.

While it's true that embracing the pink things of stereotypical girlhood isn't a radical gesture meant to overturn the way society is structured, it can be a confident gesture. When younger women wearing "Girl Rule" T-shirts and carrying Hello Kitty lunch boxes dust off the Le Sportsacs from junior high and fill them with black lipstick and green nail polish and campy sparkles, it is not as totems to an infantilized culture but as a nod to our joyous youth. Young women are emphasizing our real personal lives in contrast to what some feminist foremothers anticipated their lives would—or should—be: that the way to equality was to reject Barbie and all forms of pink-packaged femininity. In holding tight to that which once symbolized their oppression, Girlies' motivations are along the lines of gay men in Chelsea calling each other "queer" or black men and women using the term "nigga."

In creating a feminism of their own, though, Girlies are repeating a pattern as old as the patriarchy: rebelling against their mothers, for instance, Debbie Stoller, who was quoted calling Gloria Steinem a dinosaur in the dumb and now defunct Gen-X magazine *Swing* or Katie Roiphe writing books that seem to be a direct response to her 1970s-feminist mother Anne Riophe. In the same way that Betty Friedan's insistence on professional seriousness was a response to every woman in an office being called a girl, this generation is predestined to fight against the equally rigid stereotype of being too serious, too political, and seemingly asexual. Girlie culture is a rebellion against the false impression that since women don't want to be sexually exploited, they don't want to be sexual; against the necessity of brass-buttoned, red-suited seriousness to infiltrate a man's world; against the anachronistic belief that because women could be dehumanized by porn (and we include erotica in our definition), they must be; and the idea that girls and power don't mix.

Although rebelling appears to be negative, we think it's natural—and the result leads to greater diversity and, in turn, produces a stronger feminist movement. For example, it's important that Andrea Dworkin identify herself as "a feminist, not the fun kind," but if it was ever implied that she was the *only* kind, the movement might feel a little Antioch, as in rigid. (Antioch College is famous for a 1992 policy that required verbal consent for every step of a possible seduction, for example, Do you want me to touch your breast?) Similarly, the Spice Girls make for a pretty thin definition of *feminist* because they are only the fun kind. And yet preteen girls dancing around freely in their living rooms or at concerts singing "Wannabe," rock music made just for them, can be nothing short of empowering.

Girlie doesn't so much identify different issues for young women as say that this generation of feminists wants its own institutions and a right to its own attitudes and interpretations. Familiarity with porn, sexual aggressiveness, and remaining single and childless until pretty late in life play out in their take on issues such as censorship, date rape, and day care. The fact that most of the Girlies are white and straight, work outside the home, and belong to the consumer class provides some explanation for why they choose to promote certain issues. The Second Wave, our mothers, had Ms. (and So-journer and Lilith and Our Bodies, Ourselves) and NOW and the fight for the ERA. We have Bust (and Bitch and the now defunct HUES and webzines and fanzines) and the Third Wave Foundation, Riot Grrrls and Queen Latifah and Lilith Fair and, well, we still have the fight for the ERA, and Ms., So-journer, and Our Bodies, Ourselves.

Where Girlie stops short of being the path to a forceful movement is that it mistakes politics for a Second Wave institution as well, rather than seeing it as inherent in feminism. This disconnect—politics versus culture—was on display at the 1997 Media and Democracy Forum, where Girlie debuted as a topic of conversation.

* * *

The point is that the cultural and social weapons that had been identified (rightly so) in the Second Wave as instruments of oppression—women as sex objects, fascist fashion, pornographic materials—are no longer being exclusively wielded against women and are sometimes wielded by women. Girlie presumes that women can handle the tools of patriarchy and don't need to be shielded from them. Protective labor laws that were part of the original ERA limited the jobs women could do. They were changed by 1970s feminists to promote egalitarian labor laws, which presumed that women could really do the police, car-assembly, and late-night work that men could do. Similarly, Girlie is replacing protective cultural "rules" with a kind of equality. "These days putting out one's pretty power, one's pussy power, one's sexual energy for popular consumption no longer makes you a bimbo," wrote Elizabeth Wurtzel in her 1998 glory rant Bitch. "It makes you smart." Madonna is in control of her sexual power, rather than a victim of it; she wields it the way she could a gun or a paintbrush or some other power tool that is usually the province of men. And she is enjoying it, which is her luxury and her strength. When Riot Grrrls screamed versions of IlovefuckingIhatedanger from rock clubs and fanzines and song lyrics in the early 1990s, or when women rappers like Lil' Kim "objectified" men's bodies right down to their dicks, they presumed some sort of strength in the social arena. But where did that strength come from?

* * *

Girlie, like all strands of the women's movement, is hindered by a divorce from history: specifically, the history of other versions of Girlie that have existed, women who have reinvented the image of feminism and brought new life to the movement. But when the image change is complete, the inequality remains. And it is the inequality and injustice based on gender that feminism addresses. But, when we are separated from our political history, it is primarily the reinventions that continue, as if women's aesthetics were what we wanted to transform rather than women's rights. Much of the story of the Second Wave is fragmented, mythologized, or difficult to find. In some ways, Girlie can't be blamed for its shortsightedness; the story of women wasn't part of school when we were growing up. But it is our fault that we haven't sought out our history.

This fuzzy sense of where we've been plays out when something like *Bust* or Bikini Kill or the phrase "girl power" turns masses of females on to feminism—and then peters out after the first rush. Having no sense of how we got here condemns women to reinvent the wheel and often blocks us from creating a political strategy.

* * *

As feminists, *we* love Girlie because it makes feminism relevant and fun and in the moment. Because we love it, we want to maximize its bloom, and see if it can thrive in a political context. . . . A lot of what Girlie radiates is the luxury of self-expression that most Second Wavers didn't feel they could or should indulge in. Other women wouldn't choose the knitting, miniskirts, or Barbies, anyway. But Girlies culture can be a trap of conformity, just with a new style. "Culture is always tied to material movements; you are not going to create a revolution through culture," says Pam Warren of the band the Coup, responding to the depoliticization of hip-hop.

With Girlie, there is danger that Spice Girls Pencil Set Syndrome will settle in: Girls buy products created by male-owned companies that capture the slogan of feminism, without the power. Kathleen Hanna describes it this way: "The thing that disturbs me now, with the commercialization, is I fear that young girls will be encouraged to stop there. That young girls will go buy their Spice Girls notebook and not go to the library or the gay or feminist bookstores. But, deep down, I think people are smarter than that and when they experience girl power in the real form, they'll get excited and seek out more information."

* * *

The mature Girlie feminist is somewhere between the woman who believes she must be grimly vigilant or she'll get screwed, and the bold

Minx/Bust/Jane girls, who want it all but don't necessarily want to figure out how to change anything. If we're strong enough to handle sexy clothes and Barbie dolls, then we should be strong enough to read Andrea Dworkin and other analyses of power, and still feel in touch with why we love skinny rocker boys or false eyelashes. The feminist transformation comes from the political theory *and* the cultural confidence. We can't afford to overlook the real barriers to women's liberation.

"All of that Girlie stuff feels right to me," says Lisa Silver, the feminist and journalism professor at New York University who worked with Betty Friedan. She is more comfortable with the women who create *Bust* than with the red-suited businesswomen. Silver sees the "spark" in Girlie and believes that pro-sexy representations underscore that women have a sexuality and can be as lustful as men. "However, Girlie as an ideology," continues Silver, "it is not a rally point. It's something we can all connect on—but now what? What do we believe? With the old feminists, they had something to work toward, like the ERA with all of its problems. All of the pro-pornography, pro-strippers, that's all fine, but ultimately, to my mind, so *what*? Unless it leads to something else."

Without a body of politics, the nail polish is really going to waste.

Biography

Excerpt from their chapter in *Manifesta*. Omissions are noted by asterisks.

Jennifer Baumgardner is a former editor at *Ms.* and writes regularly for *The Nation*, *Nerve*, and *Out*. Amy Richards is a contributing editor at *Ms.*, and a cofounder of The Third Wave Foundation.

PART FOUR

RELIGION

CHAPTER THIRTEEN

Multiplication and Division: Feminist Theology from 1980 to 2000

Shannon Craigo-Snell

The development of feminist theological discourse over the past two decades has been marked by multiplication and division. While feminist theology continues to be concerned with several of the issues Gayle Kimball discussed twenty years ago, it has changed significantly and structurally in the intervening years. In fact, it is no longer accurate to attempt a description of feminist theology; one must speak of feminist theologies instead. The field of feminist theology now includes a cacophony of voices engaged in struggles to critique, challenge, reject, and renew religious traditions. Further, feminist scholarship is burgeoning within many connected disciplines, including biblical studies, religious ethics, liturgical studies, and philosophy of religion. At the same time, the increasing diversity and particularity of feminist theologies has contributed to a profound questioning of several concepts central to early feminist theology. The notion of women's experience, the status of normative ethical claims, and even the belief that "women" can or should form a stable group, are being questioned by contemporary feminist theologians.

Feminist Discourse and Political Change

Feminist theology, like all forms of feminist discourse, has its roots in the political struggle to change the world. Earlier feminist theologians sought to concretely improve the daily lives of women by changing the way we think about the divine, formulate religious meaning, and understand ourselves in relation to the sacred and to religious traditions. Their efforts and those of many others have significantly benefited women in many communities and engendered some important changes in some religious structures. For example, growing numbers of women have been ordained into different Christian denominations, assuming leadership within their communities and contributing to the slow process of transforming their religious traditions. Throughout the 1950s, 1960s, and 1970s, several Protestant denominations decided to ordain women.[1] Women are now ordained clergy in Methodist, Presbyterian, American Baptist, Disciples of Christ, Congregationalist, and other denominations.[2] Before the 1970s, less than 3 percent of ordained clergy in the United States were women.[3] By 2000, that percentage had reached 10 to 12, with women comprising 25 to 30 percent of ministerial students.[4]

While there has been considerable improvement in the status of women within several religious traditions in the past twenty years, it would be inaccurate simply to portray these changes as part of a steady progress. There have been numerous setbacks, and obstacles continue to block gender equality. Further investigation of the example of women's ordination within Christian churches shows that the setbacks have been significant. Within the last twenty years, the two largest Christian denominations in the United States, the Southern Baptist Convention and the Roman Catholic Church, have both turned away from earlier movement toward gender equality, choosing to reject the ordination of women.[5]

The Southern Baptist Convention, the largest Protestant denomination in the United States, accepted the ordination of women in local churches in 1965. In 1984, they reversed this decision.[6] Many Roman Catholic women were encouraged by the statements issuing from the Second Vatican Council, an assembly of bishops that convened from 1963 to 1965 and made several positive steps regarding issues of social justice and equality. Vatican II condemned discrimination on the basis of sex as "contrary to God's intent."[7] When seen as the beginning of a new movement toward equality within the church, Vatican II offered significant hope for women. However, in the years following the Council, much of the hoped-for movement failed to take place. Subsequent church statements rejected the ordination of women, first in 1977 and then in 1994, when Pope John Paul II stated, "The church has no authority whatsoever to confer ordination on women and this judgment is to be definitely held by all the church's faithful."[8] While this statement does not completely foreclose further discussion of the matter, the tone of optimism and hopefulness that marked conversations about women in the Catholic church in the 1960s and 1970s is no longer present.

Resistance to women's progress has taken many different forms in different settings. Within the United States, hindrances have included both a backlash against feminism and an assimilation of certain aspects of feminism into mainstream American culture. The backlash against feminism denigrates and combats feminist efforts to advocate for women. At the same time, the mainstream acceptance of an extremely abbreviated form of feminism—the bare notion that women should have career opportunities equal to men's—serves to distract attention from the larger structural issues of oppression and thereby depoliticize feminism. Both responses to feminist movements make use of the small number of women who have achieved financial and professional success, either by ridiculing them as unwomanly or by celebrating them as signs that the feminist battle has been fought, won, and may now be forgotten. Both tactics personalize feminism and camouflage the unjust social structures that sustain the economic, political, physical, cultural, and religious oppression of women.

Multiplications

Many of the multiplications and divisions that the field of feminist theology has undergone in the past twenty years have resulted from feminists' efforts to live up to and into their own principles and commitments. For example, earlier feminists condemned the way in which men universalized their own experience, speaking and writing as if their own perspective on the world was completely objective and their lived reality was the norm. This universalization silenced women by ignoring, devaluing, or discrediting their different experiences and perspectives and by hindering their ability to shape culture and religious tradition in accordance with their own lived reality.[9] In the 1960s and 1970s many white, middle-class, educated feminists replicated this mistake, universalizing their own experiences as normative for all women without attending to issues of race, class, or sexual orientation. Eager to foster unity for political action, white feminists declared and embraced a "sisterhood" among women that effectively silenced many women, including women of color and women from different socioeconomic backgrounds. In 1984, bell hooks published *Feminist Theory: From Margin to Center*, which criticized middle-class, white feminism's silencing of other women, its maintenance of a unified party line, its focus on achieving social equality with men, and its willingness to equate feminism with lifestyle and identity choices rather than political action.[10] Hooks did not reject feminism, but called it to be true to its own principles and commitment to end sexist oppression, which, she argued, requires attention to all forms of domination and group oppression, including racism and classism.[11]

With varying degrees of success, feminists have responded to this criticism by trying to better manifest their own principles, both in speaking one's own truth and in making space to hear the voices of other women. In describing what is particularly feminist about feminist theology, Serene Jones notes that feminist theology has a "commitment to listening" to the voices of others.[12] From its beginnings, feminist theology was understood to be funded by women's experience, to be both conceived in and accountable to women's lived reality, and to be committed to hearing and honoring voices that had been silenced. Its foundational concerns demand diversity. Women from many different cultural contexts and social locations have challenged the failures to meet this demand and added their distinctive voices to the expanding conversation of feminist theologies. Some have chosen to identify their theological contributions with names that acknowledge and celebrate their social and cultural specificity. Theologians such as Delores Williams, Emilie Townes, Renita Weems, and Kelly Brown Douglas name themselves as "womanists," a term defined by Alice Walker.[13] Ada Maria Isasi-Diaz adopted the term *mujerista* for herself and other Latina theologians.

Diversity within the field of feminist theology is expanding in at least four directions. First, theologians from around the world are working out of their own cultural and geographical contexts, often in dialogue with others around the globe. Feminist theologians from Asia (e.g. Kwok Pui-Lan and Chung Hyun Kyung), Africa (including Mercy Amba Oduyoye and Musimbi R.A. Kanyoro), Latin America (Elsa Tamez, Maria Pilar Aquino, and others), and elsewhere are reshaping feminist theological discourse into a truly global enterprise.

Second, increasing numbers of feminists are working within and across numerous religious traditions. Women are engaging Judaism (such as Judith Plaskow and Ellen Umansky), Buddhism (Rita Gross, S. Boucher, A. C. Klein), Islam (Riffat Hassan and Amina Wadud-Muhsin), Native American traditions (Paula Gunn Allen and S. Wall), Wicca (Cynthia Eller, Starhawk, M. Adler), and many other traditions.[14]

Third, part of the expanding richness of feminist theology has been the use of a variety of theoretical approaches (e.g., trauma theory and postcolonial theory).[15] While the relationship between feminist theology and theory has been contentious at times, many feminist theologians use theory to help understand more fully the forces at play in women's oppression. Ongoing conversations with different types of theory increase both the breadth and depth of feminist theology, stretching it into interdisciplinary conversations and helping it to focus more sharply on particular elements of structural oppression.

A fourth area of expansion in feminist theology is the field of ecofeminism. Ecofeminism begins by addressing the relationship between the oppression of women and the ecological destruction perpetrated by hierarchical, androcentric Western culture. Broadening their analysis to include philosophy, economics,

science, and technology, ecofeminists explore interconnection and interde-
pendence within a framework of unity and diversity. Some ecofeminists reject
religion as inherently oppressive or unhelpful, but others are doing creative constructive theology within Christianity and goddess traditions.[16]

Divisions

The expansion of the field of feminist theology and its multiplication into
numerous feminist theologies are the great triumph of the past twenty years,
won through what Beverly Wildung Harrison calls an "academic-political
practice of inclusion."[17] She writes of herself and the feminists of her generation, "Our goal was not so much to perfect our theories individualistically
but to broaden concrete participation in the work of constructing and expanding women's theological 'knowledge.'"[18] However, this success does not
come without difficulties. As women from many different backgrounds begin
to speak of their own particular experiences, the assumption of unity built on
similarity begins to crumble. Women struggling for survival in underdevel-
oped countries may have far more in common with the men who struggle beside them than with affluent white women in overdeveloped countries in the
Northern West. Is the fact that we are all women enough to establish us as a
unified and stable group? The answer is not clear, especially given that "womanhood" has itself come into question. The radical diversity of experience
among women from different cultural contexts makes it difficult to locate
some common characteristic or experience that makes us all "women."

Feminists have long been involved in challenging cultural assumptions about
what it means to be a woman. As the cultural patterns that enforce certain behaviors as womanly are ever more thoroughly analyzed, the question of what actually constitutes womanhood arises. Earlier feminists observed that Western
patterns of thought organize the world into a hierarchy of dualisms in which one
member of each pair is more highly valued than the other. Thus men are stereotypically understood to be strong, active, and rational, while women (their opposites) are seen as weak, passive, and emotional. One of the first moves that
feminists made to disrupt the oppressive effects of this way of thinking was to el-
evate the side of the dualisms associated with women, to honor and embrace
those characteristics that have been seen as feminine.[19] However, feminists in
many fields quickly began to suspect that embracing the stereotypically feminine actually undergirds and reinforces the dualistic, hierarchical thinking that
had been identified as oppressive.[20] While such strategies might affirm the space
created for women in Western thought as valuable, they have few resources for
rejecting the fact or processes of women's confinement. They can grant respect

to women who are stereotypically feminine, but cannot honor women who do not fit that model, cannot open up new opportunities and roles for women, and cannot seriously question the cultural patterns that proclaim and enforce a singular model of womanhood.

Difficulties with this strategy led many feminists away from essentialist views of woman—views that see all women as possessing certain common, innate, identifiable characteristics—toward constructivist views, which understand the female self as being formed in and through social and cultural relationships over time, such that women differ widely according to location and experience.[21] Within a constructivist view, one can interpret the fact that many women in the West are stereotypically feminine not as an indication that these characteristics are necessarily part of what it means to be a woman, but rather as evidence that Western culture encourages females, from the time they are infants, to become, understand, and enact their gender in a stereotypical, proscribed fashion.

If the word "woman" does not refer to a person possessed of a whole package of essential characteristics, but rather to a person who has been (and is being) socially constructed within particular, culturally defined expectations and limitations, then grouping half the population of the world together on the basis of the similarity of womanhood seems problematic, since it is unclear what constitutes or funds the assumed similarity. Analysis of how our cultural indoctrination affects our understanding and interpretation of anatomical and hormonal differences between men and women makes it difficult to rely on biology as a clear marker.[22] Even if biology were a clear marker, would the category of "woman" thus defined be meaningful enough to fund the political and analytical work that feminists ask of it? Some feminists suggest that it might be more useful to describe "women" as a historical group or a social class.[23] However womanhood is defined, it is clear from the debate that womanhood can no longer be assumed as a clear and necessarily meaningful category.

While the concepts of "women" and "women's experience" have been vastly important to the field of feminist theology, increasing respect for differing particularities and theoretical considerations of social construction both challenge these unifying themes.[24] If we avoid universalizing accounts of the human person in order to hear the different voices of women around the world describe their own realities, how do we begin to understand the different truths they tell? Who is the arbiter of truthfulness, once the image of a bearded white man has been toppled from the sky? Should we refrain from telling religious truths that make universal or metaphysical claims? Or ought we to reassess the categories of religious truth and meaning altogether?

Shaping the Larger Theological Discourse

One of the ways that feminist theologies have shaped the larger theological discourse in the past two decades has been by raising and attending to such concerns. Shifting understandings of the self and of truth open onto questions as abstract as the nature of the divine and as concrete as how to make normative claims or how to engage in political struggle for a desired end. Feminist theologians have explored and debated all of these issues and demanded that other theologians also attend to the challenges of talking about God in a pluralistic, diverse, postmodern context.

The influence of postmodernism has deepened feminist theologians' criticism of dualistic thinking in many ways.[25] Twenty years ago, feminist theologians addressed the issue of language primarily to advocate inclusive language in religious services and discuss difficulties in translating sexist biblical texts. They also began the process of naming the silencing of women within religious traditions. This naming continued, as feminist theologians have addressed the ways that women have not had the power to shape the language and culture of their religious traditions.[26] Postmodern feminists such as Luce Irigaray take a different (though not unrelated) approach, examining the ways that language itself is ordered in hierarchical dualisms, which then become imbedded in our processes of knowing and interpreting reality.

Furthering feminist analysis of dualism, Irigaray demonstrates that when Western culture defines women as the opposite of men, it relies on a worldview in which all things can be hierarchically ordered, or as she writes, a logic of "sameness."[27] Within the logic of the same, everything can be compared as better or worse; there are no "apples and oranges" situations in which comparisons do not apply. Thus women, when viewed as the opposite of men, are really understood to be weaker, distorted reflections of men. On a deep level, this logic of sameness relies on the idea that everything in the universe is a weak, distorted reflection of one singular Truth, one Absolute Good. This implicates the traditional monotheistic conception of an omniscient, omnipotent God as the anchor that stabilizes and guarantees the entire hierarchical structure of comparison, and raises anew the question of whether monotheistic religion is fundamentally incompatible with feminism. Yet in this context, the difficulty is not primarily that traditional monotheism images God as male, but rather that its monotheistic structure grounds a linguistic framework and worldview that limit our ability to enact, acknowledge, and embrace difference and multiplicity.

In conversation with postmodernism, the feminist theological discussion of language has gone in new directions: identifying language itself as a location in which the subordination of women is propagated and envisioning ways of funding new language that could contain the multiplication of women's voices. In *The Power to Speak: Feminism, Language, God*, Christian theologian Rebecca Chopp writes:

> Women will be forever strangers unless their words and their voices revise the social and symbolic rules of language, transforming the law of ordered hierarchy in language, in subjectivity, and in politics into a grace of rich plenitude for human flourishing. . . . [W]omen must find ways of resisting the codes, the concepts, the values, and the structures that are subject to this two-term system. In this fashion women may not so much balance or equalize the hierarchy as change its monotheistic ordering of the "one" as opposed to the "other" into a multiplicity, allowing differences and connections instead of constantly guaranteeing identities and oppositions.[28]

In this quote, we see again the contemporary feminist emphasis on allowing and enabling the voices of many women to be heard, in all their difference and particularity. It is also clear that the changes in thought and behavior that move toward a joyful multiplication of voices come hand in hand with serious intellectual and theological difficulties. Concepts basic to the theological enterprise—such as truth, the self, history, and language—no longer appear stable, even as sites of debate.

Unity in Discourse and Difference

Perhaps the most surprising aspect of feminist theology at the turn of the millennium is that, while it has been both multiplied and divided by the changes of recent decades, it has not been utterly fragmented. The unifying factors that had been assumed, such as essentialist understandings of womanhood or women's experience, have all come into question, yet women continue to choose to be in unity with other women, at least to the degree that they continue to be part of feminist discourse and political action. This chosen solidarity embraces difference while struggling with the real difficulties difference can involve. For example, women debate whether or not "women" constitute a stable collective group. Yet even while arguing that we have more differences than similarities, many women choose to engage in this debate with other feminists—choosing to be part of a collective group of women committed to advocacy for women.

Contemporary feminist theologies move toward this different kind of unity in a number of ways. In *The Church in the Round: Feminist Interpretation of the*

Church, Letty Russell envisions a church where diversity is not in conflict with unity, but is rather held together by hospitality. She writes, "Hospitality is an expression of unity without uniformity, because unity in Christ has as its purpose the sharing of God's hospitality with the stranger, the one who is 'other.'"[29] Some scholars choose to embody this kind of unity by working in collaboration with other women, who may or may not have similar views.[30] Particularly in postcolonial literature, there are women of many different faiths writing together or publishing side by side.[31] Beverly Wildung Harrison writes of "'networking' toward ever new and shifting solidarities" as the "the(a)logical mode of practice par excellence."[32] In large part this different kind of unity—a unity that allows and embraces real difference—is formed when feminist theologians attend to the pragmatic political concerns that lie at the heart of all feminist discourse, struggling against the oppression of women.

Conclusion

In the past twenty years, the field of feminist theology has abundantly multiplied into a growing conversation of increasing particularity, diversity, and pluralism. This multiplication has been accompanied by division, as several of the basic concepts and modes of discourse that once stabilized and unified feminist theology have come into question. The understanding of women as a stable group, the idea of all women having similar experiences, any account of life or truth that can be seen as universalizing one's own limited perspective: these topics and conversations have been rendered problematic by the concrete difficulties of encountering differences as well as by postmodern theoretical considerations. Yet in the face of these conceptual challenges as well as political resistance, feminist theologians continue to creatively embody a fluid and multiple unity in commitment to the liberation of women.[33]

Notes

1. Rosemary R. Ruether, "Christianity," in *Women in World Religions*, ed. Arvind Sharma, 232 (Albany: State University of New York Press, 1987).

2 Ann Braude, *Women and American Religion*, (New York: Oxford University Press, 2000), 120.

3. Braude, *Women and American Religion*, 115.

4. Braude, *Women and American Religion*, 120.

5. Braude, *Women and American Religion*, 120.

6. Braude, *Women and American Religion*, 121–22.

7. Braude, *Women and American Religion*, 111.

8. Braude, *Women and American Religion*, 121.

9. Such considerations were part of the impetus toward inclusive language in religious rituals and translations: The differences between women's and men's realities are erased when women are subsumed under "generic" masculine terms. These considerations also lead women to be wary of camouflaging the deeper androcentric bias in such texts and services by changing pronouns to superficially include women.

10. bell hooks, *Feminist Theory: From Margin to Center* (Boston: South End Press, 1984), 1–31.

11. hooks, *Feminist Theory*, 24–25.

12. Serene Jones, *Feminist Theory and Christian Theology: Cartographies of Grace* (Minneapolis: Fortress Press, 2000), 14.

13. Alice Walker, *In Search of Our Mothers' Gardens: Womanist Prose* (San Diego: Harcourt Brace Jovanovich, 1983), xi–xii. Walker's definition reads as follows:

> Womanist 1. From *womanish*. (Opp. of "girlish," i.e., frivolous, irresponsible, not serious.) A black feminist or feminist of color. From the black folk expression of mothers to female children, "You acting womanish," i.e., like a woman. Usually referring to outrageous, audacious, courageous or *willful* behavior. Wanting to know more and in greater depth than is considered "good" for one. Interested in grown-up doings. Acting grown up. Being grown up. Interchangeable with another black folk expression: "You trying to be grown." Responsible. In charge. *Serious*. 2. *Also*: A woman who loves other women, sexually and/or nonsexually. Appreciates and prefers women's culture, women's emotionally flexibility (values tears as natural counter-balance of laughter), and women's strength. Sometimes loves individual men, sexually and/or nonsexually. Committed to survival and wholeness of entire people, male *and* female. Not a separatist, except periodically, for health. Traditionally universalist, as in: "Mama, why are we brown, pink, and yellow, and our cousins are white, beige, and black?" Ans.: "Well, you know the colored race is just like a flower garden, with every color flower represented." Traditionally capable, as in: "Mama, I'm walking to Canada and I'm taking you and a bunch of other slaves with me." Reply: "It wouldn't be the first time." 3. Loves music. Loves dance. Loves the moon. *Loves* the Spirit. Loves love and food and roundness. Loves struggle. *Loves* the Folk. Loves herself. *Regardless*. 4. Womanist is to feminist as purple is to lavender.

14. Because the term "feminist" originally referred to a movement shaped by middle-class white women, some of these authors do not use the term "feminist" to refer to their own work, while they continue to be part of the large discourse concerning the liberation of women. Some useful anthologies that give a sense of the field are *With Passion and Compassion* (Maryknoll, NY: Orbis Books, 1988), edited by Virginia Fabella and Mercy Amba Oduyoye; *The Power of Naming: A Concilium Reader in Feminist and Liberation Theologies* (Maryknoll, NY: Orbis Books, 1996), edited by Elisabeth Schüssler Fiorenza; *Feminist Theology: A Reader* (Louisville, KY.: Westminster/John Knox Press, 1990), edited by Ann Loades; *Feminist Theology from the Third World: A Reader* (Maryknoll, NY: Orbis Books, 1994), edited by Ursula King; *Freeing Theology: The Essentials of Theology in Feminist Perspective* (San Francisco: HarperSanFrancisco, 1993), edited by Catherine Cowry Lacuna; *Feminist Theological Ethics: A Reader* (Louisville, KY.: Westminster/John Knox Press, 1994), edited

by Lois K. Daly; *After Patriarchy: Feminist Transformations of the World Religions* (Maryknoll, NY: Orbis Books, 1991), edited by Paula M. Cooley, William R. Akin, and Jay B. McDaniel; and *Feminism and World Religions* (Albany, NY: State University of New York Press, 1999), edited by Arvin Sharma and Katherine K. Young.

15. Jones's *Feminist Theory and Christian Theology* is a good example, as is *Horizons in Feminist Theology: Identity, Tradition, and Norms*, edited by Rebecca Chopp and Sheila Greeve Davaney. Trauma theory, or trauma studies, is an interdisciplinary field that analyzes the ways in which acts of traumatic violence harm individuals and communities. Postcolonial theory is an exploration of how the period of European colonization shapes, and is suppressed in, contemporary understanding of self, language, and other.

16. Rosemary Radford Ruther, "Feminism in World Christianity," in *Feminism and World Religions*, ed. Arvid Sharma and Katherine K. Young, 223 (Albany: State University of New York Press, 1999); Ivone Gebara, "Ecofeminism," in *Dictionary of Feminist Theologies*, ed. Letty M. Russell and J. Shannon Clarkson, 76–78 (Louisville, Ky.: Westminster John Knox Press, 1996). Other texts of related interest are *The Body of God: An Ecological Theology* (Minneapolis: Fortress Press, 1993), by Sallie McFague; *Gaia and God: An Ecofeminist Theology of Earth Healing* (San Francisco: HarperSanFrancisco, 1992), by Rosemary Radford Ruether; *Longing for Running Water: Ecofeminism and Liberation* (Minneapolis: Fortress Press, 1999), by Ivone Gebara; and *Women Healing Earth: Third World Women on Ecology, Feminism, and Religion* (Maryknoll, NY: Orbis Books, 1996), edited by Rosemary Radford Ruether.

17. Beverly Wildung Harrison, "Feminist Thea(o)logies at the Millennium: 'Messy' Continued Resistance or Surrender to Post-Modern Academic Culture?" in *Liberating Eschatology: Essays in Honor of Letty M. Russell*, ed. Margaret A. Farley and Serene Jones, 158 (Louisville: Westminster John Knox Press, 1999).

18. Harrison, "Feminist Thea(o)logies at the Millennium," 158.

19. Gayle Kimball discussed this in her original chapter.

20. Kimball touched on this briefly and mentioned androgyny as an exciting possibility for subverting dualistic gender roles. Androgyny is not a significant theme in contemporary feminist theology. The idea of androgyny—combining the masculine and the feminine—upholds the essentialist view that certain characteristics are inherent to women and others to men. At the same time, the feminists who used this term affirmed the possibility of altering or erasing the gendered allocation of such characteristics, thereby acknowledging some role for social construction of gender identity. As Kimball wrote, "The concept of androgyny is an exciting one, in which women will be socialized for example, to be assertive and men to be open with their emotions." Discussion of androgyny as a hopeful strategy waned as debate between essentialist and constructivist views clarified the underlying issues. Contemporary feminists whose strategies would be similar to Kimball's, such as socializing women to be more assertive, would likely reject the term androgyny as indicating an essentialist view. If women can be socialized to be more assertive, then assertiveness is not an essentially masculine trait, and there is no need to call an assertive woman androgynous.

21. For a clear discussion of this debate, see Jones, *Feminist Theory and Christian Theology*, 22–48. Even those who hold an essentialist view that certain qualities are

inherent to women have gained a greater respect for the role of social construction in the formation of the self.

22. Through her book *Gender Trouble: Feminism and the Subversion of Identity* (New York: Routledge, 1990), Judith Butler has significantly shaped contemporary conversations regarding the sources, stability, and status of gender identity.

23. Jones, *Feminist Theory and Christian Theology*, 7.

24. Similar challenges face broader understandings of the self. Constructivist views of the human person imply a deep critique of Enlightenment notions of the self as an autonomous, rational, free subject. They also cast suspicion on any attempt to give a universal, metaphysical account of the human person, and instead call for more particular descriptions. For discussion of some of the difficulties attending feminist theological anthropology and constructive approach to the topic, see *Changing the Subject: Women's Discourses and Feminist Theology* (Minneapolis: Fortress Press, 1994) by Mary McClintock Fulkerson.

25. Postmodernism is a sustained critique of modernity, focused on exposing the unstated, repressed conditions and assumptions of modern cultural and intellectual discourse. The relationship between the field of feminist theology and postmodernism is fluid and interesting. In many ways, foundational principles of feminist theology coincide with postmodern sensibilities, such that one may look back at earlier feminist theology and see ideas and themes that became prominent in postmodern thought. Feminist theology began to be more directly in conversation with postmodernism in the 1980s. See Harrison for an interesting account of similarities and divergences.

26. Judith Plaskow gives an excellent description of this in relation to the Jewish tradition in *Standing Again at Sinai: Judaism from a Feminist Perspective* (San Francisco: HarperSanFrancisco, 1990). See also *The Power of Naming* (Mary Knoll, NY: Orbis Books, 1996), edited by Elisabeth Schüssler Fiorenza.

27. See Luce Irigaray, *Speculum of the Other Woman*, trans. Gilligan C. Gill (Ithaca, N.Y.: Cornell University Press, 1974), 259, 263, 275, 320–21.

28. Rebecca Chopp, *The Power to Speak: Feminism, Language, God* (New York: Crossroad, 1989), 2.

29. Letty Russell, *Church in the Round: Feminist Interpretation of the Church* (Louisville, Ky.: Westminster John Knox Press, 1993), 173. Russell is drawing upon insights in Thomas W. Ogletree, *Hospitality to the Stranger: Dimensions of Moral Understanding* (Philadelphia: Fortress Press, 1985).

30. This is one reason for the large number of anthologies in feminist theology, several of which are listed in note 14.

31. See *Postcolonialism, Feminism, and Religious Discourse* (New York: Routledge, 2002), edited by Laura E. Donaldson and Kwok Pui-lan.

32. Harrison, "Feminist Thea(o)logies at the Millennium," 161.

33. I am grateful for the suggestions and criticisms of Cynthia Hess, Serene Jones, Letty Russell, and Ludger Viefhues.

CHAPTER FOURTEEN

~

The Goddess/Wiccean Movement: Interview with Z Budapest

Gayle Kimball

GK: You mentioned your life work was "Priestessing a feminist/womanist community." How has that developed and changed over the last two decades?

ZB: I am no longer a dimple-cheeked agile young women with an attitude. I am a new Crone groping confidently for the third destiny. While I was having other plans, like becoming a great Hungarian novelist, LIFE has directed the essence of what I was to bring back the ancient Goddess into women's lives. LIFE is the final editor. What she writes is often better than what I have thought up. She writes bolder herstories.

For the past thirty years I acted as priestess, as well as a writer, initiator, and conceptualizer. Priestess is the oldest profession by the way, not prostitution. What does it mean? I facilitated hundreds of circles of women with a spiritual content and experience. I taught women how to pray to the Goddess from the heart. I was the closest to this information. I had all the stars, the Aquarian sun, the Libra moon, humanitarian and equality minded; it all hung together imperceptibly. Plus, I had a psychic mother who prayed on the winds to our ancestors. I inherited the witchy genes that manifested early in my life.

When I was four years old I could frighten away Russian soldiers from our bunker during World War II in Budapest. Even as a toddler, I had certainty that I could pray aloud to the heavens for a protection with my skinny little arms outstretched. The soldiers were undone by this picture. They knew I was in contact with God. I have always prayed the Big Prayer to the Goddess Boldogasszony. She was a fairy queen for the Hungarians who birthed a girl, not a boy. We renamed her for political reasons. Mary got assimilated into the local tradition, all the churches were finally to Mary, or her mother Anna, or her friend St. Katherine, or our homegrown saints St. Elisabeth and

St. Teresa. There are no churches built in my country to Jesus Christ that I have ever seen.

This prayer is older than Hungarian Christianity. Boldogasszony (Glad Woman) was the power over everything and it saved us many times during the war. I still do this prayer in Hungarian when I do healing work. It goes like this in mirror translation: "Now is the time to help me, oh Maria! You merciful Virgin Mother! The deep prayers of your children you never, never deny. Where humans cannot help, you alone have the power to deliver. Where the need is keen and hopeless, your power alone can turn the tides. Show us that you are our mother! Now help us oh Maria! You merciful Virgin Mother!"

GK: The archetype of the great mother, to use Jungian terminology, always surfaces, despite patriarchy's efforts to suppress her. What do you think about the appearances of Virgin Mary in Mexico, the United States, and various parts of Europe?

ZB: All healing sites are connected with the Mother of God. All springs, healing baths, and rivers are the Goddess. She is everywhere and pervades the entire culture. I think humanity noticed that the Mother of all Gods actually does good things for us, heals the sick, gives hope to the hopeless, and warns of pending disasters. She is a working God, a God who never deserted us. A true Good God. Eventually it will be normal to love nature, to love peace.

GK: What is the evolution of your personal relationship with and understanding of the Goddess?

ZB: I am still a work in progress. Nothing can be more powerful; nothing is more exuberant in the evening, nothing more worthy to dress up for than a ritual circle with a sacred fire and a few hundred women ready to dance and pray. Nothing compares to the oneness we feel when imagining the Goddess together. When women imagine the world, the world actually gets better. When blending action to our inner life, we are shapers of the new mythology that has bigger power then any president. Imagination and humor has toppled the powerful before.

The spiritual revolution is imperceptible, a stealth revolution. The Goddess is coming in little pieces, a woman at a time. The great awakening is in its almost maturity, we're almost all getting it. LIFE doesn't mind discord or unpleasantness, or even death. LIFE doesn't mind because she made more of us yesterday. It's a huge continuum. LIFE runs the show.

Our Zeitgeist (Right now Pluto in Sagittarius) is the humanistic coming to consciousness as the human race. Women always stand for all of humanity, since we have created everybody from scratch; there are only two kinds of people on Earth, the mothers and her children. This is why the Madonna with child is essentially the symbol of our human race. This is the image that occurs in every culture over and over again.

GK: What do you see as the focus of young women today?

ZB: They want to make everyone feel included, not hate each other. They enjoy a gender continuum; the whole arch from extreme masculine and feminine to androgyny they see as "cool." They don't hate each other for sexual orientation. They're kick ass wonderful, they know more than we did. My sons' girlfriends were feminists; I used to be girlfriend bait. Young women we were before them, looking for a mission in life.

A young woman like Julia Luna Hill loves nature and acts on her beliefs; that's what I hope they all find, a noble mission. More women are graduating from universities with degrees, streaming into white-collar jobs. Women will run this country in ten years. They still need women's study groups, women's centers and bars, as existed in the 1960s and 1970s, although women's centers do exist in the universities and you don't have to pay rent for Internet chat rooms.

GK: Is the Sisterhood of the Wicce still an organization? What about other wiccean organizations around the United States and other countries? Are there still goddess and wiccean conferences, newsletters and magazines?

ZB: Oh yes there are! The organizations and their public visibility have moved to the Internet. You type in Witchcraft, or Goddess, and hundreds of things will pop up, including my own website, and the Dianic University. The space where the Aquarian Age can grow up is the Internet.

In the 1980s, I started the Women's Spirituality Forum, our own San Francisco Bay Area nonprofit, and lead it still. We organize women's festivals and celebrations. We come together in a special place—the redwood forest; we circle to celebrate the seasons eight times a year. For example, Halloween is the New Year when the new calendar begins. We mourn people we lost, lament, speak out, then play music to come back to the present. We use the spiral dance, the most ancient symbol, the Milky Way, spiral down to the center to the house of death, commune with ancestors, and bring them offerings. We spiral back out, purified; the soul comes out as we hold hands with the women and spiral in and out. We dance for health, for peace, what ever the high priestess puts out. She sends a kiss around, a group hug, and then we do final chanting and release it into the universe. (For more details see *The Holy Book of Women's Mysteries*, available only on my website.)

Each holiday is different as we celebrate the seasons. Winter solstice is where they stole Christmas (it used to be January 6 and still is for the Greek Orthodox church). Pick a holiday and revive it with friends in your own tradition. We opened up Pandora's treasure chest, but there's tons more to do to create a culture with meaning. When everyone feels included, there's no war.

At a recent festival, we did a big Peace Ritual where we entwined a sword with olive branches and offered it to the Goddess, left it overnight in the woods. We burned rose buds in the sacred fire. Working on the ethereal plane is important because manifestation begins there and then we kick it into the physical world. Women's mysteries, where we celebrate the moons and the seasons, are the fastest growing religious activity in the pagan movement. We're creating a new mythology, leaving behind patriarchal gods. Old Testicles and New Testicles have been cast away. The goddess represents plurality; the life force is one but it enjoys diversity. The impulse of life has to be diverse.

GK: What have you published over the decades since the first edition of the women's culture book?

ZB: I published seven more books since the first one, *The Feminist Book of Lights and Shadows,* which is now *The Holy Book of Women's Mysteries* and twice as long. I published with Harper and Row *The Grandmother of Time,* about the lost Earth holidays, and *Grandmother Moon* about the lost lunar holidays.

For example, in Rome, March 17 was Liberale, the celebration of freedom, when slaves were allowed to speak their mind, the foremother of speakouts. The Greek festival of Astarte was the coming together of male and female principles. One of my favorites is Hillaria, the Roman laughing day, the original Easter celebration.

Goddess in the Office was the book for the 1980s as women went to work in heels and rode home in sneakers. They were on the edge, the first inheritors of the second wave's fruits of feminism. It's still my best seller. I created for them magical spells to do in the office. It aligns office work with the universe, each day has a meaning; I include a scent, color, and gemstone for each day as a way to align your consciousness.

Goddess in the Bedroom is for working women when they return home. It suggests varying your posture in intercourse: When the woman is on top she controls the rhythm of the thrusting. Being a wild woman allows you to revel in your lovemaking. Lesbian sex focuses on the whole body, a spiritual and emotional experience. I also write about solo sex, bedtime stories, and fairy tales from Hungary.

Summoning the Fates was about TIME and Fate and planets and herstory and the three Weird Sisters who rule over life, death, and beauty. A sister book about the Spirit of our Times is the *Celestial Guide for Every Year of Your Life,* which came out in 2003, focusing on the transpersonal planets and how they mature our spirits. For example, if you have a Saturn return you can't unchoose it. It must be lived. The first Saturn return is age twenty-eight to thirty; it flips bright women out because things are unclear until the dust settles around age thirty-three and they see their second destiny and its life mission. The third destiny from sixty to ninety is the most important. More and more I am looking at online publishing, and an online business selling new books and CDs of the old ones. Being an Aquarian, I like change.

GK: Do you think it would make a difference if more women were political and religious leaders? What about Margaret Thatcher, Golda Meir, Indira Gandhi, and others who don't seem to lead any differently than men? You hoped for revolution; is it on its way?

ZB: Those leaders were better than men, but were token women and had no role models, almost like orphans without mommies. They only had the ancient queens to look to, and that was too archaic. At least they all fought short wars and won; short wars equal less corruption. They were there first and made sure there will be more women leaders, letting down the mythical roots. We need generations of women leaders, before we can develop the most excellent ones we admire. We need woman leaders who also make mistakes; how else do they develop? Call together the wives and sisters of all the male leaders in power now and see what they are thinking.

How about the women who have brought down male corruption? In 2002, women exposed Oracle, like Debbie Leibrock. Sharon Watkins brought down Enron, and special agent Colleen Rowley exploded the CIA. Are these women/sisters not our frontrunners? Our noble generals? They don't have to be witches; we are all used by LIFE.

The culture changes, right under our feet, and then the rest follow. We listen to music from the all ages now and from all countries that had a recording machine. We watch TV about historical events reenacted, we look and watch ourselves from around the world. Humanity is watching, bonding, witnessing themselves; the world is shrinking. Bitterness issues are being worked on. Women must resolve their own inner conflicts and step up and take more responsibility for what's going on in the world. The questions of war and peace must be addressed publicly by women. We also must lift our voices and dare to call on the men to take responsibility for themselves as a group.

GK: What's your focus for the future?

ZB: For the future I say let PAX, the Goddess of PEACE, manifest with us. Without Peace there is nothing, because all evolution stops when war scorches earth and her culture. All resources are sucked away. Women and children once again go back to the bottom of the list. Have you asked yourself why we never ask how is the Iraq war going to pay for itself? There is unlimited money to kill, and here hospitals are closing down, schools too. Stupefying our population is only good for cheap labor. There are seven million more women voters registered than males, why don't we use our votes to rule out all wars? Let a woman be elected president.

I conceived of "The Global PAX Project," creating infomercials for PEACE. Pax is the only one who doesn't have her fifteen minutes of fame. I think Pax should have infomercials where the women solve problems the men could not. Peace should be not politics; it is the basis for commerce and arts and civilizations.

Women must be visible in the media where our realities blend. "If it's not on TV, it didn't happen," said Flo Kennedy, the civil rights lawyer. Waiting for the male leadership to make peace when they didn't do so for 5,000 years is like waiting for fish to grow legs. Now we are in position to make female issues mainstream. And Pax is the number one female issue.

The big picture is that patriarchal wars must fail and become obsolete. I thought this would be done by now, thirty years after women's liberation, thirty years after women coming into consciousness.

After wars there is no victory for anyone, mothers cry and bury their children on both sides; there is only famine, and poverty. The reasons for the wars are quickly forgotten, or never had any (weapons of mass destruction in Iraq) but its takes three generations to recover from a major war.

Women voters are the Sleeping Goddesses, snoozing on their sides. They need to wake up, to use the vote in a block. Only once did we vote with power, when women put Bill Clinton in the White House. We need another gender gap, to vote out war, to vote in as many women as possible. Then we'll have generations of women with earthy powers as well as spiritual ones, supporting each other, growing out of self-hatred and self-defeat into diverse expressions of freedom and culture.

Biography

Zsuzsanna Budapest was born in Budapest, Hungary. Her mother was a medium and a practicing witch who supported herself and her daughter with her art, as a sculptress. Her mother Masika's themes always celebrated the Triple Goddess and the Fates, and Z grew up respecting and appreciating Mother Nature as a God. Z immigrated to the United States in 1959, became a student at the University of Chicago, married, and gave birth to two sons. When she entered her Saturn cycle at the age of thirty, she became involved with the women's liberation movement in Los Angeles and became an activist herself, staffing the Women's Center there for many years.

There she recognized a need for a spiritual dimension so far lacking in the feminist movement and started the women's spirituality movement. She founded the Susan B. Anthony Coven Number l, the first feminist witches' coven, which became the role model for thousands of other spiritual groups being born and spreading across the nation. She wrote *The Holy Book of Women's Mysteries*, originally published in 1975 as *The Feminist Book of Lights and Shadows*. This book was the first hands-on book to lead women into their own spiritual/Goddess heritage.

Z was arrested in 1975 for reading Tarot cards to an undercover policewoman. She lost the trial but won the issue, and the law against psychics was struck down nine years later. Z has led rituals, lectured, taught classes, given workshops, written articles tirelessly, and published in hundreds of women's newspapers across the country. She has powerfully influenced many of the future teachers and writers about the Goddess.

Today Z lives in the San Francisco Bay Area, travels a lot giving workshops and lectures, but always makes time to smell the roses. Her books include *Celestial Wisdom, Summoning the Fates, The Holy Book of Women's Mysteries, Rasta Dogs, Grandmother Moon, Grandmother Time, The Goddess in the Office,* and *The Goddess in the Bedroom*. Find her Dianic University online at www.zbudapest.com; e-mail at zb@zbudapest.com.

PART FIVE

ORGANIZATIONS

CHAPTER FIFTEEN

~

Feminist Health Movement: Interview with Dido Hasper

Gayle Kimball

GK: I'm interested in women's health organizations because they are one of the few groups left that are run by women. We've seen a decrease in women's bookstores, schools like the Feminist Studio Workshop, and record producers like Olivia. Can you think of other feminist all-women organizations?

DH: There's Breast Cancer Action and the National Women's Health Network.

GK: Why the shrinkage overall?

DH: Resources in general. It's really hard to compete in the world, and to keep putting the time and energy and care into maintaining the organization. For us, we've had to do a lot of things to get through; we went without payroll, had to reduce staff, and came close to going under when MediCal changed over to managed care in 1997. We figured if we could keep going for five years they'd figure they needed us. We changed emphasis, reworked the clinic to be responsive to our clients, in general looked at every part of our organization. Every day we said there are eighty-five people paid by this organization; we were constantly on the edge financially, borrowing from one account to cover another, but we're determined to keep going. Most people wouldn't have been able to put up with it.

It had to do with our past, our present, and our goals. We've always been mission driven, committed to deliver the kind of health care every woman could use. Shauna Heckert and I have been running the center since 1978 and, for twenty-five years, we have brought different things to the codirectorship. Also, our board of directors is made up of women who've been in the women's health movement and worked in the health centers, such as Carol Downer,

Cindy Pearson, Megan Seely, and others united to keep the health center going in any way we could. The board was willing to work with us during that horrible period. Just at the right time we'd get a little bit of funding here and there, and started to build the well-women health clinic at the other three clinic sites.

Now we're seeing more women than ever before. At our four clinics in Northern California we see 600 women a week. We see them mainly for birth control, also pregnancy screening, adoption, and infertility. The other sites are Redding, Sacramento, and Santa Rosa under the umbrella of the Chico Feminist Women's Health Center. Each clinic is called Women's Health Specialists.

GK: When we last talked there was an active federation of feminist health centers with six members, but there's been shrinkage here too, correct?

DH: There isn't really an active federation now. We bring representatives of other clinics to our board meetings. People didn't feel like they could commit the resources necessary to keep it going. The Federation stopped meeting around 1996. It's been really hard.

There's no clinic in Los Angeles; they had a fire, tried to recover, and never could. San Diego is now part of Planned Parenthood; there's no longer a clinic in Concord, and Tallahassee closed about a year ago. Atlanta, yes, Detroit no, Berlin, yes. Portland just closed, Eugene closed last year. Washington State FWHC has three branches, in Renton, Yakima, and outside of Seattle.

A lot had to do with changes in health care. When managed care came in, it made the MediCal population a commodity. Different health insurance plans thought they'd make a fortune on it, but many didn't and got out of the business. Many patients got assigned to a clinic for their primary care without having a choice. We did contract with the health plans, which was part of the name change from Feminist Women's Health Centers to Women's Health Specialists, as we couldn't contract with the "f" word. There was a period when half of the plans went out of business and left us with unpaid claims. We are women-controlled clinics, considered specialty clinics because we provide abortion services. We weren't allowed federal money because we did abortions. Nationally, rates of abortions have declined over the years. Other services have grown, such as the well-woman clinic and birth control clinic. Well-woman means vaginal infections, annual exams, pap smears, pregnancy screening, testing for cervical lesions, etc.

We offer all types of birth control in our clinics. Though barrier methods like the cap and the diaphragm are much safer, most women get birth control pills, then Depo-Provera and the hormone patch. We've always offered all methods of birth control with informed consent.

Stigma about abortion has pushed people away from barrier methods like the cervical cap and diaphragm. The Centers for Disease Control said the safest birth control method is a barrier and up to two abortions a year as backup. But it's a different time today, and women feel they have failed if their birth control fails.

GK: In the early days, lay health workers wore long skirts and flipped them up to teach a group how to do self-exam with speculums and the center was a collective.

DH: Today you will still see a lay health worker at Women's Health Specialists, who will provide the education and some screening. We have nurse practitioners and doctors rather than lay health workers doing the pelvic exams and prescribing birth control. We are still a woman-controlled clinic. There is not a doctor at the top. We continue to keep the woman who is getting health care the most important decision maker. And we don't approve of doctors or nurse practitioners deciding for women what would be the best birth control or health option. We know today, with twenty-eight years of experience that, given all the information, the woman will make the best decision for herself.

We're not a collective now. We ran out of the resources it took to keep us collective. The many hours of meetings, and information sharing to ensure that every person in the collective had all the information needed to make decisions and policy, became impossible over the years. It became unwieldy for new staff to get caught up, and only equally committed people could actively participate in the collective. We recognized we had to have a different structure because we'd run out of money and time and people to continue the collective. Now we have a clinic administrator, executive director, clinic managers, etc. We try to do things by committee with people from different parts of the health center who have different perspectives. It doesn't work for only one person to do a task, because no one else will learn it or know it. We're directed by our mission statement and have the board to make critical decisions. Directors of the four clinics phone, e-mail, and fax, and management travels to the other clinics on a regular basis. We sometimes have a meeting with all centers.

One of the things that keeps us different from patriarchal organizations is that the consumer controls the way the health care is going to be delivered, not the doctors. Monday through Friday the lay people are running the clinic, making sure it's mission driven. It's what the woman wants, and she's the boss of her health care. One of the things we've found is if we have managers who've come up through the ranks, have been health workers, that works out much better. Another reason we're different is Shauna Heckert and I still work the clinics, do trainings, and see how things are going. In addition, our six phone counselors offer free information; that's still going strong: (530) 891-1911 or (800) 714-8151.

GK: You've been in this job for a long time. How have you personally changed your style and approach?

DH: I'm a different feminist director today out of being forced to do it differently. I would still prefer to have a collective, as bulky and hard as they are. But we haven't been able to afford to do that for a long time. Now it's really important to have great communication so all staff feel a part of things. We share information via meetings, emergency get togethers, bulletin boards and I work the clinics and talk to people. We sometimes type up information and put it with the paycheck.

We still aim to recognize and develop incoming leadership. It's been a very interesting change. With the women's health movement behind us, our generation never thought of not giving our all to our movement. We postponed childbirth, quit school, and put all of our energy into the movement. Young women don't look at it that way; there is no women's health movement. A lot of women who come to work have families or are single moms. They don't have the resources, the time, or the support to do it the way we did. The women's health movement and self-help empowered us to take steps and ask questions, to grab the turf and start our own clinics. Without that movement ,there is far less support.

GK: Who uses the clinic services, and for what? Do the young women have a feminist consciousness?

DH: In Chico we see a wide range, as we have a doctor working with us who sees pre- and peri-menopausal women. But the largest numbers are in their twenties, then early thirties and late teens. In all of our clinics, the clients reflect the community. In Sacramento, women are poorer and less healthy. Though I think across the board, we are seeing less healthy women because they have no place to go.

A certain amount of young women whose mothers are feminists, they're ahead of the game; their sex education and health education are not of the street variety. There's a whole other group whose mothers never talked about anything. But universally, women are anxious when they come for health care, and the more we can do to normalize their experience and give them information about their bodies, the better they feel. Women are poorer than they were when we started.

It's surprising how many women say, "This clinic is so great, what I say really matters, you care." They don't necessarily recognize that it's because we are a woman-run clinic, but they know the difference. Most people come to us from referrals from friends or family. Word gets around that they can receive respectful, dignified, and confidential care with us.

People are more knowledgeable consumers in some cases. For example, before the FDA approved RU486 (the abortion pill), people were aware of it, called wanting to know about it. When the patch came out, people were calling us about it immediately. Many young women have a feminist consciousness, but don't label it as such.

GK: Is abortion still a hot issue for the clinics?

DH: Obnoxious protesters are still a threat abortion providers face around the country. Chico has a few consistent hasslers. They're terrible in Sacramento at the Saturday abortion clinics. We had to go to court and get an injunction to get the sheriffs to do their job. Protesters block cars, obstruct access, and scream; try to stop the clients.

GK: Relationship with local doctors was a problem. Has it gotten better?

DH: When we settled the antitrust suit for local docs to provide backup care, they were afraid of lots of demand. But it's very rare that we need backup care, we've moved into a pretty good situation, with better communication with our physicians and the local backup docs.

GK: What about NARAL's [National Abortion Rights Action League] effectiveness?

DH: I don't like their fund-raising approach. Although they've done some great things over the years, I'm upset that they've done a lot of fund-raising in the name of supporting local clinics, but have never given us anything. For years people would tell us FWHC is great; I sent my donation to Planned Parenthood or NARAL. Since about five years ago, we've been getting foundation funding for certain projects. That's really helpful.

GK: When the health centers were a collective, personnel problems were time consuming.

DH: I think that our personnel problems are different, as we've gotten better at putting out what our goal and mission are, making it clear to people. Our goal is to have staff who agree with us, but there is a wide area of agreement. We probably have workers who don't call themselves feminists. Being pro-choice and respecting women are our bottom line. The antis burned down the Redding clinic three times, put chemicals in the Chico clinic, fire bombed the Sacramento clinic, etc. This really changed the way we organized ourselves around abortion rights, rather than woman-controlled health care. Someone can't work here if they're not pro-choice. Workers need to be pro-choice, pro-woman, nonjudgmental, and agree with our mission. Young women can start working here and find out they are feminists though they never realized it before. There are workers who don't identify as feminists, but really like the women we serve, want to help them, and agree with the mission. We lost the large-scale feminist movement, became small, and went into different arenas.

We had a male nurse working in the abortion clinic; he was good at following the lead. We had a transsexual nurse (woman) and male doctors. We had a man who is a bookkeeper and worked out quite well.

GK: You used to provide child care at work, but don't now. How do you help workers balance work and family?

DH: We provided child care on site until our kids were in third and fourth grade. The state didn't like us having it; they wanted us to be a full-fledged child care. We became a co-op center. It took money, time, and energy, so finally we decided to take all our kids to a local school center and enrolled them as a group. They made a lot of changes at the center; the kids thought they owned child care, as they had hired and fired their workers. Now we rely on providing flexibility to our workers as much as we can. We have no space for child care at this center. It doesn't have the same appeal as it once did.

People have brought babies to work, which worked fine. For the most part more of the administrative and professional staff has brought babies in. Health workers are not going to carry a baby around while getting a woman ready for their exam. We also substitute for each other. We have flextime and have had job sharing.

GK: The Federation produced two books. Any more?

DH: We wrote one more book, *A New View of a Woman's Body*. It's a picture book about women's health, anatomy, and a broader definition of the clitoris. It goes deeper than the traditional view, which is important in how women experience orgasm. The clitoris has been superficialized. We're understanding more about the different aspects that contribute to orgasm, how to achieve more satisfactory orgasms. An old book, *How to Stay Out of the Gynecologist's Office*, is about self-help, home remedies. The third book is *Women Centered Pregnancy and Birth*, all the things that can happen, what's usual and what's not, and what to do. Ginny Cassidy Brinn wrote the last book with the help of others; the earlier two were collectively authored. It was extremely hard, writing has so much to do with personal tastes, why you love this book and I hate that one. It was an experience I'll never forget, so heartening when it meshed.

GK: Two decades ago, your goals were more contact with Third World liberation movements and a more united women's movement.

DH: We haven't moved away from that. We still try to travel, like going to Cuba. We got a donation, and just sent two of our staff to Cuba to learn about a health care system where no one is in want. But it's still not in the hands of the Cuban people, the doctors run it; the nurses are the right hand of the doctors.

We were just talking about Iraq, talking about imperialism, how awful it is. I wish I could say we were spending a lot of time on it, but again, most of our time is spent delivering the health care. We do have contact with women all over the world, our books are translated into German and Japanese, etc.

The woman's movement is more united in some ways in national organizations like the National Women's Network and the Feminist Majority. There are not as many peaks and valleys; it's more middle of the road. There's not as much passion, discussion, or different perspectives.

GK: What do you predict for the future?

DH: I'd like to see pharmaceutical companies prohibited from direct contact with patients, not advertising on the airways, and have to be nonprofit. Each woman could get as much information as she needed to make every health decision for herself; a revolution where companies change what they think is important to get across to the consumer. We need information, not to be told exaggerations and sold wares. I hope more consumer-centered care would spread to all aspects of health care. There should be more access to alternative health care. I hope for more feminism, more women's movement, more women-controlled everything, but it doesn't seem like it's going so well for women. I'd like to see more feminist moms raising sons, like I am.

Biography

Dido Hasper (1949–2004) was the founding director of the Chico Feminist Women's Health Center (CFWHC). CFWHC is the base of four Women's Health Specialists clinics offering women-controlled reproductive health services. Thirty years ago, working with a group of nine nonprofessional women, Hasper created a woman-centered clinic offering abortion and birth control in a community where none was available. The group wanted to bring health care to women's lives without the shame attached to their sexuality or sexual health care.

Hasper worked consistently to bring health care decision making to those receiving the care, and to empower women with all the options available to them to reclaim our bodies as our own. She developed a mentoring program to foster leadership by working-class women.

Hasper coauthored and coordinated the collective writings of the Federation of Feminist Health Centers' *Women's Health in Women's Hands*, which produced the basic material later used to write *A New View of a Women's Body*, *How to Stay Out of the Gynecologist's Office*, and *Women-Centered Pregnancy and Birth*. Hasper remained a leader in the women's health movement and the Feminist Women's Health Center until the time of her death. She is survived by her son and daughter.

Index